11.95

FOUR ARGUMENTS FOR THE *ELIMINATION* OF TELEVISION

FOUR ARGUMENTS FOR THE *ELIMINATION* OF TELEVISION

BY

Jerry Mander

QUILL

NEW YORK 1978

Grateful acknowledgment is made for permission to excerpt from the following:

A Choice of Futures: To Enlighten or Inform? by Fred Emery and Merrelyn Emery, the Centre for Continuing Education, the Australian National University, P.O. Box 4, Canberra, A.C.T. 2600. Copyright © 1975. Reprinted by permission of the authors.

"Body Thinking: Psychology for Olympic Champs," article by Dr. Richard Suinn in *Psychology Today*, July, 1976, pp. 38-42. Reprinted by permission of Psychology Today Magazine. Copyright © 1976 by Ziff-Davis Publishing Company.

"Fact or Fiction," article by Bill Davidson in *TV Guide*, March 20, 1976, pp. 4-8. Excerpted with permission from TV GUIDE® magazine. Copyright © 1976 by Triangle Publications, Inc., Radnor, Pennsylvania.

News from Nowhere by Edward J. Epstein. Reprinted by permission of Random House, Inc. Copyright © 1973 by Edward J. Epstein.

Seeing with the Mind's Eye by Mike Samuels, M.D. and Nancy Samuels. Reprinted by permission of Random House, Inc., and The Bookworks. Copyright © 1975 by Mike Samuels, M.D., and Nancy Samuels.

"The Effects of Light on the Human Body," article by Richard J. Wurtman in *Scientific American*, July, 1975, pp. 69-77. Copyright © 1975 by Scientific American, Inc. All rights reserved. Reprinted by permission of W. H. Freeman and Company.

"The Scary World of TV's Heavy Viewer," article by George Gerbner and Larry Gross in *Psychology Today*, April, 1976, pp. 41-89. Reprinted by permission of Psychology Today Magazine. Copyright © 1976 by Ziff-Davis Publishing Company.

"The Science of Photobiology," article by Kendric C. Smith in *BioScience*, January, 1974. Copyright © 1974 by BioScience. Reprinted by permission of BioScience and the author.

"There Is a Bias in Television Journalism . . . ," article by John Birt in *TV Guide*, August 9, 1975, pp. 3-7. Excerpted with permission from TV GUIDE® Magazine. Copyright © 1975 by Triangle Publications, Inc., Radnor, Pennsylvania.

Printed in the United States of America

19 20

Library of Congress Cataloging in Publication Data

Mander, Jerry.
    Four arguments for the elimination of television.

    Bibliography: p.
    1. Television broadcasting—Social aspects—United States. 2. Television broadcasting—Psychological aspects. I. Title.
HE8700.8.M35   301.16′1   77-12558
ISBN 0-688-03274-5
ISBN 0-688-08274-2 pbk.

THIS BOOK IS DEDICATED

TO MY PARENTS,

EVA MANDER

AND

HARRY MANDER

CONTENTS

INTRODUCTION

FOUR ARGUMENTS FOR THE *ELIMINATION* OF TELEVISION

Argument One
THE MEDIATION OF EXPERIENCE

Argument Four

THE INHERENT BIASES OF TELEVISION

CONTENTS

Postscript
IMPOSSIBLE THOUGHTS

INTRODUCTION

I

THE BELLY OF THE BEAST

IF this book has any basis in "authority," it lies in the fifteen years I worked as a public relations and advertising executive. During that time, I learned that it is possible to speak through media directly into people's heads and then, like some otherworldly magician, leave images inside that can cause people to do what they might otherwise never have thought to do.

At first I was amused by this power, then dazzled by it and fascinated with the minutiae of how it worked. Later, I tried to use mass media for what seemed worthwhile purposes, only to find it resistant and limited. I came to the conclusion that like other modern technologies which now surround our lives, advertising, television and most mass media predetermine their own ultimate use and effect. In the end, I became horrified by them, as I observed the aberrations which they inevitably create in the world.

Adman Manqué

In retrospect, I can see that an absurd little revolt against my family led me into advertising work. My parents wanted me to choose a profession or to take over my father's business. They felt that while advertising was already a lucrative field by the time I was seeking a way into it in the late 1950s, it was still very chancy for Jewish boys. They were certainly right about that. Directly out of the Wharton School of Business and then Columbia Graduate Business School, I was denied a job in a Park Avenue ad agency because "your hair is a little kinky; you might want to try Seventh Avenue." Seventh Avenue was what I was fleeing.

My parents carried the immigrants' fears. Security was their primary value; all else was secondary. Both of them had escaped pogroms in Eastern Europe. My father's career had followed the path familiar to so many New York immigrants. Lower East Side. Scant schooling. Street hustling. Hard work at anything to keep life together. Early marriage. Struggling out of poverty.

Curiously, success came to him during the Depression. He founded what later became Harry Mander and Company, a small service business to the garment industry, manufacturing pipings, waist bands, pocketing and collar canvas.

One of the reasons for my father's success during hard times was World War II. He was beyond draft age and so was free to do a successful trade in servicing the manufacture of military uniforms. After the war, the business grew in new directions as the economy spurted forward into an era of rapid growth. Nonetheless, I decided his business wasn't for me.

I had planned something much flashier for myself, something with greater glamour. It was snobbery, I suppose. By then, when I thought about my "career"—always a hot topic around our house—certain images would fly through my mind. Since so many of the images were from the ads of the period, the world of advertising seemed appropriate. There was something about that life-style, those big cars, the great white yachts, the polished people on them and the life of leisure and pleasure: The Dream.

It wasn't so much that I was especially interested in wealth or that I ached to have all the goodies that were being shown in the ads of the 1940s and 1950s. I didn't want to own the cars and yachts so much as I wanted to be like the people who did. More, I wanted to help create those images, to be around models, artists, photographers and writers whom I imagined to be the sleek and sophisticated people.

Despite some early setbacks, such as that Park Avenue experience, by 1966 much of my dream was realized. By then I had already concluded a successful career as head of a theatrical publicity agency and joined a celebrated San Francisco ad agency, which became Freeman, Mander and Gossage.

We concentrated on so-called class clients. Triumph, Land Rover and Rover cars. Eagle shirts. Paul Masson wines. KLH audio equipment. *Scientific American*. Advent Corporation. Alvin Duskin dresses. Random House publishing.

Ours was the most elegant office in town. I was commuting coast to coast weekly, taking five-day vacations in Tahiti, eating *only* in French restaurants, jetting to Europe for a few days' skiing.

At some point, not very long into this new career, I began to realize a kind of hollowness in myself. I caught myself smiling pasty smiles. I noticed that despite all this I was not having a good time.

I think I hit an emotional bottom in 1968 while cruising through the Dalmatian Straits, observing rocky cliffs, rolling seas, dazzling sky, and colors as bright as a desert.

Leaning on the deck rail, it struck me that there was a film between me and all of that. I could "see" the spectacular views. I knew they were spectacular. But the experience stopped at my eyes. I couldn't let it inside me. I felt nothing. Something had gone wrong with me. I remembered childhood moments when the mere sight of the sky or grass or trees would send waves of physical pleasure through me. Yet now on this deck, I felt dead. I had the impulse to repeat a phrase that was popular among friends of mine, "Nature is boring." What was terrifying even then was that I knew the problem was me, not nature. It wasn't that nature was boring. It was that nature had become irrelevant to me, absent from my life. Through mere lack of exposure and practice, I'd lost the ability to feel it, tune into it, or care about it. Life moved too fast for that now.

If one seeks critical moments to explain later acts, even the writing of books, then perhaps that was one such moment for me. It was clear that I had chosen a fraudulent path toward an equally fraudulent image of a very cold sort of "happiness." On balance, though, this Big Moment was probably less significant than a slowly evolving political awareness that it was no accident that I was feeling the way I was.

Engulfed by the Sixties

One of my partners in the ad agency was Howard Gossage, a genius of sorts who for years before he died in 1969 agonized about the absurdity of working in such a profession. "I'd hate to go to my grave and be remembered as the man who invented Beethoven sweatshirts or competitions for paper airplanes."

He loved to tell the story of the retired adman who once said to him: "I got out of this business when I woke up one day and didn't give a damn whether they sold more Quaker Oats than I sold Cream of Wheat."

Gossage knew that there was more to the problem of advertising work than the way it emphasizes trivia. He would rage about the function itself, speaking of it as an invasion of privacy on an order far more extreme than the merely rude telephone solicitation, the door-to-door salesperson or even

16

the computer file on your credit. It was an invasion of the mind, which altered behavior, altered people.

Advertising expresses a power relationship, Gossage said. One person, the advertiser, invades; millions absorb. And to what end? So that people will buy something! A deep, profound and disturbing act by the few against the many for a trivial purpose.

Still thrilled by the life I was living, such considerations did not at first seem all that significant. But the period was the 1960s.

While I was showing clients through my paneled offices, a lot of people only slightly younger than I were lying about on the floors of San Francisco auto showrooms, restaurants and hotels, demanding that these places hire blacks. Across the Bay in Berkeley, students were stopping classes to insist upon participation in university policies. Thousands of others were standing in front of trains carrying war materials for Vietnam or blocking entryways to draft induction centers.

Living in the Bay Area in those years, one could scarcely avoid reflection and even involvement in these goings-on. In my own case, the involvement soon became direct.

Since I had been a publicist, I knew many reporters and had a feeling for the nuances of influencing media. Because of that, and through friendship with a number of politically inclined actors in a satirical troupe called The Committee, I began to meet many protest leaders and found myself serving as a part-time media advisor for some of the demonstrations. Like many young lawyers I was part of what was called "the liberal support group."

I rarely went so far as actually to demonstrate, or even to visit a demonstration. Instead I hosted evening meetings in my office to discuss what was happening. The main concern was how to influence the press to carry stories emphasizing issues rather than disruptions or violence.

Here was a typical problem: A group of demonstrators

would occupy a hotel lobby, demanding that blacks be hired at front-desk jobs, rather than bussing dishes in the coffee shop. Newspapers and television would run enormous stories about the demonstrations while editorially denouncing the tactics as "counterproductive to what might be worthy aims." The stories concentrated upon sloppy-looking demonstrators, moments of violence, and lengthy statements by officials about law and order. In an entire week's news coverage there might be one passing reference to the fact that for forty previous years the hotel hadn't hired a black person in a visible job.

I had no theory of media in those days, and I don't think I was of great service as an advisor. Yet it was clear to me that these demonstrations were *not* counterproductive. They produced the first news stories ever on such subjects, leading slowly to reforms which might never have happened otherwise. Obviously the media needed awakening quite as much as everyone else did.

Another realization was dawning upon me. As I commuted mentally between the interests of the demonstrators I talked to in the evenings and the interests of my commercial clients, I grew more and more impressed with the effect that the mere possession of money has upon the kind of information that is dispensed through the media.

My evening clients, speaking of social issues, needed to organize hundreds of people into confrontative acts which could get them extensive, if often unfavorable, coverage. Or, if they chose less confrontative routes, they could spend weeks of time and all their hard-won nickels and dimes to organize press information programs which would, at their most successful, net them a few inches in the back of the newspaper.

Meanwhile, any of my daytime clients, speaking for commercial purposes, could and did buy advertising space and time worth tens of thousands of dollars. Then they would do it again the following week.

I already knew that, in America, all advertisers spent more than $25 billion a year to disseminate their information. Now, however, I was beginning to pay attention to an obvious, yet little noticed, aspect of this situation. Virtually all of the $25 billion was being spent by people who already had a great deal of money. These were the only people who could afford to pay $30,000 for one page of advertising in *Time* ($54,000 by 1977) or $50,000 for one minute of prime television time ($125,000 by 1977). Ordinary people and small businesses, even those which are successful by most standards, can rarely afford any advertising beyond the want ads, or a small local retail display. Only the very rich buy mass national advertising. And they do this to become richer. What other motive could they possibly have?

A. J. Liebling once said, "Freedom of the press is limited to those who own one." I was learning that access to the press was similarly distorted by the possession of wealth. People with money had a 25-billion-to-nearly-zero advantage over people without money. The rich could simply buy access to the public mind while the not-rich had to seek more circuitous routes.

Twenty-five billion dollars is nearly as much as the whole country spends on higher education every year. I began to realize that a distortion was taking place in the quality and kind of information offered to the public. To a larger and larger extent, people's minds were being occupied by information of a purely commercial nature. As an advertising executive, I was instrumental in furthering this distortion.

The ecology movement pushed me over the edge. Our agency was hired first by the Sierra Club and then by Friends of the Earth and other organizations. Unlike most other do-good groups, these at least had a little money to buy an occasional one-shot ad on some critical issue. (During the early 1970s, all environmental groups together spent about

$500,000 per year in advertising in order to offset an average of about $3 billion in corporate expenditures on the same subjects. This ratio was relatively small, only 6,000 to 1, which may help explain the early success of the environmental movement.)

I found myself writing ads about keeping dams out of Grand Canyon, halting the overdevelopment of cities, stopping the development of SSTs, and urging people to stop buying and wearing furs.

The ads attacked the prevailing life-style of the country, which certainly included my own. They spoke of an inevitable conflict between corporate growth and the health of the planet. They encouraged a habit of mind which could grasp the inter-relationships between all natural systems, including humans. They described a growing environmental destruction which reflected itself in individual lives as well as in economic policies.

As I wrote these ads and thought about them, it got harder and harder to separate my new perspective from an awareness that it was in conflict with our corporate work. On Tuesday, I was writing about the impact cars and other technologies had upon the environment, and on Thursday I was promoting the sale of cars.

The crunch came one day in 1969 when a young *Wall Street Journal* reporter named Henry Weinstein called about doing a story on our agency's public-service work. By that time we had gained public attention for having invented a new style of advocacy advertising. Our ads were characterized by coupons urging changes in policy. The coupons could be torn out by readers and sent to corporations and government agencies. They produced enormous volumes of mail on conservation issues that until then had been considered the province of bird watchers and little old ladies in tennis shoes.

The ads had not only affected policy, they catalyzed and organized the public, because they allowed a new level of involvement. By mailing them, people became more committed to the issue. For once they were doing something more than feeling bad. A number of senators and congressmen publicly gave the ads credit for determining the outcome of several issues, and in *The New Advertising* Robert Glatzer went so far as to credit them with "starting the whole ecology boom."

Weinstein told us that the *Journal* was interested in the way we had developed this technique. However, when the story appeared on the front page, we learned he was a cagier reporter than we'd realized. While praising our work, he went to considerable lengths to reveal our misgivings about our conflicting roles. He cited my own anxiety at doing ads for an auto account, British Leyland Motors (Rover, Land Rover, Triumph), at a time that I was making speeches that said automobiles were at the heart of so many problems.

Leyland didn't like this. Within two hours of the story's appearance we were fired. The next day's *Journal* carried the headline:

AD MAN NEED WORRY NO MORE ABOUT AUTO ACCOUNT

I could describe fifty less spectacular incidents similar to this one involving struggles with clients over corporate policies that I was beginning to see as antithetical to simple rules of human well-being, or justice or planetary survival. They finally added up to a single generalization: Corporations are inherently uninterested in considerations aside from the commercial.

We began to feel that our balancing act was draining us personally. At last we saw that it was doomed to fail. Maintaining commercial accounts in the hope of using the income from them to finance other projects about which we cared more deeply was not going to work out.

We soon decided to dissolve the agency, and I began to work with a number of other people to establish a foundation-funded, non-profit advertising and public relations office. The first in the country, it was called Public Interest Communications and it was devoted solely to working for community organizations which are largely excluded from media. The project was launched in 1972 with a grant from the Stern Fund. It succeeded for a little while in performing useful services for ecologists and farm workers, consumer groups, Indian rights activists and peace groups. But keeping it alive proved difficult. The problems were much like those we had faced at Freeman, Mander and Gossage.

Whereas I had formerly spent a major part of my day keeping the agency going by caring for the needs of corporations, at Public Interest Communications we spent a majority of our time seeking grants from the few foundations interested in media reform.

Even worse, there was a feeling that everything we were doing was ineffective. A nameless juggernaut was advancing unretarded. We felt as if we were throwing snowballs at tanks. Through enormous concentrated effort, we might stop a dam on one river; meanwhile, a dozen other dams would be built. If the production of an American SST was halted, European SSTs would land at American airports. If an energy crisis developed, rather than signaling the limits of planetary resources, or the absurdity of the way we lived, it produced new drives toward nuclear power and more strip mines.

We were not the only ones with this problem. The Vietnam War was halted, but the arms race and military aid to rightwing regimes advanced. Nixon was thrown out, but government reform came down to a lame Senate ethics bill. Unemployment was growing and welfare lines with it, yet in the end economic reform measures always seemed to hurt the very segments of the population they purported to help while the rich got richer.

One young activist told me, "We seem to be running on a

treadmill; as we advance, we are always in the same place."

Every issue had to be fought as though it were the first one. People seemed unable to connect one issue to another, to find common threads in, say, a struggle against high-rise office buildings and nuclear power plants and colonial wars. Specific victories were possible, but overall understanding of the forces that were moving society seemed to be diminishing.

People's minds seemed to be running in dogged, one-dimensional channels which reminded me of the freeways, office buildings and suburbs that were the physical manifestations of the same period. Could one be affecting the other? Could life within these new forms of physical confinement produce mental confinement? For the first time, I began to think this might be possible.

We were told we had the highest literacy rate in the history of the world and the best-informed population, and yet the information seemed to be less well processed. As mass media grew until it too became a kind of environment, I began to think that it might not really be contributing to any pool of useful knowledge.

I was confused by this emerging perception and at first took a traditional view of what needed to be done. It meant we all had to work harder to reach more people with every message. Since in any specific struggle we might be outspent by several hundred times, we needed to be more clever, more creative.

That led me to think that the problem was too much information. The population was being inundated with conflicting versions of increasingly complex events. People were giving up on understanding anything. The glut of information was dulling awareness, not aiding it. Overload. It encouraged passivity, not involvement.

Then I began seeing some amazing statistics about television.

The Replacement of Experience

The first really shocking burst of figures appeared in newspapers in the early 1970s.

It was reported that in the generation since 1945, 99 percent of the homes in the country had acquired at least one television set. On an average evening, more than 80 million people would be watching television. Thirty million of these would be watching the same program. In special instances, 100 million people would be watching the same program at the same time.

The average household had the set going more than six hours a day. If there was a child, the average was more than eight hours. The average person was watching for nearly four hours daily. And so, allowing eight hours for sleep and eight hours for work, roughly half of the adult nonsleeping, nonworking time was spent watching television. Considering that these were average figures, they meant that half of the people in this country were watching television even more than that.

As these numbers sank in, I realized that there had been a strange change in the way people received information, and even more in the way they were experiencing and understanding the world. In one generation, out of hundreds of thousands in human evolution, America had become the first culture to have substituted secondary, mediated versions of experience for direct experience of the world. Interpretations and representations of the world were being accepted as experience, and the difference between the two was obscure to most of us.

I heard many people say, "Television is great; there are so many things on TV that we'd never otherwise experience." People were seeing television images of Borneo forests, European ballets, varieties of family life, distant police actions, current events, or re-creations of historical crises, and they were believing themselves to be experiencing these places, people and events. Yet the television image of the Borneo forest or the news or historical events was surely not the experience of them and not to be relied upon to the same extent. It was only the experience of sitting in a darkened room, staring at flickering light, ingesting images which had been edited, cut, rearranged, sped up, slowed down, and confined in hundreds of ways. Were people aware of the difference?

Despite my work in advertising, I had never yet made any thorough investigation of the power of images themselves. I did not know how people's minds related to imagery, whether they could separate one kind of image—that which is directly experienced—from another kind, which has been processed and altered, and which arrives out of context. It was not clear whether people ascribed the same credibility to both, either consciously or subconsciously, and how this changed the quality of their understanding.

Nonetheless, it was obvious to me from my own work that something was going wrong with what people were understanding and what they weren't. A new muddiness of mind was developing. People's patterns of discernment, discrimination and understanding were taking a dive. They didn't seem able to make distinctions between information which was preprocessed and then filtered through a machine, and that which came to them whole, by actual experience. Perhaps seeing was believing in a way that overrode the conscious mind. At the same time, no one was even writing about how the machine changed the information. Very few people understood it. Only advertisers studied the way the machine altered data, because it was the basic work of advertising to alter and confine information *in advance* so that it would have the desired effect. Hundreds of thousands of dollars were spent discovering how to do this.

Slowly I began to see how the ubiquitousness of television, combined with a general failure to understand what it did to

25

information, might affect the political work we were doing. If people were believing that an *image* of nature was equal to or even similar to the experience of nature, and were therefore satisfied enough with the image that they did not seek out the real experience, then nature was in a lot bigger trouble than anyone realized. Or, if people believed that images of historical events or news events were equal to the events or were even close approximations of them, then historical reality was in big trouble. As television became the major mental and physical experiential field for most of the people in the country, as it began to merge with environment, the confusion of television information with a wider, direct mode of experience was advancing rapidly.

The Unification of Experience

Because so many of us were confusing television experience with direct experience of the world, we were not noticing that experience itself was being unified to the single behavior of watching television. Switching from channel to channel, believing that a sports program was a significantly different experience from a police program or news of an African war, all 80 million viewers were sitting separately in dark rooms engaged in exactly the same activity at the same time: watching television.

It was as if the whole nation had gathered at a gigantic three-ring circus. Those who watched the bicycle act believed their experience was different from that of those who watched the gorillas or the flame eater, but everyone was at the circus. Worse, as we all watched from our separate living rooms, it was as if we sat in isolation booths, unable to exchange any responses about what we were all going through together. Everybody was engaged in the same act at the same time, but we were doing it alone.

What a bizarre situation!

26

It was suddenly possible for an entire nation of 200 million people to be spoken to as individuals, one to one, the television set to the person or family, all at once. I was chilled at the thought, realizing that these conditions of television viewing—confusion, unification, isolation, especially when combined with passivity and what I later learned of the effects of implanted imagery—were ideal preconditions for the imposition of autocracy.

At that time, however, my own definitions of the nature of autocracy were confined, like those of most Americans, to the model of single, charismatic leaders. Hitler. Stalin. Chiang. Franco. Mao. Differences among these were submerged in the model of the powerful leader, enforcing his will, ruling absolutely. *That* was autocracy. Television seemed to be the perfect instrument to help bring on that kind of control.

My fears were encouraged one day in 1971, as I sat around my office reading the morning *New York Times* and noted a small item. It concerned a Pentagon proposal to President Nixon that an electronic gadget be attached to every television set in the country. Capable of being activated directly by the president, it would switch on every set in the country at once. It was to be used, of course, only in case of extreme national emergency. My mind flew into a paranoid pattern:

It's 4:00 A.M. Two hundred million people are awakened by the national anthem. Where is it coming from? What's that light over there? It's the TV set. There's the President!

"My fellow Americans, it is with extreme regret that I awaken you from your well-earned rest. Yet we are all met with a crisis so grave as to require it.

"An exhaustive investigation by your law enforcement agencies has uncovered a massive conspiracy to destroy our democracy, a conspiracy which enjoys at least the tacit support of thousands of students, journalists, attorneys and even certain judges and elected officials.

"As your Commander in Chief, I have ordered the immediate arrest of the terrorists and the individuals in their support groups, whatever their official rank or prestige.

"I have also invoked the implied powers of the President to govern in such times of grave crises, free of the usual encumbrances.

"I am hopeful and confident that these emergency measures, taken to safeguard our democracy, will be short-lived.

"Thank you, Godspeed and good night."

The set switches off by itself. Was that a dream? Back to sleep.

A few months later I saw a follow-up story in the *Times* that said the Pentagon proposal had been scrapped. Apparently the administration felt people might "misinterpret the intentions" of such a project.

In retrospect, I know that my scenario was fantastic and unsophisticated, deriving from my simpleminded notion that autocratic interventions can take place only through a single leader or a coup. But whatever the intentions of the Pentagon and President Nixon, who has since asserted that presidents may create their own laws, it was clear that the existence of the technology itself had created a new potential.

We can all be spoken to at the same time, night or day, from a centralized information source. In fact, we are. Every day, a handful of people speak, the rest listen. Brutal and heavy-handed means of confining awareness, experience and behavior may actually be a thing of the past. In many ways, television makes the military coup and mass arrests of my imagination unnecessary. We can begin to grasp the irrelevance of such acts now that a more subtle coup is underway.

It takes place directly inside the minds, perceptions and living patterns of individual people. A technology makes it possible, and perhaps inevitable, while dulling all awareness that it is happening.

II

WAR TO CONTROL THE UNITY MACHINE

MARSHALL McLuhan did not help us very much in our early efforts to understand television. By the time he was popular in the mid-1960's we had already been through the Army-McCarthy hearings, the Kennedy-Nixon debates and then the Kennedy funeral which had plugged eighty million people into the same experience at the same time.

None of these events had caused the slightest ripple of alarm, but rather produced a rush to praise our new electronic unity. The mass viewing of the funeral, particularly, was hailed in religious terms, like some kind of breakthrough in the evolution of consciousness: everybody unified in grief, transcending the conditions of their individual lives. Human ingenuity had now advanced to the point where technology could produce a nationwide, one-mind experience, previously thought to reside only in the realm of the mystic.

McLuhan, who saw so much, could have helped us see through that crap. Instead, because of his celebration of our electronic connection, our planetary-tribal village, he effec-

29

tively encouraged support for the techno-mystical-unification theme.

His words entered the arena of talk show patter and word-play. "Hot and cool." "The medium is the message." People struggled to find concrete meaning in these phrases. They became the basis of hundreds of conferences and thousands of cocktail party debates. Most people were satisfied that they understood something if they grasped that, because of tele-vision, we were now vibrating together to the same electronic drumbeat. Joyful at what looked like a new and positive unity, we failed to perceive, nor did McLuhan help us become con-scious of three critical facts, 1) it was only one drumbeat, 2) this drum could be played only by a handful of players, 3) the identity of the players was determined by the tech-nology itself.

McLuhan is not a person who presents his arguments in political terms, so perhaps he can be forgiven for failing to drop the other shoe, to tell us what should have been the most urgent meaning of the medium. Perhaps he was as dazzled as the rest of us mortals, suffering the same reaction to this new technology as the deer staring at the headlights of the on-coming car. Like the religious one-minders before him, he drew no distinctions between one sort of unification and an-other, leaving the rest of us to sort it out. But we didn't.

At that moment, anyone interested in social, psychological, educational or political processes should have dropped every-thing and begun intensive study of the effects of this new phenomenon which was capable of unifying everyone within a new, reconstructed experience. Instead, all factions saw it opportunistically.

Everyone with a message to deliver—government, corpo-rations, the military, community groups, gurus, teachers and psychologists—began drooling at the possibility of gaining access to this incredible machine that could put pictures into millions of people's heads at once. It was clear that as life increasingly moved away from the streets, community centers and marketplaces, one message on television—thirty seconds on the Cronkite news—was worth more than a thousand hours of organizing or whistle-stop political touring or hundreds of newspaper ads.

A war began for control of the machine and its use. All competing factions shared the idea that if they could gain access to it, television could communicate their message as well as any other, that television technology was only a neutral instrument. Intent on changing other people's minds, they did not consider that television might change those who used it. All joined in an implicit conspiracy to increase the use of television.

Advancing from the Sixties to the Fifties

My own feelings about the effects of television began to progress beyond the Nixon-Pentagon sort of fantasy as I observed its effects on community groups and Movement people who, believing in its neutrality, sought to use it.

I watched and participated as they changed their organizations' commitments from community organizing, legal reform processes or other forms of evolutionary change to focus upon television. Educational work was sacrificed to public relations work. The goal became less to communicate with individuals, governments or communities than to influence media. Actions began to be chosen less for their educational value or political content than for their ability to attract television cameras. Dealing directly with bureaucracies or corporations was frustrating and fruitless. Dealing with communities was slow. Everyone spoke of *immediate* victory.

A hierarchy of press-oriented actions developed. Press conferences got coverage once. Rallies brought more attention than press conferences. Marches more than rallies. Sit-ins more than marches. Violence more than sit-ins.

31

A theory evolved: Accelerate the drama of each successive action to maintain the same level of coverage. Television somehow demanded that. As the stakes rose, the pressure mounted to create ever more outrageous actions.

The movements of the 1960s had become totally media based by the 1970s. The most radical elements were up to the challenges of the theory of accelerated action. They "advanced" to kidnappings, hijackings, bombings. The sole purpose of these actions was often no more than media exposure.

Sensing that television was now the country's main transmitter of reality, individuals began to take personal action to affect it.

A young Chicano man hijacked a plane to obtain a five-minute TV interview about the ill treatment of his people.

A young man in Sacramento took some bank employees hostage so that a TV news team would report that neither he nor his father could get a job.

Lynette Fromme shot at President Ford, she said, so the media would warn big business to cease destroying the planet.

The SLA kidnapping of a newspaper heiress signaled the final stage of abstraction. It exhibited a warped genius in that it allowed the SLA to demand successfully that their communiqués would be published unedited.

However, because it owed its whole life to the media, existing nowhere else, the SLA was subject to cancellation at any time, and it was cancelled most thoroughly, like a series with slipping ratings getting the ax.

Less radical elements did not suffer the SLA's dramatic demise, but the cycle of fast rise/fast fall was similar for many. Ralph Nader bloomed in the media and then became tiresome. The ecology movement, fitting the holocaust model of TV news, burst upon the scene and then declined. Watergate excited expectations of government reform, but then it was old news.

Once the U.S. was out of Vietnam, the once hot antiwar

movement was off the tube. A few years later Jimmy Carter was able to appoint some of the architects of the war to high positions in government. It was as though the war hadn't happened, or was merely another action-packed drama, replaced by next season's schedule, with the same actors playing new, equally believable, roles.

Meanwhile, those seriously committed Movement people of the 1960s who were not willing to go on to terrorism began dropping out, moving to farms in Vermont and Oregon. Or, and I know many who have done this, they got jobs writing television serials. They justified this with the explanation that they were still reaching "the people" with an occasional revolutionary message, fitted ingeniously into the dialogue.

"The people," however, were as they had been for years, sitting home in their living rooms, staring at blue light, their minds filled with TV images. One movement became the same as the next one; one media action merged with the fictional program that followed; one revolutionary line was erased by the next commercial, leading to a new level of withdrawal, unconcern and stasis. In the end, the sixties were revealed as the flash of light before the bulb goes out. The seventies became an advanced version of the fifties. And as we shall see in Chapter Seven, it was all made inevitable by the thirties.

Style Supersedes Content

The changes wrought upon movements by the emergence of television were similar to the changes in traditional political process.

Richard Nixon, probably the first major public figure to understand television deeply, realized that four hours of TV debate with Kennedy had turned probable victory into slim defeat. He understood that TV appearances were more important than personal ones. By the time he ran again, he had revised his image. He became the "new Nixon."

Even though many people understood that his change was only cosmetic, he won. This confirmed for me the idea that something in the nature of television imagery allows form to supersede content. Once elected, Nixon made his first appointments—Ziegler and Haldeman—from advertising, the field that pioneered conveying pseudocontent in place of substance.

By his third campaign, Nixon appeared *only* on television; never in public. McGovern, meanwhile, made the mistake of trying to deliver "content" through a medium predisposed to resist it.

Having used the media so well, Nixon developed a fatal arrogance about it. He and Agnew may have been right in claiming that their various transgressions were nothing special in American political history. But like the SLA, they forgot that they themselves were media illusions. The gravest mistake that can be made by a media creature is to assault the machine. The machine doesn't care about its fantasies. A new one will do. Bringing Nixon down was just as good for ratings as supporting him. Better. More action. The only goals of the machine are to continue to be the real power behind the throne, no matter who is king, and to remain the primary factor in all public perception. Television has the power to create presidents, and it has the power to destroy them.

Lyndon Johnson apparently also understood this power. So fiercely did he desire to dominate television that he kept three sets going in his offices at all times. He never succeeded in controlling mass media, but he did have a few dazzling moments. For example, the Gulf of Tonkin incident never happened, but it was carried as legitimate by every news outlet. That convinced both Congress and the public and gave Johnson the approval he needed to escalate the Vietnam War.

This event was later exposed as only one of the many non-events pushed through the media to sell us that war. It occurred to me that the very fact that this could be done at all—fictional news about fictional military events expanding faraway wars that no one watching the images could observe firsthand—was cause for serious alarm about the power of the media to pursue fictitious realities.

Johnson was finally done in by his personal style. It turned out to be better television to caricature his way of speaking and his bawdy behavior, to make him a cartoon or folk character than to present him in a favorable light.

By the 1976 campaign, politicians had to become successful media artists or fail politically. That campaign was unique in that it displayed no content at all, only form. It was a contest between images and advertising stereotypes.

We were offered the charismatic Western hero, charming and brave though an underdog: Reagan. The truth-saying revivalist in corporate packaging: Carter. The guru, speaking aphorisms, standing for a new, albeit aggressive, consciousness like David Carradine's *Kung Fu* hero: Brown. The old reliable, trusted, venerable warrior in the image of Cronkite: Humphrey. And the President, a television image merely by virtue of being president, investing himself with an apparent authority based solely on that image: Ford.

All of the candidates found their vote-getting power in their images and left content out as confusing and irrelevant. They were correct to do this. As we shall see, a campaign run on content could not possibly work on television.

Carter learned the lesson well. In May 1977, *The New York Times* released an entertaining Carter memo which showed that his organization consciously formalized his re-election plans to emphasize style over content. Carter already uses television as it has never been used before, delivering his homespun appeals directly to the people at home in their living rooms *before* dealing with Congress or journalists. His talents for leadership, already sharpened from the evangelist model he started with, are growing with his knowledge of technology.

During the years that television was coming into its own as the central factor in American personal and political life, its basic nature and the effects it had on human beings and their institutions were rarely examined. The problems that people did discuss were concentrated in three main areas: commercialism, access and programming.

Thinking that television could be reformed so that its potential for good would be realized, media reformers sought new laws, government control and regulatory policies. I was among the media workers who fought to limit the domination of advertisers and the effect of advertising on network policies. We worked to offset the emphasis on ratings, an emphasis detrimental to the needs of the public. Many of us fought for access channels so community groups could offer an occasional alternative to the consumer society. We hoped that in this way all segments of society, and all points of view, would gain access to the public mind, fulfilling what looked like a democratic potential of the medium.

Others fought on other fronts. Psychologists, parents' groups and educators lobbied against the dominance of sensational, superficial, irrelevant and violent programs. They sought programs with "prosocial values." They especially wanted new emphasis on humanistic and educational shows for children. These groups saw no reason why such values as cooperation, loving and caring could not be as appropriate for television programming as violence and competition.

It went on and on. Historians lobbied for more documentaries, believing that television had no greater inherent limits to its ability to present historical truth than the media that had preceded it. They succeeded in getting legislation requiring that TV networks permanently store their news and documentary footage. Now we can look to a future in which the present era will be understood in terms of the television treatment of it.

Ecologists assumed television could be a potentially useful tool in expanding knowledge of how our species interacts with natural forces.

Political radicals believed television could stimulate deeper understanding of complex issues.

Indian groups believed it was possible to build sensitivity to their culture and philosophy through TV. They shared this belief with other groups that sought civil rights—blacks, homosexuals, women's groups and so on.

At some point in the early 1970s, I began to be at odds with the assumption that television was the ideal medium for all these groups. I noticed that, unlike commercial advertising messages, many of these alternative views somehow didn't work on television. They lost body, became "flat." Aside from this, it was clear that while the organizations were focusing all their communications efforts through television, they themselves were being negatively affected.

One day in 1971, I raised the point with two different groups. One was seeking the educational reform of colleges, and the other was lobbying for new neighborhood zoning laws.

I told them that I felt their intense desire to attract television coverage was damaging their organizations and that they were failing to get their message through anyway. They were losing their roots, their grounding. I wondered aloud if more wasn't being lost than gained.

The answer was, "Listen, everybody's watching television. We can reach everyone if we handle things the right way."

I pointed out that when a message is squeezed through a

twenty-second news spot, so much can be lost that what is left will fail to move anyone enough to make them turn off the set and actually do something. Meanwhile, the viewers will believe that they have learned everything they need to know on that subject and will be bored the next time they hear it.

Each group responded the same way. They brought up the civil rights and antiwar movements. These surely "worked" on television, so what was I trying to say? This stopped the discussion both times.

Only later did I understand that both the civil rights and antiwar movements were exceptions which proved the point. Adopting confrontational tactics in an escalating cycle of action and reaction, they got extensive coverage and became the model for all movements seeking rapid success.

But should *all* movements use such tactics to get their time on the tube? Were the street demonstrations and violent clashes that produced television coverage for some movements appropriate for neighborhood or educational reformers? For ecologists? For consumer groups? The handicapped? Perhaps so. They certainly brought the cameras out. But what became of their messages when groups did this? What became of the organizations? Finally, what did this suggest about the so-called neutral, or even benign, nature of the medium? Did this not mean that television, in effect, was determining the style and content (or lack thereof) of all political action, that movements were becoming derivative of the needs of the technology?

I didn't know the answer to these questions, and I realized that no one else seemed to be even addressing them.

But what really drove me onward to investigate television was an experience I had while working with the Hopi Indians. I think it will be worth describing this experience in its full detail because its complexity is part of its point.

Television at Black Mesa

It was during the summer of 1972, just as I was closing down Freeman, Mander and Gossage, that I was asked to help some traditional Hopi elders who were fighting a strip mine on their reservation at Black Mesa, Arizona.

Black Mesa was sacred ground to the traditional Hopis. To rip it open and remove its contents was a violation of their most ancient religious tenets.

The problem at Black Mesa was typical of what has happened on many Indian reservations. The traditional Hopi Indians had always refused to deal with the Bureau of Indian Affairs, which functions as overlord on all reservations, and so they had been pushed aside. In their stead, the Bureau had created a tribal council composed mainly of Indians who no longer lived on the reservation. The tribal council members were not really even Hopis anymore; they were Mormons. Most had moved to Salt Lake City, had businesses there, and returned to the reservation only for their council meetings. They agreed with the BIA that their job was to sell off Indian resources and land at the best possible price, thereby helping Indian people turn into Americans more quickly. The sale of strip mine rights to a coal company was simply part of the logic of this process.

The traditional "government" which had preceded the tribal council was not really a government at all. It was a kind of informal grouping of religious leaders from the dozens of independent clans which together formed the Hopis. They did not sit in a hierarchical arrangement over the rest of the Hopis; they functioned more as teachers or as guides to the religious conceptions.

The religion itself was based on what we would now think of as ecological laws of balance. The land was alive, the

39

source of life. To rip it up and ship away its contents was so outrageous as to be unthinkable. To the Mormon-American Hopis, however, strip mines were indeed thinkable.

Eventually the traditionals realized that while they were ignoring the BIA and the tribal council, the land was being destroyed and the religion with it. The elders decided to fight. To fight they needed to learn white legal systems, white tactics, and white means of manipulating media. To learn these, they had to restructure their minds and conceptions. And so to fight the enemy, the traditional Hopis began the process of self-destroying what remained of their own Indianness.

At some point television news discovered the struggle. Network crews were flown out from Hollywood. They shot images of the deserts, images of the fifty-foot cranes, images of the older men and women standing picturesquely near their kivas. Following the network news guidelines for "good television" they sought a "balanced report." They interviewed members of the Bureau of Indian Affairs, members of the tribal council, and representatives of the coal company, all of whom discussed the issues in terms of contracts, rights, jobs and energy.

These opinions were juxtaposed with shots of some of the elderly Hopis, standing in the desert, speaking of the Great Spirit being represented in all things.

The newsmen added some footage of Hopi sacred dances and some images of the Hopi's most spiritual place, the kiva. The elders limited how far the reporters could go into their religion. It is against the Hopi religion, for example, to allow ceremonies and "power objects" to be photographed. The elders felt that to photograph these things "steals their aura." (As we will see in Chapter Fourteen, this may not be a silly notion.) They also felt that exposing their ceremonies to people who have not been trained to understand them—a process that takes Hopi apprentices many years—would undermine the meaning of the ceremonies.

A week later, I watched the report on television. It got four minutes on the evening news. It was an earnest report. The reporters revealed that their sympathies lay with the traditionals, but they had created—as they had no choice but to do—a formula story: Progress vs. Tradition. Forty million Americans obtained their first, and perhaps only, views of the Hopi people in the form of images of cranes juxtaposed with Indians in suits and ties, responsible government officials concerned about jobs, and a lot of old savage-looking types in funny clothes, talking about a religion which says that to dig up the land is dangerous for the survival of every creature on the planet. These forty million viewers also saw a white, modishly dressed TV newsman explain the crosscurrents in the struggle, and plaintively ask whether something of an earlier culture couldn't be permitted to remain. "From Black Mesa, Arizona, this is John Doe reporting." This was followed by a commercial for Pacific Gas and Electric on the growing energy crisis and the need to tap all energy resources. The next story on the news was about a bank robbery.

I turned off the television set and wondered what effect this story had had on viewers. Did it help the Hopis? Would any good come from it?

It was certain that the old people had not come through as well as the businessmen, the government officials and the reporter's objective, practical analysis. The old people just seemed tragic, and a little silly, if poignant. They were attempting to convey something subtle, complex, foreign and ancient through a medium which didn't seem able to handle any of that and which is better suited to objective data, conflict and fast, packaged information.

I wondered, had I been shooting that story myself for the evening news, if I could have done a better job of it. Could I

have been able to explain to white America that to care about
what was going on down there they would have to have cared
about the Hopi perception of reality; the Hopi mind and its
integration with natural forces? Viewers would have had to
care about the landscape, the spaces, the time, the wind, the
color, the feel of the land and the sacred places and things.
How could I have conveyed something through the medium
so that anyone would have cared, when everyone was sitting
at home in darkened living rooms, watching television? It
was time travel that needed to be conveyed. How could I
have carried a viewer from home through time and space to
another reality which can only make sense if experienced directly? I decided that my report would have been no better
than this Hollywood crew's had been. In fact, theirs was
probably as good as could have been done within the limits
of the medium. But in the end, the Hopis were hurt, not
helped. Their struggle was revealed, perhaps, but they themselves were further fixed into the model of artifact. The
medium could not be stretched to encompass their message.

On the other hand, what if I had four minutes, or even
one minute, to convey the essence of a product? A car? A
stereo set? A toy? Could I accomplish that efficiently?

I certainly could. It suddenly became obvious to me that a
product is a lot easier to get across on television than a desert
or a cultural mind-set.

Understanding Indian ways enough to care about them
requires understanding a variety of dimensions of nuance and
philosophy. You don't need any of that to understand a product, you do not have problems of subtlety, detail, time and
space, historical context or organic form. Products are inherently communicable on television because of their static quality, sharp, clear, highly visible lines, and because they carry
no informational meaning beyond what they themselves are.
They contain no life at all and are therefore not capable of

dimension. Nothing works better as telecommunication than images of products. Might television itself have no higher purpose?

The Illusion of Neutral Technology

Most Americans, whether on the political left, center, or right, will argue that technology is neutral, that any technology is merely a benign instrument, a tool, and depending upon the hands into which it falls, it may be used one way or another. There is nothing that prevents a technology from being used well or badly; nothing intrinsic in the technology itself or the circumstances of its emergence which can predetermine its use, its control or its effects upon individual human lives or the social and political forms around us.

The argument goes that television is merely a window or a conduit through which any perception, any argument or reality may pass. It therefore has the potential to be enlightening to people who watch it and is potentially useful to democratic processes.

It will be the central point of this book that these assumptions about television, as about other technologies, are totally wrong.

If you once accept the principle of an army—a collection of military technologies and people to run them—all gathered together for the purpose of fighting, overpowering, killing and winning, then it is obvious that the supervisors of armies will be the sort of people who desire to fight, overpower, kill and win, and who are also good at these assignments: generals. The fact of generals, then, is predictable by the creation of armies. The kinds of generals are also predetermined. Humanistic, loving, pacifistic generals, though they may exist from time to time, are extremely rare in armies. It is useless to advocate that we have more of them.

If you accept the existence of automobiles, you also accept the existence of roads laid upon the landscape, oil to run the cars, and huge institutions to find the oil, pump it and distribute it. In addition you accept a sped-up style of life and the movement of humans through the terrain at speeds that make it impossible to pay attention to whatever is growing there. Humans who use cars sit in fixed positions for long hours following a narrow strip of gray pavement, with eyes fixed forward, engaged in the task of driving. As long as they are driving, they are living within what we might call "roadform." Slowly they evolve into car-people. McLuhan told us that cars "extended" the human feet, but he put it the wrong way. Cars *replaced* human feet.

If you accept nuclear power plants, you also accept a techno-scientific-industrial-military elite. Without these people in charge, you could not have nuclear power. You and I getting together with a few friends could not make use of nuclear power. We could not build such a plant, nor could we make personal use of its output, nor handle or store the radioactive waste products which remain dangerous to life for thousands of years. The wastes, in turn, determine that *future* societies will have to maintain a technological capacity to deal with the problem, and the military capability to protect the wastes. So the existence of the technology determines many aspects of the society.

If you accept mass production, you accept that a small number of people will supervise the daily existence of a much larger number of people. You accept that human beings will spend long hours, every day, engaged in repetitive work, while suppressing any desires for experience or activity beyond this work. The workers' behavior becomes subject to the machine. With mass production, you also accept that huge numbers of identical items will need to be efficiently distributed to huge numbers of people and that institutions such as advertising will arise to do this. One technological process cannot exist without the other, creating symbiotic relationships among technologies themselves.

If you accept the existence of advertising, you accept a system designed to persuade and to dominate minds by interfering in people's thinking patterns. You also accept that the system will be used by the sorts of people who like to influence people and are good at it. No person who did not wish to dominate others would choose to use advertising, or choosing it, succeed in it. So the basic nature of advertising and all technologies created to serve it will be consistent with this purpose, will encourage this behavior in society, and will tend to push social evolution in this direction.

In all of these instances, the basic form of the institution and the technology determines its interaction with the world, the way it will be used, the kind of people who use it, and to what ends.

And so it is with television.

Far from being "neutral," television itself predetermines who shall use it, how they will use it, what effects it will have on individual lives, and, if it continues to be widely used, what sorts of political forms will inevitably emerge. These will be the subjects taken up in the main body of this book.

Before the Arguments: A Comment on Style

Before going on with the four arguments, I think it will be useful to remark that they involve a deliberate change in pace from what you have read till now. This introduction was written to move along the surface from point to point fairly quickly, à la *television-time,* as it were. Its purpose was to give you a rapid summary of my own changing perspectives on the medium, up to the moment I began to feel that there was much more to the problem than I understood, leading me temporarily to quit all other activities and delve further into television.

It was only after a long while and many half-steps of change in viewpoint that I finally faced the fact that television is not reformable, that it must be gotten rid of totally if our society is to return to something like sane and democratic functioning. So, to argue that case, especially considering that it involves a technology accepted as readily and utterly as electric light itself, is not something that ought to be done rapidly or lightly. Nor can such a case be confined to the technology itself, as if it existed aside from a context.

What follows, therefore, proceeds in what might be called *book-time* through four dimensions of television's role and impact. Each of them can be observed separately from the others, but they also intertwine and overlap each other.

The first argument is theoretical and environmental. It attempts to set the framework by which we can understand television's place in modern society. Yet, this argument is *not* about television itself. In fact, television will be mentioned only occasionally. It is about a process, already long underway, which has successfully redirected and confined human experience and therefore knowledge and perceived reality. We have all been moved into such a narrow and deprived channel of experience that a dangerous instrument like television can come along and seem useful, interesting, sane and worthwhile at the same time it further boxes people into a physical and mental condition appropriate for the emergence of autocratic control.

The second argument concerns the emergence of the controllers. That television would be used and expanded by the present powers-that-be was inevitable, and should have been predictable at the outset. The technology permits of no other controllers.

The third argument concerns the effects of television upon individual human bodies and minds, effects which fit the purposes of the people who control the medium.

The fourth argument demonstrates that television has no

democratic potential. The technology itself places absolute limits on what may pass through it. The medium, in effect, chooses its own content from a very narrow field of possibilities. The effect is to drastically confine all human understanding within a rigid channel.

What binds the four arguments together is that they deal with aspects of television that are not reformable.

What is revealed in the end is that there is ideology in the technology itself. To speak of television as "neutral" and therefore subject to change is as absurd as speaking of the reform of a technology such as guns.

FOUR
ARGUMENTS
FOR THE
ELIMINATION
OF
TELEVISION

ARGUMENT ONE

THE
MEDIATION
OF
EXPERIENCE

As humans have moved into totally artificial environments, our direct contact with and knowledge of the planet has been snapped. Disconnected, like astronauts floating in space, we cannot know up from down or truth from fiction. Conditions are appropriate for the implantation of arbitrary realities. Television is one recent example of this, a serious one, since it greatly accelerates the problem.

III

THE WALLING
OF
AWARENESS

DURING a six-month period in 1973, *The New York Times* reported the following scientific findings:

A major research institute spent more than $50,000 to discover that the best bait for mice is cheese.

Another study found that mother's milk was better balanced nutritionally for infants than commercial formulas. That study also proved that mother's milk was better for human infants than cow's milk or goat's milk.

A third study established that a walk is considerably healthier for the human respiratory and circulatory systems, in fact for overall health and vitality, than a ride in a car. Bicycling was also found to be beneficial.

A fourth project demonstrated that the juice of fresh oranges has more nutritional value than either canned or frozen orange juice.

A fifth study proved conclusively that infants who are touched a lot frequently grow into adults with greater self-confidence and have a more integrated relationship with the world than those who are not touched. This study found that touching, not merely sexual touching, but *any* touching of one person by another, seemed to aid general health and even mental development among adults as well as children.

The remarkable thing about these five studies, of course, is that anyone should have found it necessary to undertake them. That some people did find them necessary can only mean that they felt there was some uncertainty about how the answers would turn out.

And yet, anyone who has seen a mouse eating cheese or who has been touched by the hand of another person already knows a great deal about these things, assuming he or she gives credence to personal observation.

Similarly, anyone who has ever considered the question of artificial milk versus human milk is unlikely to assume that Nestle's or Similac will improve on a feeding arrangement that accounted for the growth of every human infant before modern times.

That any people retain doubts on these questions is symptomatic of two unfortunate conditions of modern existence: Human beings no longer trust personal observation, even of the self-evident, until it is confirmed by scientific or technological institutions; human beings have lost insight into natural processes—how the world works, the human role as one of many interlocking parts of the worldwide ecosystem—because natural processes are now exceedingly difficult to observe.

These two conditions combine to limit our knowledge and understanding to what we are told. They also leave us unable to judge the reliability or unreliability of the information we go by.

The problem begins with the physical environment in which we live.

Mediated Environments

When he was about five years old, my son Kai asked me, "Daddy, who built Mt. Tamalpais?"

Kai's question shocked me. I said, "Nobody built Mt. Tam-alpais; it grew up out of the Earth thousands of years ago. No person could build a mountain."

I don't think this satisfied him, but it did start me on a new train of thought.

I think that was the first moment that I really looked around at the urban world in which he and I and the rest of our family and the majority of the people in this country live. I wanted to know how he could have gotten the notion that human beings are responsible for the construction of mountains. I soon realized that his mistaken impression was easy to understand; it was one that we all share on a deeper level.

Most Americans spend their lives within environments created by human beings. This is less the case if you live in Montana than if you live in Manhattan, but it is true to some extent all over the country. Natural environments have largely given way to human-created environments.

What we see, hear, touch, taste, smell, feel and understand about the world has been processed for us. Our experiences of the world can no longer be called direct, or primary. They are secondary, mediated experiences.

When we are walking in a forest, we can see and feel what the planet produces directly. Forests grow on their own without human intervention. When we see a forest, or experience it in other ways, we can count on the experience being directly between us and the planet. It is not mediated, interpreted or altered.

On the other hand, when we live in cities, no experience is directly between us and the planet. Virtually all experience is mediated in some way. Concrete covers whatever would grow from the ground. Buildings block the natural vistas. The water we drink comes from a faucet, not from a stream or the sky. All foliage has been confined by human considerations and redesigned according to human tastes. There are no wild animals, there are no rocky terrains, there is no cycle of bloom and decline. There is not even night and day. No food grows anywhere.

Most of us give little importance to this change in human experience of the world, if we notice it at all. We are so surrounded by a reconstructed world that it is difficult to grasp how astonishingly different it is from the world of only one hundred years ago, and that it bears virtually no resemblance to the world in which human beings lived for four million years before that. That this might affect the way we think, including our understanding of how our lives are connected to any nonhuman system, is rarely considered.

In fact, most of us assume that human understanding is now more thorough than before, that we know more than we ever did. This is because we have such faith in our rational, intellectual processes and the institutions we have created that we fail to observe their limits.

I have heard small children ask whether apples and oranges grow in stores. "Of course not," we tell them. "Fruit grows from the ground somewhere out in the countryside, and then it's put into trucks and brought to the stores."

But is this true? Have you seen that? Do you have a sense that what you are eating was once alive, growing on its own?

We learn in schools that fruit grows from the ground. We see pictures of fruit growing. But when we live in cities, confined to the walls and floors of our concrete environments, we don't actually see the slow process of a blossom appearing on a tree, then becoming a bud that grows into an apple. We learn this, but we can't really "know" what it means, or that a whole cycle is operating: sky to ground to root through tree to bud ripening into fruit that we can eat. Nor do we see particular value in this knowledge. It remains an idea to us, an abstraction that is difficult to integrate into our consciousness without direct experience of the process. Therefore we don't develop a feeling about it, a caring. In the end how can our children or we really grasp that fruit growing from trees has anything to do with humans growing from eating the fruit?

We have learned that water does not really originate in the pipes where we get it. We are educated to understand that it comes from sky (we have seen that, it is true!), lands in some faraway mountains, flows into rivers, which flow into little reservoirs, and then somehow it all goes through pipes into the sinks in our homes and then back out to—where? The ocean.

We learn there is something called evaporation that takes the water we don't need up to the sky. But is this true? Is there a pattern to it? How does it collect in the sky? Is it okay to rearrange the cycle with cloud seeding? Is it okay to collect the water in dams? Does anyone else need water? Do plants drink it? How do they get it? Does water go into the ground? In cities it rolls around on concrete and then pours into sewers. Since we are unable to observe most of the cycle, we learn about it in knowledge museums: schools, textbooks. We study to know. What we know is what we have studied. We know what the books say. What the books say is what the authors of the books learned from "experts" who, from time to time, turn out to be wrong.

Everyone knows about night and day. Half the time it's dark, half the time it's light.

However, it doesn't work that way in our homes or outside in the streets. There is always light, and it is always the same, controlled by an automatic switch downtown. The stars are obscured by the city glow. The moon is washed out by a filter of light. It becomes a semimoon and our awareness of it inevitably dims.

We say it is night, but darkness moods and feelings lie dormant in us. Faced with *real* darkness, we become frightened, overreact, like a child whose parents have always left the light

57

on. In three generations since Edison, we have become creatures of light alone.

❖   ❖

One evening during 1975, I went with my family to a small
park in the middle of San Francisco to watch a partial eclipse
of the moon. We saw it rise above the buildings, but it had
little power. Hundreds of street lamps, flashing signs, and
lighted buildings intruded. The street lamps, those new mercury-vapor arcs that give off a harsh pinkish-white light, were
the worst problem. It was difficult to feel anything for the
moon seen through this pinkish filter. The children became
bored. We went for an ice cream.

Later that same evening, I went alone to a different park
on a high hill. I imagined the city lights gone dark. I turned
them off in my mind. Without the buildings diverting me, I
gained the briefest feeling for how the moon must have been
experienced by human beings of earlier centuries, why whole
cultures and religions were based upon it, how they could know
every nuance of its cycle and those of the stars, and how they
could understand its connection with planting times, tides, and
human fertility.

Only recently has our own culture produced new studies
confirming the moon's effect on our bodies and minds, as well
as its effect on plants. Earlier cultures, living without filters, did
not need to rediscover the effects. People remained personally
sensitive to their connections with the natural world. For most
of us, this sensitivity and knowledge, or science, of older
cultures is gone. If there are such connections, we have little
awareness of them. Our environment has intervened.

Not long after the eclipse I just described, my wife, Anica,
was told by her ninety-year-old grandmother that we should
not permit our children to sleep where the moonlight could

bathe them. Born in preindustrial Yugoslavia and having spent most of her life without technology, the old woman said the moon had too much power. One night, our oldest son, Yari, who was eight at the time, spent an evening at a friend's house, high on a hill, sleeping near a curtainless south-facing window. He called us in the morning to tell us of a disturbing thing that had happened to him during the night. He had awakened to find himself standing flush against the window, facing the full moon. He had gotten out of bed while still asleep, walked over to the window, and stood facing the moon. Only then did he wake up. He was frightened, he said, more by the oddness of the experience than any sense of real danger. Actually, he thought it rather special but didn't like having an experience different from what is expected and accepted, which is *not* to experience the power of the moon. He had been taught that what he had just been through couldn't happen; he wished it hadn't and it hasn't since.

Yari, like most of the rest of us, does not wish to accept the validity of his personal experience. The people who define the moon are now the scientists, astronomers and geologists who tell us which interactions with the world are possible and which are not, ridiculing any evidence to the contrary. The moon's cycle affects the oceans, they say, but it doesn't affect the body. Does that sound right to you? It doesn't to me. And yet, removed from any personal awareness of the moon, unable even to see it very well, let alone experience it, how are we to know what is right and what is wrong? Most of us cannot say if, this very evening, the moon will be out at all.

Perhaps you are a jogger. I am not, but friends have told me how that experience has broken them out of technologically created notions of time and distance. I have one friend in San Francisco who runs from his Russian Hill apartment to Ocean Beach and then back again, every morning. This is a distance of about eight miles. There was a time, he told me, when the idea of walking, or bicycling that distance seemed impossible to him. Now the distance seems manageable, even easy. Near, not far. He has recovered a personal sense of distance.

I have made similar discoveries myself. Some years ago I decided to walk to work every day instead of driving. It changed getting to work into a pleasurable experience—no traffic jams or parking hassles—and I would stop now and then for coffee and a chat with a friend. More important, it changed my conception of distance. My office was twenty blocks from my home, about a thirty-minute walk. I noticed that walking that distance was extremely easy. I hadn't known that my previous conception of twenty blocks was one which technology had created. My knowledge was car-knowledge. I had become mentally and physically a car-person. Now I was connecting distance and range to my body, making the conception personal rather than mechanical, outside myself.

On another occasion, while away on a camping trip with my two children, I learned something about internal versus institutional-technological rhythm.

The three of us were suffering an awful boredom at first. My children complained that there was nothing to *do*. We were all so attuned to events coming along at urban speed in large, prominent packages, that our bodies and minds could not attune to the smaller, more subtle events of a forest.

By the second day, however, the children began to throw rocks into a stream and I found myself hearing things that I hadn't heard the day before: wind, the crunch of leaves under foot. The air was somehow clearer and fresher than it seemed to have been the day before. I began to wander around, aimlessly but interestedly.

On the third day, the children began to notice tiny creatures. They watched them closely and learned more about their habits in that one day than I know even now. They were soon imitating squirrels, birds, snakes, and they began to invent some animals.

By the fourth day, our urban-rhythm memory had given way to the natural rhythms of the forest. We started to take in all kinds of things that a few days before we hadn't noticed were there. It was as if our awareness was a dried-out root system that had to be fed.

Returning to the city a few days later, we could feel the speedup take place. It was like running to catch up with a train.

Sensory-Deprivation Environments

The modern office building is the archetypal example of the mediated environment. It contains nothing that did not first exist as a design plan in a human mind. The spaces are square, flat and small, eliminating a sense of height, depth and irregularity. The decor is rigidly controlled to a bland uniformity from room to room and floor to floor. The effect is to dampen all interest in the space one inhabits.

Most modern office buildings have hermetically sealed windows. The air is processed, the temperature regulated. It is always the same. The body's largest sense organ, the skin, feels no wind, no changes in temperature, and is dulled.

Muzak homogenizes the sound environment. Some buildings even use "white noise," a deliberate mix of electronic sounds that merge into a hum. Seemingly innocuous, it fills the ears with an even background tone, obscuring random noises or passing conversations which might arouse interest or create a diversion.

The light remains constant from morning through night, from room to room until our awareness of light is as dulled as our awareness of temperature, and we are not aware of the passage of time. We are told that a constant level of light is good for our eyes, that it relieves strain. Is this true? What about the loss of a range of focus and the many changes in direction and intensity of light that our flexible eyes are designed to accommodate?

Those who build artificial environments view the senses as single, monolithic things, rather than abilities that have a range of capacity for a reason. We know, for example, that our eyes can see from the extremely dark to the extremely bright, from far to near, from distinct to indistinct, from obvious to subtle. They perceive objects moving quickly and those that are still. The eye is a wonderfully flexible organ, able to adjust instantly to a dazzling array of information, constantly changing, multi-leveled, perceiving objects far and near moving at different speeds simultaneously. A fully functioning visual capacity is equal to everything the natural environment offers as visual information. This would have to be so, since the interaction between the senses and the natural environment *created* the ranges of abilities that we needed to have. Sight did not just arrive one day, like Adam's rib; it coevolved with the ingredients around it which it was designed to see. When our eyes are continually exercised, when flexibility and dynamism are encouraged, then they *are* equal to the variety of stimuli that night and day have to offer. It is probably not wise always to have "good light" or to be for very long at fixed distances from anything. The result will be lack of exercise and eventual atrophy of the eyes' abilities.

When we reduce an aspect of environment from varied and multidimensional to fixed, we also change the human being who lives within it. Humans give up the capacity to adjust, just as the person who only walks cannot so easily handle the experience of running. The lungs, the heart and other muscles have not been exercised. The human being then becomes a creature with a narrower range of abilities and fewer feelings about the loss. We become grosser, simpler, less varied, like the environment.

The common response to this is that if we lose wide-spectrum sensory experience, we gain a deeper mental experience. This is not true. We only have less nonmental experience so the mental life seems richer by comparison. In fact, mental life is more enriched by a fully functioning sensory life.

In recent years, researchers have discovered some amazing things about the connections between mental and physical life by doing sensory-deprivation experiments. In such experiments, a human subject is cut off from as much sensory information as possible. This can be accomplished, for example, by a totally blank environment—white walls, no furniture, no sounds, constant temperature, constant light, no food and no windows. A more thorough method is to put the blindfolded subject inside a temperature-controlled suit floating in a water tank with only tubes to provide air and water, which are also at body temperature. This sensory-deprivation tank eliminates the tactile sense as well as an awareness of up and down.

Researchers have found that when sensory stimuli are suppressed this way, the subject at first lives a mental life because mental images are the only stimulation. But after a while, these images become disoriented and can be frightening. Disconnected from the world outside the mind, the subject is rootless and ungrounded.

If the experience goes on long enough, a kind of madness develops which can be allayed only by reintroducing sensory stimuli, direct contact with the world outside the subject's mind.

Before total disorientation occurs, a second effect takes place. That is a dramatic increase in focus on any stimulus at all that is introduced. In such a deprived environment, one single stimulus acquires extraordinary power and importance. In the most literal sense, the subject loses perspective and cannot put the stimulus in context. Such experiments have proven to be effective in halting heavy smoking habits, for example, when the experimenter speaks instructions to stop smoking or describes to the subject through a microphone the harmful, unpleasant aspects of smoking.

These experiments have shown that volunteers can be programmed to believe and do things they would not have done in a fully functional condition. The technique could be called brainwashing.

It would be going too far to call our modern offices sensory-deprivation chambers, but they are most certainly sensory-reduction chambers. They may not brainwash, but the elimination of sensory stimuli definitely increases focus on the task at hand, the work to be done, to the exclusion of all else. Modern offices were designed for that very purpose by people who knew what they were doing.

If people's senses were stimulated to experience anything approaching their potential range, it would be highly unlikely that people would sit for eight long hours at desks, reading memoranda, typing documents, studying columns of figures or pondering sales strategies. If birds were flying through the room, and wind were blowing the papers about, if the sun were shining in there, or people were lolling about on chaise lounges or taking baths while listening to various musical presentations, this would certainly divert the office worker from the mental work he or she is there to do. In fact, if offices were so arranged, little business would get done. This is why they are not so arranged. Any awareness of the senses, aside from their singular uses in reading and sometimes talking and listening, would be disastrous for office environments that require people to stay focused within narrow and specific functional modes.

Feeling is also discouraged by these environments. Reducing sensual variations is one good way of reducing feeling since the one stimulates the other. But there is also a hierarchy of values which further the process. Objectivity is the highest value that can be exhibited by an executive in an office. Orderliness is the highest value for a subordinate office worker. Both of these are most easily achieved if the human is effectively disconnected from the distractions of her or his senses, feelings and intuitions.

With the field of experience so drastically reduced for office workers, the stimuli which remain—paper work, mental work, business—loom larger and obtain an importance they would not have in a wider, more varied, more stimulating environment. The worker gets interested in them largely because that is what is available to get interested in.

Curiously, however, while eschewing feeling and intuition, business people often cannot resist using them. They come out as aberrations—fierce competitive drive, rage at small inconveniences, decisions that do not fit the models of objectivity. Such behavior in business sometimes makes me think of blades of grass growing upward through the pavement.

A more poignant example, perhaps, is that modern offices have proven to be such hot sexual environments. Aside from the occasional potted plant, the only creatures in offices with which it is possible to experience anything are other humans. With all other organic life absent and with the senses deprived of most possibilities for human experience, the occasional body which passes the desk becomes an especially potent sensual event, the only way out of the condition of suspended experience, and the only way to experience oneself as alive. In fact, the confinement of human beings within artificial environments may be a partial explanation of our new culture-wide obsession with and focus on sex.

I have been speaking mainly of cities. This has only been because their effects are most obvious. I don't want to create the impression that suburbs, retirement communities, recreational communities and the like offer any greater access to a wider range of experience.

Those places do have large trees, for example, and more small animals. The sky is more visible, without giant buildings to alter the view. But in most ways, suburban-type environments reveal less of natural processes than cities do. Cities, at least, offer a critical ingredient of the natural world, diversity, albeit a diversity that is confined to only human life forms. It does not nearly approach the complexity of any acre of an ordinary forest.

In suburbs the totality of experience is plotted in advance and then marketed on the basis of the plan. "We will have everything to serve the recreational needs of your family: playgrounds, ball fields, golf course, tennis courts, bowling alleys and picnic grounds." This, plus a front lawn, a back lawn, two large trees, and an attentive police force makes up the total package. Human beings then live inside that package.

Places formerly as diverse as forest, desert, marsh, plain and mountain have been unified into suburban tracts. The human senses, seeking outward for knowledge and stimulation, find only what has been prearranged by other humans.

In many ways the same can be said of rural environments. Land which once supported hundreds of varieties of plant and animal life has been transformed by agribusinesses. Insect life has been largely eliminated by massive spraying. For hundreds of square miles, the only living things are artichokes or tomatoes laid out in straight rows. The child seeking to know how nature works finds only spray planes, automated threshers, and miles of rows of a single crop.

Rooms inside Rooms

There are differences of opinion about what the critical moments were that led human beings away from the primary forms of experience—between person and planet—into secondary, mediated environments. Some go back as far as the control of fire, the domestication of animals, the invention of agriculture or the imposition of monotheism and patriarchy.

In my opinion, however, the most significant recent moment came with the control of electricity for power, about four generations ago. This made it possible to begin moving nearly all human functions indoors, and made the outdoors more like indoors.

In less than four generations out of an estimated one hundred thousand, we have fundamentally changed the nature of our interaction with the planet.

Our environment no longer grows on its own, by its own design, in its own time. The environment in which *we* live has been totally reconstructed solely by human intention and creation.

We find ourselves living inside a kind of nationwide room. We look around it and see only our own creations.

We go through life believing we are experiencing the world when actually our experiences are confined within entirely human conceptions. Our world has been thought up.

Our environment itself is the manifestation of the mental processes of other humans. Of all the species of the planet, and all the cultures of the human species, we twentieth-century Americans have become the first in history to live predominantly inside projections of our own minds.

We live in a kind of maelstrom, going ever deeper into our own thought processes, into subterranean caverns, where nonhuman reality is up, up, away somewhere. We are within a system of ever smaller, ever deeper concentric circles, and we consider each new depth that we reach greater progress and greater knowledge.

Our environment itself becomes an editor, filter and medium between ourselves and an alternative nonhuman, unedited, organic planetary reality.

We ask the child to understand nature and care about it, to know the difference between what humans create and what the planet does, but how can the child know these things? The child lives with us in a room inside a room inside another room. The child sees an apple in a store and assumes that the apple and the store are organically connected. The child sees streets, buildings and a mountain and assumes it was all put there by humans. How can the child assume otherwise? That is the obvious conclusion in a world in which all reality *is* created by humans.

As adults, we assume we are not so vulnerable to this mistake, that we are educated and our minds can save us. We "know" the difference between natural and artificial. And yet, we have no greater contact with the wider world than the child has.

Most people still give little importance to any of this. Those who take note of these changes usually speak of them in esoteric, aesthetic or philosophical terms. It makes good discussion at parties and in philosophy classes.

As we go, however, I hope it will become apparent that the most compelling outcome of these sudden changes in the way we experience life is the inevitable political one.

Living within artificial, reconstructed, arbitrary environments that are strictly the products of human conception, we have no way to be sure that we know what is true and what is not. We have lost context and perspective. What we know is what other humans tell us.

Therefore, whoever controls the processes of re-creation, effectively redefines reality for everyone else, and creates the entire world of human experience, our field of knowledge. We become subject to them. The confinement of our experience becomes the basis of their control of us.

The role of the media in all this is to confirm the validity of the arbitrary world in which we live. The role of television is to project that world, via images, into our heads, all of us at the same time.

IV

EXPROPRIATION
OF
KNOWLEDGE

A T the moment when the natural environment was altered beyond the point that it could be personally observed, the definitions of knowledge itself began to change. No longer based on direct experience, knowledge began to depend upon scientific, technological, industrial proof.

Scientists, technologists, psychologists, industrialists, economists and the media which translate and disseminate their findings and opinions became our source. Now they tell us what nature is, what we are, how we relate to the cosmos, what we need for survival and happiness, and what are the appropriate ways to organize our existence.

There is little wonder, therefore, that we should begin to doubt the evidence of our own experience and begin to be blind to the self-evident. Our experience is not valid until science says it is. (Mother's milk is healthy!)

It is also of little wonder that we feel removed from participation in most of the larger issues which shape our lives. We feel removed because we *are* removed.

As we continue to separate ourselves from direct experience of the planet, the hierarchy of techno-scientism advances. This creates astounding problems for a society that is supposed to be democratic.

In democracies, by definition, all human beings should have a say about technological developments that may profoundly change, even threaten, their lives: nuclear power, genetic engineering, the spread of microwave systems, the advance of satellite communications, and the ubiquitous use of computers, to name only a few. And yet, in order to participate fully in discussions of the implications of these technologies one must have training in at least physics, psychology, biology, philosophy, economics, and social and political theory. Any of these technologies has profound influence in all those areas. Because most of us are *not* so trained, all discussion takes place among our unelected surrogates, professionals and experts. They don't have this full range of training either, but they do have access to one or another area of it and can speak to each other in techno-jargon—"tradeoffs," "cost-benefits," "resource management"—and they therefore get to argue with each other over one side of the question or the other while the rest of us watch.

That their technological training and the language they use excludes from their frame of reference a broader, more subtle system of information and values rarely seems to occur to them.

The alternative to leaving all discussion to the experts would be to take another route entirely. That would be to define a line beyond which democratic control—which is to say full participation of the populace in the details of decisions that affect all of us—is not possible, and then to say that anything which crosses this line is taboo. Yet, the notion of taboo is itself taboo in our society, and the idea of outlawing whole technologies is virtually unthinkable.

San Francisco ecologist Gil Baillie, in a brilliant article in the 1975 edition of *Planet Drum,* argues that taboo systems of earlier cultures were not quite the darkly irrational frameworks we now believe them to have been. Most often they reflected knowledge taken from nature and then modified by human experience over time. Their purpose was to articulate and preserve natural balances in a given area or within a given group of people at a particular time. They were statements about when too far is too far. This sensitivity to natural balances, which was the basis of virtually every culture before our own, has now been suppressed by our modern belief that science and technology can solve all problems and that, therefore, all technologies which can be created ought to be. The question of natural balance is now subordinated. Evolution is defined less in terms of planetary process than technological process. The planet and its information are now considered less relevant than human ingenuity, an idiotic and dangerous error shielded from exposure only by the walls of previous assumption and the concrete of the physical forms within which we live.

Ivan Illich, a leading critic of the expropriation of knowledge into a nether world of experts and abstraction, argues in *Medical Nemesis* that professional medicine may be causing more harm than good. We go to doctors as we go to mechanics. They speak a language that remains impenetrable to us. We take their cures on faith.

Illich remarks that this may be producing more illness than cure: It has separated people from knowledge about keeping themselves healthy, a knowledge that was once ingrained in the culture. Although some of our techno-scientific methods work, some do not, and the doctors who use them may not understand them or may be inexpert in their use. The doctors, Illich believes, are also taking the validity of techno-medicine on faith. *Their* source is usually the chemical and drug industry, which has a stake in disrupting natural healing methods. How else could they sell their chemicals?

Direct Education

As a child I wondered how human beings learned which plants were edible and which were not. How did our ancestors learn about poisons, or cures for poisons, without any doctors around? I assumed it was trial and error because that was the way it was explained to me. A group of cave people or Indians came upon a new plant. One of them tasted it and keeled over dead. That's how they knew not to eat that plant again. Doubtless this was one method, but from what I can gather this "taste method" was not the primary means for acquiring this knowledge. It certainly could not account for the finely detailed knowledge Indians have of plants.

How was an Indian to know that eating juniper berries would make one's liver function better, one's skin color change and one's energy increase? None of these effects could be immediately apparent. The effects might take days or weeks or longer. And yet they knew it.

Writing in the Winter 1975 edition of *Indigena*, a Brazilian Indian woman, Carmem de Novais, reports that the Indian people of the Amazon jungle "have been able to identify, locate and use plants for curing specific ailments as well as for arrow poisons and fish-stunning substances." While Western science has not yet arrived at a chemical contraceptive that does not harm women, she says, "the Amazon people have been using medicinal plants as a successful contraceptive method for many thousands of years.

"The medicines developed and produced through 'modern technology' are usually extracted from medicinal herbs and plants. The major sources of information about plants and their medicinal uses are the people who live in harmony and very close to the cycles of Mother Earth. The drug companies would take many years if they were to research all the plants by themselves in an attempt to discover their medicinal uses." De Novais mentions Indian medicines such as coca, ipecac, quinine, curare, among others, and traces how some of these led to anesthetics such as procaine and novocaine, and to cures for amebic dysentery, malaria, heart disease, and poisons, and to treatments for nerve disorders, epilepsy and others. All of these were first used by Indians.

"The drug companies secure an adequate supply of the basic plant material, sometimes buying off Indian land for production, and sell the drugs derived from these plants to the world and to the people who first told them about them as well," de Novais notes. "They make great profits from their 'discoveries' without any monetary reward to the Indians from whom they acquired their 'drug secret.'" Quite the opposite in fact. By taking over the land and turning the Indians into laborers, while introducing the money system and imposing Western-style medicine, the drug companies put the Indians in the position of having to buy the medicines they formerly had in abundance.

The question remains: How did the Indians know about the curative powers of plants in the first place?

While researching the portion of this book that deals with the consequences of humans ingesting as much artificial light as we do now, particularly television light, I came upon an odd report in the *New England Journal of Medicine*. A team of doctors discovered that infant jaundice could be cured by ordinary sunlight. This discovery led to a spurt of articles on the possibility that natural light might be healthy for humans. What a revelation!

The doctors had undertaken their study of the effects of sunlight on jaundiced infants when a day nurse remarked that the infants near the open window were improving faster than those who were away from it. Then, while working on the study, someone discovered that over seven thousand years ago, Egyptians treated jaundiced infants by placing them in the sunlight and feeding them an herb that had a beneficial interaction with the sun's rays.

The article did not ask, but I couldn't help wondering how the Egyptians, stranded back there in time, discovered this important effect of sunlight and herb on jaundice without grants from the National Science Foundation.

One explanation for the knowledge of earlier cultures, expounded by such people as the popular German writer Erich Von Daniken, is that humans—white with red hair—had arrived from outer space and taught the ignorant savages everything they knew. This kind of explanation, aside from its implicit racism and its entertainment value, is an indication of how far we all are from understanding knowledge systems that are based on direct experience.

Recently, I had the chance to see some time-lapse films of plants by Dr. John Ott. Time-lapse photography makes it possible to see plants moving. It reveals them constantly straining for light like baby birds with their mouths open. Tendrils climb, crawl and wave around. Stems swell, inflate, then relax, like an inhaling and exhaling lung. Plants vibrate and pulsate in response to the immediate condition of their environment.

In one particular sequence, passionflowers blossomed in an excruciating process of slowly mounting intensity. The bud began to turn into a flower, the petals took form and slowly burst out from the bud that contained them. Suddenly there was another burst of energy as the petals released themselves upward, stretching and straining every tiny tip, exhibiting a fullness of expression clearly analogous to orgasm and what even looked like plant pleasure.

From this perspective, it is obvious that plants are alive in more or less the way humans and other animals are. Our failure to see plants as living creatures, and to appreciate ourselves as some kind of sped-up plant, is the result of limited human perception, a sign of the boundaries of our senses or the degree to which we have allowed them to atrophy, *or* the

74

fact that we have become too speedy to perceive the slower rhythms of other life forms.

It is a cliché among naturalists that *the* most critical ingredient of their work is patience. The researcher has to slow down sufficiently to wait and wait and watch until cycles of activity which were previously invisible become visible. The longer one waits, and the slower one's rhythms, the more one is able to perceive the tiny details of natural growth.

Pretechnological peoples do not have to go through a slowing-down process. Surrounded by nature, with everything alive everywhere around them, they develop an automatic intimacy with the natural world. Beyond intimacy, there is the sense that events of the forest, or desert, are not actually separate from oneself, that humans are just part of a larger living creature: the planet. This was not merely a way of speaking for Indian peoples; it was a definite fact. They meant it and would give evidence of it. Things that grow are put into our bodies so that we grow. The air goes into us and out. The water goes through us. Warm air outside warms us inside and vice versa. We can imagine that we are *not* connected to things in this way only when our connections are blocked, altered or stunted.

For Indian people, the plants, weather, terrain, soil, water, and their interactions were part of the body of which they themselves were also a part. They experienced these natural forces as they did themselves.

In *Wizard of the Upper Amazon* F. Bruce Lamb records the apparently true account of Manuel Cordova de Rios, a Peruvian rubber cutter, kidnapped by the Amaheuca Indians for invading their territory and forced to remain with them for many years. Rios describes the way the Indians learned things about the jungle, which was both the object of constant study and the teacher. They observed it first as individuals, experiencing each detail. Then they worked out larger patterns together as a group, much like individual cells informing the larger body, which also informs the cells.

In the evenings, the whole tribe would gather and repeat each detail of the day just passed. They would describe every sound, the creature that made it and its apparent state of mind. The conditions of growth of all the plants for miles around were discussed. This band of howler monkeys, which was over here three days ago, is now over there. Certain fruit trees which were in the bud stage three weeks ago are now bearing ripe fruit. A jaguar was seen near the river, and now it is on the hillside. It is in a strangely anguished mood. The grasses in the valley are peculiarly dry. There is a group of birds that have not moved for several days. The wind has altered in direction and smells of something unknown. (Actually, such a fact as a wind change might not be reported at all. Everyone would already know it. A change of wind or scent would arrive in everyone's awareness as a bucket of cold water thrown on the head might arrive in ours.)

Rios tells many of the Indian stories concerned with "personalities" of individual animals and plants, what kinds of "vibrations" they give off. Dreams acted as additional information systems from beyond the level of conscious notation, drawing up patterns and meanings from deeper levels. Predictions would be based on them.

Drugs were used not so much for changing moods, as we use them today, but for the purpose of further spacing out perception. Plants and animals could then be seen more clearly, as if in slow motion (time lapse), adding to the powers of observation, yielding up especially subtle information as to how plants worked, and which creatures would be more likely to relate to which plants. An animal interested in concealment, for example, might eat a plant which tended to conceal itself.

Reading these accounts made it clear to me that all life in

the jungle is constantly aware of all other life in exquisite detail. Through all this, the Indians gained information about the way natural systems interact. The observation was itself knowledge. Depending on the interpretation, the knowledge might or might not become reliable and useful.

Each detail of each event had special power and meaning, understood as part of a larger pattern of activities and forces. The understanding was so complete that it was only the rare event that could *not* be explained—a twig cracked in a way that did not fit the previous history of cracked twigs—that was cause for concern and immediate arming.

Rios recounted the way the Indians would capture and kill pigs. They knew that the pigs were led by a single sow, and that they walked through the forest in a very widely dispersed, but specific, fanned-out pattern behind the lead sow, much as birds fly through the air in formation. The Indians knew that killing the lead sow would throw the others into a state of confusion while they worked out who the new lead sow would be. During the confusion, the Indians would kill a few pigs, being careful *not* to kill any emerging leaders. Instead, they would allow the new lead sow to emerge and lead the surviving band out of danger. Then they would take the dead leader, and cut off her head. They would plant the head just below the surface of the ground, facing in a specific direction *exactly*. If they did this just so, the entire band would return to that exact spot in precisely three moons. If they erred in any minute detail of the procedure, the band would not return, and the Indians would have to hunt for a new band.

Rios saw this work many times. No one ever asked why it worked so well; the knowledge of it was merely passed down, generation to generation, and there was always plenty of pig to eat.

Many books written by Indian people describe another method by which knowledge of plants and animals could be amplified and integrated into the observer, directly, physically: emulation. By imitating a creature, "getting inside" it, one learns to understand it better. A person imitates a plant's stance and movements, its behavioral characteristics, in order to be as it is, to integrate its mood and character into herself or himself.

This is often done tribally, or personally, in dances and ceremonies, and includes not only plants and animals but also the attitudes of wind, rain and other people.

Indian literature as well as the literature (what we call "myth") of pretechnological people, including our own European ancestors, is filled with stories of humans turning into wolves, bears, birds, snakes, or insects, in order to circumvent some otherwise insurmountable difficulty by using the knowledge of the appropriate creature. If stealth were the capacity human beings needed, a way of gaining knowledge of stealth would be to observe stealthy creatures—panthers, for example —and then imitate them. If instant strike from repose was desired as a protective ability, then the cobra was a good model. If calmness and flow were sought, observe streams. If airiness or lightness were wanted, imitate the butterfly.

Indians did not name people after particular creatures from some kind of charming aesthetic sense—Many White Buffalo, Crazy Horse, Sitting Bull. The animals and natural elements that were part of the names had concrete observable characteristics: strength, constancy, agility, slyness, fierceness and so on. Nature was not only a metaphor for human behavior, nature was literally a teacher. The way animals solved problems, or the way they moved or otherwise behaved, became the model for human behavior.

Even today, imitation and emulation inform human behavior. We read that Muhammad Ali says, "I dance like a butterfly, sting like a bee." By using such phrases, he mentally associates his own movements with those of the creatures. While he cannot behave exactly as they can, he does probably succeed in integrating some creaturely movement into himself. Of course, if he had never seen a butterfly or a bee, he could not learn anything from them.

The imitative process is automatic with children. They imitate whatever is around: parents, cats, dogs, insects, plants, cars, each other, and whatever images are delivered through the media. Of course, imitating the animal seen in the media image is not the same as imitating the animal seen in the forest.

To achieve their exquisitely detailed knowledge of the world around them, human beings living in nonmediated environments had to use all their abilities to observe themselves, the planet, and the things that grow from it. They might not have even considered the planet to be something that was actually outside them since their senses told them it was also inside them. Their world was organized along flow lines, not in separate and distinct boxes.

Knowledge results from personal experience and direct observation—seeing, hearing, touching, tasting and smelling. These are aided by several inward systems. There is instinct, for example, gathered by innumerable previous generations and carried forward in the cells. There is intuition, what Eastern religions call "knowing without seeing." In addition there are feelings, which may have been informed by prior experience. All of these—the five senses plus instinct, intuition, feeling and thought—combine to produce conscious awareness, the ability to perceive and describe the way the world is organized. Western people like to think of these human qualities as separate from one another and some as more "real" than others. Yet all of the abilities interact both between person and planet and among each other. One sense interacts with another sense, the senses interact with feelings. Intuition functions together with instinct, thought flows constantly in and out of all experience. The fully functional human being can be understood as a kind of microcosmic ecosystem inside a wider eco-system inside a wider one and so on, all systems flowing in and out of each other. As with other systems, when one thing is altered, the overall balance is altered. Changes in one aspect of human perception or experience affect all others.

When a person has all senses fully operative, we call the person "sensitive." People who live in environments that stimulate the full sensory range from the most subtle to the most obvious are more sensitive than those who don't. The senses developed in interaction with the multiple patterns and influences of the natural environment; no sensual capacity was developed by accident. No sense maintains itself if it is not used. If a sense remains unused, it atrophies.

In 1969 my wife and I visited several of the small islands that make up the larger area that colonists named Micronesia. Most of these islands are so small and so remote—hundreds of miles from each other—that many of their native cultures remain largely intact although there is an increasing U.S. military and business presence there.

On one island, we met a man who had a small motorboat. He had been to school in Hawaii, had lived in Los Angeles for a time and spoke good English. He offered to take us for a ride into the ocean to visit some tiny islands he knew about. This required taking one of two routes past the coral reef that surrounded the island. He gave us a choice. One route took many hours to where there was a break in the reef; the other way, he told us, was to follow the pattern of the waves until they are organized just so. Then he would leap the reef with the boat. We decided to go along with him on this latter route.

When we got to the island, he succeeded in spearing a few fish. We built a small fire, and he threw the fish directly into the flames. After a few minutes, he reached into the fire with his hands and turned them over. I asked him if reaching into the fire like that didn't hurt. He answered, "It hurts a little bit." We were becoming more interested in this man.

Then he started talking about the reef, a favorite subject. We asked him why he walked around on the reef with bare feet when we had been warned always to wear thick-soled sneakers because of a poisonous starfish that can deliver a painful and sometimes paralyzing wound.

He then told us words to this effect: "Yes, but if you step on one all you have to do is pick it up, turn it over, and place its underside directly on your wound. It will suck its own poison back out of you."

We asked him how he knew that, and he said, "Everybody around here knows that. Whenever there is something poisonous its antidote is never more than a few yards away. Everybody knows this. It's the same everywhere."

We asked him about his life during those years in the big cities of the world, and his story was like any story of any Indian who leaves home to participate in the life of the "developed" world. It was about fights, miserable jobs, jail, and drunkenness. Detailed knowledge of wind, rain, sun and stars only got in his way. It would have been far better for survival in *our* world to suppress those observations and to develop mental agility, persuasiveness, charm, guile and aggression.

Naïvely, we asked why he chose to sacrifice his island life for cities and for this he had no answer, except to say that his own response to cars and machines reminded him of the way the fish becomes stunned by the glint of the diver's metal face mask. At last he had come back to the island, where he remained, hoisted between cultures.

Motel Education

In 1974 I was one of thirty "leading environmental educators" invited to attend a conference at Ann Arbor,

Michigan, jointly sponsored by the Environmental Education Program of the School of Natural Resources of the University of Michigan and the Division of Technology and Environmental Education of the U.S. Department of Health, Education and Welfare.

The goal of this conference was to provide guidelines to the government on how to grant money for environmental education projects. We thirty people would decide what is good and effective environmental education and what is not. We had four days to do this.

I arrived to discover that the meeting place was a motel outside of Ann Arbor, sandwiched between two freeways. If we wished to go anywhere, we had to do so by car. The rooms we slept in had windows which did not open; they offered twenty-four-hour air conditioning or heating. The rooms in which the meetings themselves were held had no windows at all. The light was fluorescent.

The motel had a swimming pool under a glass roof. Artificial palm trees were arranged around the pool area. The glass roof did not open, but there were lounge chairs here and there and portable sunlamps on wheels.

The talk at the conference was in techno-newspeak. We spoke of "educational delivery systems," "value tradeoffs," "checklists," "guidelines," "needs assessments," "target groups," "cost effectiveness," "impact strategies" and, of course, my specialty, "education of and through the media."

During the second day of the conference, a small group of the participants interrupted the proceedings to point out that we were all receiving an environmental education directly from our environment of windowless rooms, blank walls, and fluorescent lights. While we spoke of teaching others about an organic environment out there somewhere, the artificial environment that we were in was teaching us that nature was irrelevant, separate from us, and of only intellectual value. The natural environment, if it existed for us anywhere, was only in our minds, in our memories. Our failure to recognize that this was important signified that a widespread aberration of mind had proceeded further than we preferred to believe. It was useless for us to speak of making other people sensitive to environmental values when we, a group of so-called leaders, were satisfied with an environment which totally excluded the organic environment, and did not even notice that condition.

A biologist in her sixties stood up and gave an impromptu lecture, pointing out that a serious distortion had taken place in the very concept of education, and that we were all examples of it. I will paraphrase what she said:

"There are objective educational processes in which rational modes operate. Reading a textbook certainly does transmit a kind of knowledge, but there are also subjective informational-receptive modes. Walking through forests is different from attending classes on forests because each offers information of an entirely different sort; classes on forests can never help us 'relate' to forests, or to *care* about them at all. Only being in one can accomplish that, just as the only way to know what dancing is about is to dance.

"When we are inside these motel walls, we begin to think the natural world has nothing to teach us. We environmentalists suffer the same distorted notion of education that all Western people do. We think of education as objective, quantifiable and verbal. Our own words become our basis.

"As a result we don't have a sense of the rightness or wrongness of each new technological wonder. We hear about a 'green revolution' which will feed the starving millions and we buy the expert's word, just as everyone else does. Without any experience with natural balance, we forget that things grow only so fast. If you accelerate the process artificially, something is lost.

"We read studies by scientists which say that the ozone layer is safe despite aerosols, and we read other studies by scientists which say the ozone layer is in danger. We wonder which is true? Which scientists are correct? But this wondering signifies that we have sold out our instinctive knowledge. Obviously, any artificial alteration of the ozone layer changes the volume of radiation which reaches the planet, and is harmful.

"We read that the whales are beaching themselves and we wonder why. Scientists tell us that the leader whale may have parasites in its brain, goes crazy and leads the others to the beach. Millions of people read this story and find it logical, because their knowledge of whales is confined to the length, weight, mating habits, breeding grounds, commercial uses, and optimum sustainable yield. And yet, the Solomon Islanders have long descriptions of whales and dolphins beaching themselves every year for thousands of years. The islanders say it is a human-animal communications ritual, part of a cycle which is obscure to us. I don't know if *they* are right either. I do know that whales don't have leaders—they operate in groups—and given their brain size they are probably the most intelligent mammals on Earth. I don't believe it's a parasite problem."

She concluded by saying that we have "put all of our eggs into a single basket; we have assumed that empirical objectified processes produce knowledge equal to what the environment offers as information. We have assumed our knowledge is growing. I'm not so sure."

Her speech was received with polite interest. There was general agreement that her statement was both moving and inspired—she was a grand old lady—but there was also considerable embarrassment at the silliness and romanticism of the idea that the environment—whether windowless walls, or rivers—itself teaches. Teachers teach. Education is cerebral not sensory. It was our role to help the teachers know what to teach. We were the ones who know.

The participants agreed it would have been better if the conference had been in a location nearer to nature. It would have been more *pleasant* that way. (That's what nature is: pleasant!) But as long as we were here on this important mission, we might just as well get on with the work and cease with the diversions.

One year later, I received a 548-page bound volume called an "instrument" which summarized the "emerging issues in environmental education" with details of the findings of the "experts" at this landmark meeting. The instrument was submitted to the Office of Environmental Education which, for all I know, may still be using it today.

If so, then I suppose we all will have furthered the process of moving knowledge away from natural sources and deeper into the realm of the expert. This, in turn, makes it easier for government and industry to expropriate it, alter it, and feed it back to us through the media in techno-jargon explicable only to techno-minds. With nature obscured, nearly everything we know comes to us processed and it may be right or it may be wrong. We know only what we're told. For most of us the TV news is now our source. Without any basis of comparison, as the news report changes, our understanding changes.

Mother's milk is unsanitary. Mice like cheese. Mars has life on it. Technology will cure cancer. The stars do not influence us. Nuclear power is safe. Nuclear power is not safe. Mars has no life on it. Food dyes are safe. Saccharin is safe. Technology causes cancer. Columbus proved the world was round. A little X ray is okay. The Vietnam War was not a civil war. We will have an epidemic of swine flu. Mother's milk is healthy. Technology will clean up pollution. Preservatives do not cause cancer. Economic growth is in the offing. Red food dyes are not safe. Swine flu vaccine is safe. The Vietnam War was a civil war. Hierarchy is natural. Humans are the royalty of nature. Saccharin is not safe. Swine flu vaccine causes paralysis. We have the highest standard of living. Hormones in beef cause cancer. Touching children is good for them. Too much sun causes cancer. And so it goes.

V

ADRIFT
IN
MENTAL SPACE

MANY people who experiment with mind-manifesting drugs report that while under the influence they begin to "see" the world, especially the human-made technological forms that dominate cities, as absurd and alien. People who take LSD commonly "freak out" in the presence of heavy traffic, sterile environments, abrasive sounds, or mechanical things and smells. They often describe these experiences of everyday life as "unreal."

It is part of the LSD literature that "bad trips" are more likely to occur in urban than in natural environments. Setting is critically important. People are urged to keep objects around from which they gain feelings of comfort, to play music which has been familiar and friendly in the past, or to have close friends nearby and to stay in physical contact with them. Hugging is highly recommended if the friend is deeply trusted. So are warm baths and personal conversation. These elements can accomplish what is called "grounding," meaning contact which is undeniably real, not abstract, not interpreted, not artificial, not open to question.

The radical psychiatrist R. D. Laing, among others, has said that the growing incidence of mental illness these days may be explained in part by the fact that the world we call real and which we ask people to live within and understand is itself open to question. The environment we live in is no longer connected to the mix of planetary processes which brought us all into being. It is solely the product of human mental processes. It is real, but only in the way that a theatrical play or a fun house is real. Our artificial environment is there and we can experience it, yet it has been created on purpose by other humans. It is an interpretation of reality, it no longer reveals how nature works and it cannot provide much useful information to human beings who seek to see their own lives as part of some wider natural process. We are left with no frame of reference untouched by human interpretation.

Living within this environment ultimately foists upon us a bizarre choice between two equally disconnected realities. We may decide to accept as real our artificially reconstructed human environment, ignoring that it is an arbitrary re-creation, and accepting this interpretation of reality as our own. Or we may recoil from it, allowing ourselves to see our new environment as a stage set or a series of false fronts. This is the way the schizophrenic often describes the world. Those who make the latter choice risk the dangers inherent in trying to understand the world solely through their own isolated internal mental processes.

Either choice, acceptance or rejection, separates us from the possibility of interacting with and learning from the organic reality which exists outside of human conception. But what we call sanity lies in the first choice, acceptance of the arbitrary as real.

Laing proposes, therefore, that the schizophrenic of today is not suffering a psychological problem with a personal cause so much as he or she is making an apt response to a true condition of the modern world that has a political or technological cause. The so-called sane are holding on by our teeth to an extremely flimsy and arbitrary framework of reality.

Thus far, political theorists have failed to make very much of the effect our modern environments have on us. Failing to grasp that the physical world we live in is itself arbitrary, and thereby likely to be confusing to masses of people who seek solid ground on which to stand, political observers have not made some critical deductions. Primary among these is that when people cannot distinguish with certainty the natural from the interpreted, or the artificial from the organic, then all theories of the ideal organization of life become equal. None of them can be understood as any more or any less connected to planetary truth. And so the person or forces capable of speaking most loudly or most forcefully, or with some apparent logic—even if it is an unrooted logic—can become convincing within the void of understanding.

Where political theorists have overlooked these phenomena, others have not.

Looking at today's worlds from the outside in, as it were, and extrapolating from here into the future, science fiction writers have often been politically visionary. In their analyses and uses of the relationships between artificial environments, high technology, sanity and insanity, and, therefore, the inevitability—or more accurately—the *fact* of human mind control, some science fiction writers produce work that merges with political criticism.

A second category of people who have noticed the modern human relationships with the environment is the leadership of the new popular philosophical-religious movements, such as Scientology, *est,* Arica, Mind Dynamics and others. Unfortunately these leaders do not warn us of the consequences of the confusion, but instead take advantage of it.

Noting that reality and its definitions have now entered the realm of game and are up for grabs, they become better at the game than anyone else, exploiting it, reshaping disordered, unrooted minds and tilling a new bed of mental soil from which monsters will inevitably grow.

By looking at science fiction and the new philosophical-religious movements, we can develop a model which may indicate the likely result of the technological processes that are already very far along in our world.

Science Fiction and Arbitrary Reality

A widely misunderstood Soviet film, *Solaris,* directed by André Tarkovski from the book by Stanislaw Lem, depicts problems faced by some astronauts in a space station that is orbiting the planet Solaris in a faraway galaxy.

Of an original group of eighty-five astronauts, only two are left. Most have fled, others have gone mad and been shipped back to Earth. Several have killed themselves.

The surface of Solaris is one vast ocean, which is also a single living mind. This planet-ocean-mind is playing some kind of awful mental trick on its visitors.

Back on Earth, puzzled space officials send a psychologist, Kris Kelvin, to investigate. Before leaving the planet for outer space, Kelvin spends his final weeks visiting his father in a small house deep in some woods. He immerses himself in the forest and takes long, silent walks through meadows. The film moves exceedingly slowly at this point. There are long sequences in which nothing but natural events of the forest pass by the camera lens. Nature-time.

Sometimes the camera follows Kelvin's eyes as they absorb the surroundings. It rains. He is soaked. Back at his cabin, his body is warmed by a fire.

Finally it is time to leave. Now the camera is in the front seat of the car, sitting where Kelvin is sitting. We see what he sees.

Slowly the terrain changes. Winding wooded roads give way to straight, one-lane roads. The foliage recedes from the highway. Then we are on a freeway. The environment has become speeding cars, overpasses, underpasses, tunnels. Soon, we are in a city. There is noise, light, buildings everywhere. The natural landscape is submerged, invisible. Homocentric landscapes, abstract reality prevail. From there it's a fast cut to space.

Kelvin is alone in a small space vehicle, heading toward Solaris. Earth is gone. His roots have been abandoned. Grounding, by definition, is impossible. His whole environment is abstract. His planetary home now exists only in memory.

Arriving at the space station, Kelvin understands Solaris' trick. It enters visitors' memories and then creates real-life manifestations of them. This begins to happen to Kelvin. His long-dead wife appears in his room. At first he believes it is an image of her; then he realizes it is not just an image, it is actually she. And yet, they are both aware that she is only a manifestation of his mind. So she is simultaneously real and imaginary.

Other people from Kelvin's life appear in the lab. He encounters the re-created memories of the other two astronauts; relatives, old friends, toys, scraps of long-abandoned clothing, technical equipment, potted plants, dogs, dwarfs from a childhood circus, fields of grass. Things are strewn wildly about as the visitors from Earth try to figure out what to do with all the real/unreal stuff that keeps appearing from their memories. The space station takes on the quality of a dream, a carnival, a lunatic asylum.

The scientists consider returning to Earth as the others

have. Kelvin favors this move as he feels his sanity slipping, yet he realizes that to leave means "killing" his rediscovered wife. Back on Earth she will be a memory, much as Earth has become in this space station. She understands this, and it is a source of anguish for both of them.

No one among the scientists or their mental creations can control what will happen. Without concrete reality, which is to say, contact with their planetary roots, they are adrift in their minds: insane. All information has become believable and not believable at the same time. It has become arbitrary. There is no way to separate the real from the not-real. Although the astronauts know this, since there is nothing that is not arbitrary, except each other, all information is equal. It is impossible to determine which information to act on.

Solaris has made the astronauts its subjects. They cannot defend themselves from the images the planet makes concrete. In the end, the men have no choice but to accept all information as real. Kelvin goes through a long cycle of Earth images, from childhood to his present space-station life. He is in his father's house again, but he is also in space. It rains again, but now the rain is indoors. It might as well be. He cannot distinguish. He accepts.

Finally, the message of the film is clear. The process of going insane began long before the launch into space. It began when life moved from nature into cities. Kelvin's ride from woods to city to space was a ride from connection to disconnection, from reality to abstraction, a history of technology, setting the conditions for the imposition of reconstructed realities by a single powerful force.

A generation ago both George Orwell and Aldous Huxley wrote twentieth-century classics on this same theme. Both

1984 and *Brave New World* have been analyzed and reanalyzed, but with each turn of the technology screw, they take on new levels of meaning and relevance.

In Orwell's *1984*, the central technique of oppression is the absolute control of all kinds of information, both in the traditional sense—news, books, language—and also in the sense of information from the environment.

A suffocatingly narrow language, Newspeak, is imposed. It has no vocabulary to express many ideas and human feelings, and without expression, they begin to atrophy.

Every room contains a television set which constantly floods people's minds with martial music, news of military achievements and the despicable actions of the leader of the Underground, Goldstein.

The past is completely eliminated. History is revised. Books are destroyed. Without print media, there is no evidence that anything has been different. Even keeping diaries is forbidden. People are expected to absorb and accept the new information delivered by the television sets even if it directly contradicts the news of a month ago. Since it is impossible to prove the contradiction, it is useless to try to resist. Without points of comparison, all information is equally real. The Underground, for example, or a distant war between Oceania and Eastasia, might have existed or they might not have; there is no way of knowing.

A critical element in *1984* that has been little observed by commentators is that the people are confined inside cities. For any visit to the natural landscape—*which is itself the past*—special permission is needed.

Sex is illegal, except for purposes of propagation. Pleasure is outlawed. In this way, Big Brother is able to enter and control people's experience of their internal nature, as he controls their experience of the landscape. Humor, feeling, senses and instincts are also part of the past.

The effect of all this is to purge all references to any alternative. Whatever is offered as real can no longer be faulted. Nothing is provable by direct experience because all experience is manufactured. All existence becomes arbitrary, subject to the creation of Big Brother and the Party, Orwell's Solaris.

"The Party said that Oceania had never been in alliance with Eurasia. He, Winston Smith, knew that Oceania had been in alliance with Eurasia as short a time as four years ago. But where did that knowledge exist? Only in his own consciousness, which in any case must soon be annihilated. And if all others accepted the lie which the Party imposed—if all records told the same tale—then the lie passed into history and became truth. 'Who controls the past,' ran the Party slogan, 'controls the future: who controls the present controls the past.'

". . . The Party told you to reject the evidence of your eyes and ears. It was their final, most essential command.

". . . In the end the Party would announce that two and two made five, and you would have to believe it. It was inevitable that they should make that claim sooner or later: the logic of their position demanded it. Not merely the validity of experience, but the very existence of external reality was tacitly denied by their philosophy. . . . If both the past and the external world exist only in the mind, and if the mind itself is controllable—what then?

". . . Cut off from contact with the outer world, and with the past, the citizen of Oceania is like a man in interstellar space, who has no way of knowing which direction is up and which is down. The rulers of such a state are absolute, as the Pharaohs or the Caesars could not be."

While Orwell was primarily concerned with the excesses he saw in the Soviet Union, Huxley directed *Brave New World* at Western technological society. Instead of a grim Party that ruled through fear, the brave new world had a benevolent group of corporation-type managers; satisfactions were guaranteed by "emotional engineers."

Huxley's future world resembled Orwell's in that all physical experience was rigidly limited. Orwell's list was considerably grimmer, but Huxley realized that the point was a short list rather than a grim list. Sensual pleasures were encouraged in *Brave New World*, programmed into people as infants through "hypnopaedic" messages repeated thousands of times as they slept. The messages encouraged sexual promiscuity, attendance at mass entertainments such as "feelies" (movies with tactile stimuli), and, most important, the ingestion of drugs such as "soma" for any and every unpleasant feeling or little distress.

The goal was to keep people focused on their own satisfaction and limit their needs to those that could be conveniently satisfied by the social engineers. This precluded discontent.

Most important, life was contained within planned, controlled environments. People were programmed to believe that any "natural" experience was inconvenient or disgusting. The idea of personal love or caring for one's own infant, especially to the extent of breast feeding, was made so horrible that the very thought of it would send people groping for their drugs.

There is no underground in *Brave New World*, but there are two contrasting societies. One, modeled after the Zuni and Hopi villages where Huxley lived for a time in the 1920s, is the home of the "savages," museumized remnants of the nontechnological past. The city people take helicopters to these places to observe the savages' strange and sickening ways. The second society, confined to "islands," is filled with the mistakes of the genetic and hypnopaedic assembly line, people who've expressed the cardinal aberration: dissatisfaction.

In a foreword Huxley added to later editions of the book, he mused on the trends he saw in the world: "To deal with confusion, power has been centralized and government control increased. It is probable that all the world's governments will be more or less completely totalitarian before the harnessing of atomic energy; that they will be totalitarian during and after the harnessing seems almost certain. Only a large-scale popular movement toward decentralization . . . can arrest the present tendency. . . . At present there is no sign that such a movement will take place.

"There is, of course, no reason why the new totalitarianisms should resemble the old. Government by clubs and firing squads, by artificial famine, mass imprisonment and mass deportation, is not merely inhumane . . . it is demonstrably inefficient, and in an age of advanced technology, inefficiency is the sin against the Holy Ghost. A really efficient totalitarian state would be one in which the all-powerful executive of political bosses and their army of managers control a population of slaves who do not have to be coerced, because they love their servitude. To make them love it is the task assigned . . ."

This could be achieved, Huxley believed, by new technologies offering "a greatly improved technique of suggestion," by the dissemination of drugs, by mass spectacles to unify experience and feelings, and by eugenics, which would standardize people themselves. Writing in 1932, Huxley was not aware of any *single* technology that could achieve this standardization and unification process, but he saw that technology would inevitably lead in that direction. It was *his* particular genius, I believe, to perceive that the critical element was the creation of the joyful cooperation of the people being controlled.

Huxley made the assumption, natural to the 1930s, that governments would be the main propagators of pleasure controls in the future. Only lately have we seen the emergence of trans-governmental corporations that exercise similar powers, molding living and transportation patterns, rechanneling human experience, instilling habits of mind, and using "hypnopaedic" technology to do this programming.

Huxley understood that no matter who the controllers are, their success depends on confining experience and awareness to predetermined patterns. Both Huxley and Orwell recognized that human feelings and any wilderness experience were complicated and unwieldy and revealed alternative realities. They were, therefore, dangerous to the controllers. Anything connected to natural ("savage") awareness must be ridiculed and eliminated, and all experience must be contained within controlled artificial environments. In a large society, technology is a good standardizer, and the confinement works best if technology has been enshrined.

I could go on with examples from dozens of science fiction works on the theme of technological control of reality. Sometimes it is deliberate, but sometimes, as in *Solaris*, the use of technology to produce autocracy is not so much deliberate and conscious as it is evolutionary.

As technology has evolved, step by step, it has placed boundaries between human beings and their connections with larger, nonhuman realities. As life acquired ever more technological wrapping, human experience and understanding were confined and altered. In *Solaris* these changes happen in a nonspecific order over time, until people's minds and living patterns are so disconnected that there is no way of knowing reality from fantasy. At such a point, there is no choice but to accept leadership, however arbitrary.

Such leadership may very well not plan its own success. It emerges organically at the moment when human experience has been sufficiently channeled and confined. In this cultural analogue of mass sensory deprivation, simple, clear statements assume a greater authority and profundity than they deserve.

Whoever recognizes that such a crucial moment has arrived, that people's minds are appropriately confused and receptive, can speak directly into them without interference. The people who are spoken to are preconditioned to accept what they hear, like the Solaris astronauts or the poor, puzzled masses of *1984*.

Technology plays a critical role in this process because it creates standardized arbitrary forms of physical and mental confinement. Television is the ideal tool for such purposes because it both confines experience and implants simple, clear ideas.

Seen in this way, a new fact emerges. Autocracy needn't come in the form of a person at all, or even as an articulated ideology or conscious conspiracy. The autocracy can exist in the technology itself. The technology can produce its own subordinated society, as though it were alive, like Solaris.

Eight Ideal Conditions for the Flowering of Autocracy

The three fictional works I have described, when combined with those rare political writers who approach autocratic form from the point of view of technology (Jacques Ellul, Ivan Illich, Guy Debord, Herbert Marcuse), begin to yield a system of preconditions from which we can expect monolithic systems of control to emerge. These may be institutional autocracies or dictatorships. For the moment, it will be simpler to use the dictatorship model.

Imagine that like some kind of science fiction dictator you intended to rule the world. You would probably have pinned over your desk a list something like this:

1) *Eliminate personal knowledge.* Make it hard for people to know about themselves, how they function, what a human being is, or how a human fits into wider, natural systems. This will make it impossible for the human to separate natural from artificial, real from unreal. *You* provide the answers to all questions.

2) *Eliminate points of comparison.* Comparisons can be found in earlier societies, older language forms and cultural artifacts, including print media. Eliminate or museumize indigenous cultures, wilderness and nonhuman life forms. Re-create internal human experience—instincts,

97

thoughts, and spontaneous, varied feelings—so that it will not evoke the past.

3) *Separate people from each other.* Reduce interpersonal communication through life-styles that emphasize separateness. When people gather together, be sure it is for a prearranged experience that occupies all their attention at once. Spectator sports are excellent, so are circuses, elections, and any spectacles in which focus is outward and interpersonal exchange is subordinated to mass experience.

4) *Unify experience, especially encouraging mental experience at the expense of sensory experience.* Separate people's minds from their bodies, as in sense-deprivation experiments, thus clearing the mental channel for implantation. Idealize the mind. Sensory experience cannot be eliminated totally, so it should be driven into narrow areas. An emphasis on sex as opposed to sense may be useful because it is powerful enough to pass for the whole thing and it has a placebo effect.

5) *Occupy the mind.* Once people are isolated in their minds, fill the brain with prearranged experience and thought. Content is less important than the fact of the mind being filled. Free-roaming thought is to be discouraged at all costs, because it is difficult to control.

6) *Encourage drug use.* Recognize that total repression is impossible and so expressions of revolt must be contained on the personal level. Drugs will fill in the cracks of dissatisfaction, making people unresponsive to organized expressions of resistance.

7) *Centralize knowledge and information.* Having isolated people from each other and minds from bodies; eliminated points of comparison; discouraged sensory experience; and invented technologies to unify and control

experience, *speak*. At this point whatever comes from outside will enter directly into all brains at the same time with great power and believability.

8) *Redefine happiness and the meaning of life in terms of new and increasingly unrooted philosophy*. Once you've established the prior seven conditions, this one is easy. Anything makes sense in a void. All channels are open, receptive and unquestioning. Formal mind structuring is simple. Most important, avoid naturalistic philosophies, they lead to uncontrollable awareness. The least resistible philosophies are the most arbitrary ones, those that make sense only in terms of themselves.

Popular Philosophy and Arbitrary Reality

There is considerable evidence that the science fiction vision of arbitrary reality inevitably leading to autocracy has already begun to materialize. We can see it in action in the quasi-religious philosophies that are now sweeping the country, gathering in millions of devotees.

The techniques used in gathering adherents to these burgeoning movements are startlingly similar in conception to *1984, Solaris, Brave New World* and the eight-pointed list just offered. The results are also similar. Converts effectively submit to having their minds reconstructed along simpler, flat, narrow, but, most important, unrooted channels. This allows them to embrace arbitrary information as though it were grounded in concrete reality.

In a world where alienation and confusion are common conditions, these new philosophies offer a comforting mental order that accepts and absorbs all contradictions. The danger is that once people's minds are so simplified and receptive, they become vulnerable to any leader, guru or system of forces which understands the simplicity of the code and can speak the appropriate techno-speak.

Like a mass of Manchurian candidates, the people whose minds have been retrained into passive channels by these technologically based processes are available at all times for imprinting. In this way they merge with and can accept advertising-mind, television-mind and other simplistic intrusions without the slightest belch of rejection.

I am going to be using *est* as the example to show how thinking patterns are restructured, but not because it is any worse than any of the other currently popular systems. In many ways it is benign in comparison with Scientology or the mind control used by Reverend Moon. Neither is it worse than advertising and television.

However, *est* is interesting because it operates in a realm totally outside the media while nonetheless utterly re-creating reality in an arbitrary form. In fact, its failure to realize its potential as a world movement stems from the failure of its founder, Werner Erhard, to grasp the use of the media, though he tries and tries.

The *est* training sessions are always held in huge hotel meeting rooms which have artificial light, air conditioning, no windows, and are characterized by the kind of non-decoration typical of such places.

Trainees are met by *est* graduates and trainers, all of whom wear coded name tags and amazingly similar clothes and facial expressions, cheerful like airline attendants in advertisements. Hard folding chairs are arranged in neat rows facing a stage and microphone. The instructions are absolute: no talking, no sitting with friends, no eating or drinking. In an eighteen-hour session, there is usually one short meal break, and one or two bathroom breaks. No moving around the room. No clocks. No taking notes.

There are absolute rules on exactly how to wear your own name tag, how to sit, how to hold the microphone when speaking into it, how to acknowledge other people's reports (whatever the content, what you say is "good"), how and when to look into people's eyes. Above all, you must follow instructions immediately and to the letter. If, for example, someone does not wear the name tag in exactly the prescribed manner, or shows up a minute late, he or she is publicly humiliated and threatened with expulsion. The violator is told she or he is breaking an agreement, but of course there was no real agreement in the usual sense of two parties working out a contract or understanding. This is "agreement" in the hierarchical model, as in a military situation where rules are predesigned and then imposed. You "agree" or else you are punished. *est* can't put you in the brig, so the punishment is exclusion.

All these rules break any contact with outside grounding. In this new floating environment, the trainers become the absolute authority (*1984*) and the source of all salvation, although they continually give credit for all the rules and activities to *their* absolute authority, Werner Erhard. "We do this because Werner says this is what works." What it works *for* is *never* explained because either you "get it" or you don't.

But I am happy to tell you that what you "get" in the end is training in a new pattern of thought and a floating logic.

The trainers lead the trainees through a series of long, repetitive exercises, which include the use of implanted imagery and hypnosis. These are combined with a series of games, including deliberately silly, funny games which, nonetheless, require full participation, that is, submission to the game, before one is permitted to stop. Included are self-humiliation and humiliation by the trainer. The only purpose of these is to break ordinary mental patterns and let go of earlier "tapes and records." Once that is done, new ones can replace them. This is not to say that breaking "tapes" cannot be useful therapy, but in the case of *est,* you get Werner-tapes to replace parent-tapes.

Time is a critical element in the training, because it takes quite a while before all the trainees become unified in the experience of living up to the instructions of the leadership, discovering the appropriate responses, and developing a peer-group understanding of what is expected. Meanwhile, the trainer retains a grim visage.

People who protest are told they are bringing their own belief system in, which is what they are there to *stop* doing.

People are told *not* to compare what goes on in the *est* training with anything else they have experienced—in this way *est* maintains its floating, separated quality, like the sensory-deprivation subject floating for hours in a liquid tank, or the atsronaut in the space station. Slowly the isolated environment, the endless series of instructions, the fixed patterns of behavior, the repetition and the boredom raise the volume of immediate experience, so that any connection with the world outside, including past experience, recedes and disappears as though it is the abstract and the room the real. (Solaris) The room becomes the whole world. The people in the room are all of society, embodying all values as delivered from the mountain. (Erhard) The trainers are the ultimate authorities. Reality is here and now. Nothing else exists. (*1984*)

After several days of this environmental and contextual onslaught, any confusion and resistance people brought with them gives way to the desire for acceptance, and then the construction of a new "ground of reality" can begin. When trainers say "ground of reality" they literally mean the structuring of a reality where there is none. (Space station).

Here is a summary of the new *est* reality:

Everything is belief. Everything that we see or experience of the world is only an outgrowth of our belief that what we see and experience is the way things really are. Reality, then, is nothing more than an agreement as to what is real. Therefore, problems that we may have, or problems that may exist in the world (napalm, genocide, police repression, loss of jobs or lovers, pollution and so on) are real only because we believe they are real; in fact they exist only in our minds. If we do not acknowledge them, they don't exist. So we effectively create these things with our belief systems; so do the napalmed kids, the Jews in Germany, and the laid-off factory workers.

This is a very comfortable attitude for much of today's world; people who "get it," like it. It's not only a fun game—mixing up all those perceptual tricks in one's head—but there's something that passes for mystical in the notion that one creates one's own reality, and the world doesn't really exist. It makes people feel they have special powers. It is a comfort because it simultaneously relieves trainees from making better sense of their artificial, arbitrary world, which *is* literally nonsensical and ungraspable, and at the same time it asserts that *they* determine whatever world they wish. If things don't go perfectly, well, that's the way they created it, and it must be for the best. It is simultaneously creation and submission, total responsibility and irresponsibility, involvement and noninvolvement, according to personal definition.

Now, it is certainly true that if you believe a thing is a certain way—let's say you believe yourself to be competent or beautiful, or that you will succeed in your new career—then that will make your belief more likely to become reality. Dale Carnegie taught that fifty years ago; so does every loving parent. So *est* can benefit many people who might otherwise turn themselves back at every conflict. If there were nothing attractive in *est* then obviously no one would follow it.

When people fully accept the idea that all reality exists *solely* in their own minds, and that nothing outside their minds is definitely, concretely real, each person then has unlimited personal power to create and define reality. It is now up for grabs. There is no cause. There is no effect. Relationships do not exist. Money does not exist. Jobs do not exist.

I have known several *est* trainees who carried this belief into new levels of disillusionment and a loftier sense of personal failure because they were unable to "create" food or meaningful contact with other human beings when they needed it.

More important, when these assumptions of personal creation are extrapolated out of the individual realm and applied to society and politics (a philosophy which holds a napalmed baby responsible for having created its own reality is a political philosophy), then we have something dangerous on a systemic level. Power does not exist unless one decides that it does; oppression does not exist, politics do not exist, and neither does nature.

In this denial of everyday worldly reality, all realities become totally arbitrary, creating the perfect precondition for the imposition of *any* new "ground of reality" within the void. Though it may be nonsensical or fascistic, any reality is acceptable.

From *1984*:

"Anything could be true. The so-called laws of nature were nonsense. The law of gravity was nonsense. . . . [The fallacy is to believe] that somewhere or other, outside oneself, there was a 'real' world where 'real' things happened. But how could there be such a world? What knowledge have we of anything, save through our minds? All happenings are in the mind."

Whether it is Werner Erhard or Big Brother reconstructing the mind, it is true that once mental processes are disconnected from planetary sources, or concrete realities, then all validation of truth is impossible. Everything is acceptable. One constructs one's own truth. War is peace. Hate is love. Anything can begin to make sense but only within its own self-contained, unrooted bubble of logic. Once the bubble contacts the Earth, however, the logic evaporates. There is nothing arbitrary about the reality of an earthquake or the collision of cars or the loss of a job or the stabbing to death of one person by another. Nor is there anything arbitrary about one group of people subjugating another either through military or economic means. When such events happen, then they actually happen. They are outside human definition. Reality can become arbitrary only within the confines of a mental framework. People who live in direct contact with the planet itself are not concerned with any such questions.

The difference between Erhardian religions of the present moment and Indian or nature-based religions of other cultures or earlier times is that Erhard's is abstract. Its ideas depend upon their own unrootedness. Nature-based religions, including even Zen Buddhism, are concrete, involving direct observation, totally functional and integrated perceptual systems that "see" things as they are and experience life directly: person to planet, person to person, and person to self. When American Indian religions speak of responsibility, there is no question of responsibility to self as opposed to group. The one cannot be separated from the other.

Erhard-type movements are outgrowths of the wider alienation from source that I've been describing, which makes all things possible because nothing is grounded, definite and personally verifiable. These religions would remain mere curiosities or aberrations if they did not fit so neatly the technologically created arbitrary environments, but they are growing at a wild rate. As they grow, they turn further to the right, producing *real* monsters like Reverend Moon and others, no doubt, still to come. They reset the minds of millions of people to believe that all things are arbitrary and, since this is so, that nothing actually matters, and therefore nothing needs improving.

I will quote briefly from a letter I received from a young woman, Magi Discoe, just after she completed the *est* training. The letter reports on the cathartic moment when the trainer reveals to the trainees the beauty of the concept that there is nothing to be done about anything:

"Stand by for revelation. After our minds are in the appropriate mush state, the trainer winds up for his greatest moment. He looks us over and begins, letting his voice rise to a booming crescendo: 'IT IS ALL HOPELESS,' he says to us. No use whatsoever. There is no hope. That's what is. It's not depressing or anything else, it's just hopeless. Not only that but we are hopeless. We are also machines. And so that we 'get' what machines we are, we are told to be in touch with our own little voice saying 'I am not a machine.' That's how much we are machines. We are stimulus-response machines. That's just the way it is. That's what's so.

"Up until this point no one involved in the training has smiled. Exactly when in this harangue the trainer began to smile, I am not sure. I was perceiving a difference and finally it dawned on me that the man was beginning to smile. A shared secret smile. The entire environment of the room changed at this moment. The fact that we were machines was surpassed by the fact that we were for the first time being included in the world of *est*.

"A lot of people were still functioning well enough, even after this long period, to get upset at the idea of themselves as machines. It was their last hold on resistance. By the end, however, people either stopped commenting or agreed. If people held out too long, the trainer got into a smiling tirade about *them* having to be 'right,' that all they were doing was trying to survive by making someone wrong. It was another one of those circular processes he always used which made it impossible to argue with him or even to remember, once you were swimming in his words, that it was *he* who needed to be right. *est* depended upon it. But he had all the cards from day one.

"The amazing thing is that even with everything I know about how fascism operates, after a long-enough time I lost touch with my logic and began wanting and needing the approval of this asshole and the smiling, plastic robots around him; there was a moment there when I was with them."

I don't think that Werner Erhard is a particularly dangerous person. I've met him several times. He attends a lot of San Francisco cocktail parties. He strikes me as another aggressive, success-oriented man who fell into something hot because of his years around auto showrooms, management seminars and Scientology workshops. What makes him not dangerous is that he has never figured out television. Though he would like to push *est* through television, when he gets on he goes flat. He doesn't "work" on television, to put it in his own terms. He knows the medium changes his message but he can't figure out the dimensions of the change.

Dangerous or not, Erhard and some of his contemporary gurus are tinkering with an amazingly powerful form. They have learned, as the science fiction dictators have, that if you control environment carefully enough, and confine human experience totally enough, you can shatter all human grounding. This leaves the subject in such a disconnected state, you can easily predict and control how he or she will respond to the addition of only one or two stimuli. These are, in effect, mass sense-deprivation experiments. They leave people floating without connections, their minds separated from their bodies, open to implantation of any kind of arbitrary logic. In the end, their minds have been restructured to accept whatever comes. They are clear, simple, open, receptive channels. All personal experience, irrelevant. All complexity, eliminated. All points of reference, disposed of. Floating freely in space. All information is arbitrary, the product of mind. One piece of news is equal to the next. Everything is believable and not believable at the same time. There is no reality aside from mind. The only existence is belief.

As we will see in the latter half of this book, television does the same thing in virtually the same way.

Schizophrenia and the Influencing Machine

On September 27, 1973, a young man walked into the lobby of San Francisco television station KGO-TV and began shooting. He killed an advertising salesman before he himself was killed by police.

The local media then pieced together the story. The man had been in and out of mental hospitals for several years, and his complaint was always the same. He said that a receiver had been implanted into his body in a secret operation, that it was constantly broadcasting to his mind, that he couldn't turn it off, that he was in agony, and that it was making him crazy.

His action at KGO was presumably an attempt to silence the broadcasts. He had taken a previous trip to Hawaii to escape the broadcast signal but to no avail.

Though very few mental patients go so far as to shoot up broadcasting stations, the number of disturbed people who say they can't get broadcasts out of their minds is apparently growing.

A description of this problem was offered in the *Bulletin of the Menninger Clinic* by Dr. Joseph Robert Cowen. He described a woman obsessed by television signals.

"For many months during the course of her hospitalization she made frequent reference to television. When she referred to television she would develop a look of ecstatic terror on her face. In various ways she described how she was being controlled, persecuted and tormented by television. She had clairvoyant experiences with other patients mediated by television. She variously described herself as being 'hooked' or 'taped' into television. Periodically she would tell me, 'Everything would be all right if they just wouldn't turn on the television set.' "

Dr. Cowen described his patient's distortion of the very word "television" to "tcll-a-vision." He felt this word distortion explained how she could fantasize that television was a "machine of infinite power which inexorably demands that ego alien material be told through it . . ." Cowen goes on to say, "The singling out of various instruments as the source of trouble is common in regressed states where projection is the predominant feature. With the advent of television it has become a frequent clinical feature."

Most mental institutions in this country now keep television sets operating during all waking hours to occupy their patients without a thought that this could possibly have a negative effect. Dr. Cowen does not mention whether he ever considered merely turning off the television set as the woman was asking.

In 1919, Dr. Viktor Tausk, a colleague of Freud's, wrote an amazing article called "On the Origin of the 'Influencing Machine' in Schizophrenia."

Tausk wrote that a significant number of patients described their problems as being caused by an "influencing machine" operated by alien forces. These aliens represented belief systems threatening to the patient's own and which were being forcibly implanted in the patient's mind.

The influencing machine usually has gigantic wheels, gears and other paraphernalia, Tausk says. It often has the ability to project pictures and invisible rays in some way capable of imprinting the brain. The pictures frequently emanate from a "small black box" and are flat, not three-dimensional, images. The machine and its emanations can produce feelings and thoughts in the victim, while removing other ones, according to Tausk, "by means of rays or mysterious forces which the patient's knowledge of physics is inadequate to explain. It creates sensations that in part cannot be described," says Tausk, "because they are strange to the patient himself, and that in part are sensed as electrical, magnetic or due to air-currents."

Soon, Tausk reports, the victim cannot distinguish information—feelings, thoughts, sensations, memories—that have been received from this "external" source from those that have been personally generated or are the result of personal experience and discovery.

Tausk's hypothesis, similar to Cowen's, is that patients create this machine fantasy as an outward manifestation of an internal confusion between the external and the internal worlds; the world of one's own thoughts and the concrete world outside the person.

This confusion has its roots in early childhood, Tausk says. At a certain age, a child seeks a reality beyond the parents, seeks to contact an outer world and so begins exploring. To the degree the child succeeds, it learns to integrate and process the wider world it has experienced. It can tell the difference between the impulses, images and experiences which are connected to the world outside, and those which are totally self-generated, floating, not rooted in the world. If the child has made this distinction, then the projections of his or her own mind can be distinguished and identified. This is sanity.

The schizophrenic, says Tausk, does not learn to make this distinction and cannot tell which images emanate from inside the mind and which are connected to experiences in the world. At this point, all experience, whether internally generated or the result of an interaction with the world, is equal. Projections of the mind take on the same quality as direct experience of the world. One's experience of the world becomes unreliable, as do one's own thought processes. Both become floating, unrooted. All are equally internal and equally external.

At this point, Tausk suggests, the patient will create an

"influencing machine" fantasy as a physical manifestation of the confusion. Capable of implanting images which are in the form of rays, capable of implanting alien realities outside of one's own experiences, capable of changing one's feelings, this machine "causes" the patient to fall into utter confusion about what is real and what is not, what is internal and what is external.

Doubtless you have noticed that this "influencing machine" sounds an awful lot like television. The mystery is how the phenomenon could have existed in 1919 before the apparatus was invented. Dare I suggest that television was invented by people similarly preoccupied, as an outward manifestation of *their* minds?

In any event, there is no question that television does what the schizophrenic fantasy says it does. It places in our minds images of realities which are outside our experience. The pictures come in the form of rays from a box. They cause changes in feeling and, as we will see, utter confusion as to what is real and what is not. All reality becomes ethereal, existing only in our minds.

Like the machine of Tausk's suffering patients, television is a final manifestation of an already apparent confusion. This confusion existed at the time Tausk was writing, but it has now been institutionalized by the ubiquitousness of the artificial environments we live in. A real world which cannot be questioned has been submerged beneath a reconstructed, human-created world. We live inside the manifestations of human minds. Like the child seeking outside connection, we find only the projections of other humans. We can't know the natural from the artificial, since the processes that would reveal that are nowhere visible. We are cut off, floating in space, living within a nationwide sense-deprivation tank. We see a stimulus, a light, and we cling to it. It becomes everything. It causes images in our brain. We call this experience, but we can't tell if it is *our* experience or something else. It is in our heads, but we didn't create it. We don't know if it is real or it isn't. We can't stop the broadcasts. We accept whatever comes. One vision is equal to the next. One thought is as good as the next. All information merges. All experience merges. We take everything on faith. One explanation is the same as the next one. Contradictions do not exist. We have lost control of our minds. We are all lost in space. Our world exists only in memory. Everything is arbitrary. TV is the guru speaking reality. We have merged with the influencing machine. We are the Solaris astronauts.

ARGUMENT TWO

THE
COLONIZATION
OF
EXPERIENCE

It is no accident that television has been dominated by a handful of corporate powers. Neither is it accidental that television has been used to re-create human beings into a new form that matches the artificial, commercial environment. A conspiracy of technological and economic factors made this inevitable and continue to.

VI

ADVERTISING: THE STANDARD-GAUGE RAILWAY

W E have seen how the natural environment has been transformed into secondary, artificial and abstracted forms. This process has been described as though it happened by accident, without purpose. I have been avoiding conspiracy theories.

It is true that no small group could successfully plot to dominate social and technological processes that take millennia to evolve. Yet at any one moment, some people may benefit considerably more than others from particular forms of social organization and the technologies that accompany them. These will be the people who sit at the hub of the most critical institutions at any given time. They will naturally seek to consolidate their own position by concentrating their control while widening its effect. In this way, a tendency that may have been going on for hundreds of years or longer, beyond the range of human conspiracy, gains power over time. And so the tendency, the social and technological line of development, becomes more monolithic, more dominant, more difficult to stop.

Take, for example, the growth and centralization of energy-production systems during the last few hundred years. No single human could have planned to reap the great benefits that some have gained from the evolution of wood-burning stoves into coal-burning stoves into electric utilities, gigantic power companies with nuclear facilities and multinational oil companies. Each technology grew out of the previous one. At each stage, a small number of people occupied key spots and were able to guide change in ways that would concentrate the direct benefits in their hands. By now, the energy technologies and the institutions that serve them are so large, they dominate virtually all of life and even our political and social systems, while an exceedingly small number of people have come to control them.

Meanwhile, other technological systems have also become larger and more monolithic at the same time. Transportation systems, for example, have advanced from horses to horses and buggies to railroads to cars and trucks on freeways to SSTs. Long-distance communications systems have gone from telegraph to telephone to radio to television to satellite. As these technologies grow, their power and influence grows with them, but the number of people who control them shrinks.

In a capitalist, free-enterprise economy, that the controllers of the communications systems should become personally acquainted with the controllers of the energy systems, the transportation systems and so on and eventually begin to cooperate with each other ought to be obvious and predictable. The fact that it is not obvious to most of us, at least not so obvious that we act to stop it, has allowed matters to "pop" organically into still larger and *more* monolithic patterns of domination and control at each turn of the cycle, affecting human lives and political organization.

At some point we begin to call this a conspiracy. Humans

get together and discuss how best to help each other concentrate power. But the human conspiracy didn't begin the process. It resulted from another, less personal though more basic, conspiracy: a conspiracy of technological form. The patterns of life, the social and political systems, the narrowing style of thinking about the world and the technologies that both result from and foster these trends are the ground upon which the conspiracy can grow.

In this chapter and the one which follows we shall see how television and its parent and child, advertising, have contributed to this process of concentration, and how it was inevitable from the moment of its invention that television would be used this way. Later, we will also see that no other use of television makes much sense or, in any practical way, is even possible.

The Creation of "Value"

In transforming natural environments into artificial form, the United States is the most advanced country in the world. This is not an accident. It is inherent in our economic system.

To the capitalist, profit-oriented mind, there is no outrage so great as the existence of some unmediated nook or cranny of creation which has not been converted into a new form that can then be sold for money. This is because in the act of converting the natural into the artificial, something with no inherent economic value becomes "productive" in the capitalist sense.

An uninhabited desert is "nonproductive" unless it can be mined for uranium or irrigated for farms or covered with tracts of homes.

A forest of uncut trees is nonproductive.

A piece of land which has not been built upon is nonproductive.

Coal or oil that remains in the ground is nonproductive. Animals living wildly are nonproductive.

Virtually any land, any space, any material, any time that remains in an original, unprocessed, unconverted form is an outrage to the sensibilities of the capitalist mind. Iron, tungsten, trees, oil, sulphur, jaguars and open space are searched out and transformed because transformation creates economic benefits for the transformers.

In economics this transformation has a name: "value added." Value added derives from all the processes that alter a raw material from something which has no intrinsic economic value to something which does. Each change in form, say, from iron ore in the ground to iron or steel to car to car which is heavily advertised adds value to the material. The only raw materials which have intrinsic economic value before processing are gold and silver. This is only because people have agreed on these values in order to define a value for paper money, which certainly has no intrinsic value.

It is, then, the nature of profit seeking to convert as much as possible of what has not been processed and exists in its own right into something which has the potential for economic gain.

A second element in the creation of commercial value is scarcity, the separation of people from whatever they might want or need. In artificial environments, where humans are separated from the sources of their survival, everything obtains a condition of relative scarcity and therefore value.

There is the old story of the native living on a Pacific island, relaxing in a house on the beach, picking fruit from the tree and spearing fish in the water. A businessman arrives on the island, buys all the land, cuts down the trees and builds a factory. Then he hires the native to work in it for money so that someday the native can afford canned fruit and fish from the mainland, a nice little cinder-block house near the beach with a view of the water, and weekends off to enjoy it.

The moment people move off land which has directly supported them, the necessities of life are removed from individual control. The things people could formerly produce for their survival must now be paid for.

You may be living on the exact spot where a fruit tree once fed people. Now the fruit comes from five hundred miles away and costs thirty-five cents apiece. It is in the separation that the opportunity for profit resides.

When the basic necessities are not scarce—in those places where food is still wild and abundant, for example—economic value can only be applied to new items. Candy bars, bottled or chemical milk, canned tuna, electrical appliances and Coca-Cola have all been intensively marketed in countries new to the market system. Because these products hadn't existed in those places before, they are automatically relatively scarce and potentially valuable.

Redeveloping the Human Being

Once the process of accounting for every available square inch of terrain and every raw material has begun, it is necessary to convince people to want the converted products.

On the environmental end of the equation, the goal is to turn raw materials in the ground, or the ground itself, into a commodity. On the personal end of the equation, the goal is to convert the uncharted internal human wilderness into a form that desires to accumulate the commodities.

The conversion process within the human is directed at experience, feeling, perception, behavior and desire. These must be catalogued, defined and reshaped. The idea is to get both ends of the equation in synchrony, like standard-gauge railways. The human becomes the terminus of the conversion of plants, animals and minerals into objects. The conversion of natural into artificial, inherent in our economic system, takes place as much inside human feeling and experience as it does in the landscape. The more you smooth out the flow, the better the system functions and, in particular, the more the people who activate the processes benefit. In the end, the human, like the environment, is redesigned into a form that fits the needs of the commercial format.

People who take more pleasure in talking with friends than in machines, commodities and spectacles are outrageous to the system. People joining with their neighbors to share housing or cars or appliances are less "productive" than those who live in isolation from each other, obtaining their very own of every object. Any collective act, from sharing washing machines to car-pooling to riding buses, is less productive to the wider system in the end than everyone functioning separately in nuclear family units and private homes. Isolation maximizes production. Human beings who are satisfied with natural experience, from sexuality to breast feeding to cycles of mood, are not as productive as the not-so-satisfied, who seek vaginal sprays, chemical and artificial milk, drugs to smooth out emotional ups and downs, and commodities to substitute for experience.

As long as the process of mediating between people and natural nonconsumer experience is encouraged, the big wheel keeps turning and we all turn with it.

Not long ago I learned of a laboratory experiment which mirrored this process of reshaping needs to fit environment. Some chimpanzees had been isolated, one to a room, and were being taught to communicate with a team of scientists by way of symbols. Whenever they had a need or a desire they would push buttons. If they wanted a banana, they located a button marked with a symbol of a banana, pushed it and a banana came down a chute.

Other buttons had other symbols. There was one for water

and one for changes in lighting. There was even one that requested physical affection. When the chimp pushed it, a human scientist would enter the room, hug and play with the chimp for a time, and then go back out the door.

The chimpanzees' world of experience was reduced to what they could ask for with these buttons. What could be requested, of course, was limited to what the scientists had thought to provide. Since cost was a factor in the experiment, the scientists did not attempt to duplicate the kinds of experiences the chimps formerly enjoyed in the forests. The scientists provided the experiences which were convenient for them to provide in a lab. I think there were twelve in all.

Apparently, at least for the time being, these few experiences were sufficient to keep the animals satisfied, although it is well known that there is an extraordinarily high death rate (even suicide rate) among all confined animals. This is especially true of the more intelligent ones, such as dolphins and monkeys. There is an even higher lethargy rate, as a visit to any zoo reveals.

The scientific purpose of the experiment was to demonstrate that as the scientists switched a symbol from one button to another button—let's say a banana symbol was switched from button three to button ten—the animal would notice the switch had taken place. It would "read" the symbol accurately and immediately push the newly appropriate button.

This was hailed as a significant breakthrough because it showed that these animals had the ability to abstract. That is, they were able to go through mental associative processes, just as we can, and could thereby be trained more quickly to follow the scientists' routines.

To me, however, the experiment meant only that the chimp in the lab was undergoing an accelerated version of human history, from concrete to abstract (like the Solaris astronaut proceeding from forest to space). More important and more poignant, it meant that chimpanzees, like any other confined animals, will do whatever is necessary to survive and will make the best of a bad situation that is totally out of their control.

Confinement itself, the removal of a creature from its natural habitat into a rearranged world where its ordinary techniques for survival and satisfaction are no longer operative, produces several inevitable results:

1) The creature becomes dependent for survival upon whoever controls the new environment. It will use its intelligence to learn whatever new tricks are necessary to fit that system. If it takes tricks and changes to stay alive, then that's what it takes.

2) The creature becomes focused upon (addicted to) whatever experiences remain available in the new environment.

3) The creature therefore reduces its own mental and physical expectations to fit what can be gotten.

Confined creatures that cannot fit this pattern go crazy, revolt or die.

Commodity People

While the analogy between chimps and humans is certainly not precise, neither is it farfetched. We were not suddenly captured by hunters and imprisoned in a room or a zoo, but over a period of several generations, our species has suffered a similar fate.

We have been removed from the environment within which we evolved and with which we are uniquely designed to interact. Now we interact and coevolve with only the grosser, more monolithic, human-made commercial forms which remain available within our new laboratory–space station. Because we live inside the new environment, we are not aware that any tradeoff has been made.

We have had to sacrifice the billions of small, detailed,

multispectral experiences—emotional, physical, instinctive, sensual, intuitive and mental—that were appropriate and necessary for humans interacting with natural environments. Like the Micronesian islander in Chapter Four trapped between two modes of experience, we have found that functioning on an earlier multidimensional level has become not only useless but counterproductive. If we remained so attuned to the varieties of snowflakes that we could find fifty-six varieties as the Eskimo can; or to dreams so that we could find hundreds of distinct patterns as the Senoi Indians can; or to the minute altitude strata, inch by inch above the ground, occupied by entirely different species of flying insects as the California Indians once could; all this sensitivity would cripple any attempt to get along in the modern world. None of it would get us jobs, which gets us money, which in turn gets us food, housing, transportation, products, or entertainment, which are the fulfillments presently available in our new world.

We have had to re-create ourselves to fit. We have had to reshape our very personalities to be competitive, aggressive, mentally fast, charming and manipulative. These qualities succeed in today's world and offer survival and some measure of satisfaction within the cycle of work-consume, work-consume, work-consume. As for any dormant anxieties or unreconstructed internal wilderness, these may be smoothed over by compulsive working, compulsive eating, compulsive buying, compulsive sex, and then our brands of soma: alcohol, Librium, Valium, Thorazine, marijuana and television.

Born within the walls of our reconstructed environment, unaware of any other, we are like the chimpanzee in the lab. We are making the best of a situation that seems as inevitable as it is ubiquitous. Participating in it is the only logical way to get along.

Yet there are people who do not adjust, who cannot be made satisfied or functional within these confines. They eventually fall out of the pattern. As you may have noticed, a lot of people seem to be going crazy these days. People are shooting each other as never before, walking the streets with blank stares, lying in doorways, making jail a way of life, or living off welfare. Others burst out, unable to contain their frustrations: beating children, torturing animals, forming gangs, or, on another level, among those who view these matters in terms of power, forming revolutionary movements.

These people are unable or unwilling to remake themselves to fit the given arrangement. In Huxley's world, all of them would be moved benevolently out of the system to islands. In Orwell's world they would be imprisoned and changed by torture and brainwashing. Our own world uses a combination of separation, removal and reconstruction, but there can never be any question of the enforcement of the overall model. If too many people fell out of the pattern, the whole system would be endangered. If even a small percentage of the population should step out of the cycle of button pushing—work-consume, work-consume—then we'd see the gross national product decline and the economy begin to disintegrate. After a time no one would deliver our food from afar, the buses would cease to run, jobs would disappear, hospitals would close, money would be useless, and having lost all individual skills of survival and all contact with the earth itself, people would experience craziness and a breakdown of order as the new reality.

Breaking the Skin Barrier

Given how critical it is to keep the production-consumption process flowing smoothly, advertising obviously occupies a place of considerable importance.

It has been assigned the specific duty of keeping people buying, buying, buying and therefore working, working, working to get the money to do so. It is the system invented to break the skin barrier, as it were, by entering the human being to reshape feelings and create more appropriate ones as need be.

If suburbs are capitalism's ideally separated buying units, and suburbs can be built profitably, then we must create humans who like and want suburbs: suburb-people. Since before the existence of suburbs there were no suburb-people, advertising has the task of creating them, in body and mind.

Since before the creation of electric shavers or hair dryers or electric carving knives people felt no need for these things, the need was implanted into human minds by advertising.

Advertising is the instrument of transmutation. *It* lays the standard-gauge railway track from wilderness to human feeling, assisting in the transformation of both into a unified commercial form. Unplugged from our natural connection to the environment, we are replugged into a new consumer environment.

To the degree that advertising reaches us, occupying our time and thought, it keeps us vibrating within strict limits. If forty million people see a commercial for a car, then forty million people have a car commercial in their heads, all at the same time. This is bound to have more beneficial effect on the commodity system than if, at that moment, all those people were thinking separate thoughts which, in some cases, might not be about commodities at all.

Of course, advertising people will argue against the notion that the purpose and result of their activities is to unify and homogenize people and culture. They are forever speaking of the dazzling array of choices our market system provides and how advertising provides the information we need to make choices.

It is an ominous sign that so many people can accept this argument, which confuses diversity of product choice with diversity of life-style or thoughts. It ought to be self-evident that if I choose a Ford and you choose a Volvo, we are not expressing diversity, we are expressing unity. Moreover, if you and I at any one moment are both occupied with mental images and feelings related to products—*any* products—rather than some experience which is not connected to purchasing, then in terms of the commodity system, the gross national product, and the world of advertising, we are indistinguishable; we have merged as "market."

While it might matter to Upjohn or Cutter Laboratories which drug a consumer buys, both are in agreement that they benefit whenever people seek any drug rather than a nondrug solution to a problem.

Advertising, then, serves to further the movement of humans into artificial environments by narrowing the conception of diversity to fit the framework of commodities while unifying people within this conception. The result is a singularly channeled mentality, nicely open to receiving commercial messages, ready to confuse brand diversity with diversity itself, and to confuse human need with the advertiser's need to sell commodities.

The Inherent Need to Create Need

Advertising exists only to purvey what people don't need. Whatever people do need they will find without advertising if it is available. This is so obvious and simple that it continues to stagger my mind that the ad industry has succeeded in muddying the point.

No single issue gets advertisers screaming louder than this one. They speak about how they are only fulfilling the needs of people by providing an information service about where and how people can achieve satisfaction for their needs. Advertising is only a public service, they insist.

Speaking privately, however, and to corporate clients, advertisers sell their services on the basis of how well they are able to create needs where there were none before.

I have never met an advertising person who sincerely believes that there is a need connected to, say, 99 percent of the commodities which fill the airwaves and the print media. Nor can I recall a single street demonstration demanding one single product in all of American history. If there were such a demonstration for, let's say, nonreturnable bottles, which were launched through tens of millions of dollars of ads, or chemically processed foods, similarly dependent upon ads, there would surely have been no need to advertise these products. The only need that is expressed by advertising is the need of advertisers to accelerate the process of conversion of raw materials with no intrinsic value into commodities that people will buy.

If we take the word "need" to mean something basic to human survival—food, shelter, clothing—or basic to human contentment—peace, love, safety, companionship, intimacy, a sense of fulfillment—these will be sought and found by people whether or not there is advertising. In fact, advertising intervenes between people and their needs, *separates* them from direct fulfillment and urges them to believe that satisfaction can be obtained only through commodities. It is through this intervention and separation that advertising can create value, thereby justifying its existence.

Consider the list of the top twenty-five advertisers in the United States. They sell the following products: soaps, detergents, cosmetics, drugs, chemicals, processed foods, tobacco, alcohol, cars and sodas, all of which exist in a realm beyond need. If they were needed, they would not be advertised.

People do need to eat, but the food which is advertised is *processed* food: processed meat, sodas, sugary cereals, candies. A food in its natural state, unprocessed, does not need to be advertised. Hungry people will find the food if it is available. To persuade people to buy the processed version is another matter because it is more expensive, less naturally appealing, less nourishing, and often harmful. The need must be created.

Perhaps there is a need for cleanliness. But that is not what advertisers sell. Cleanliness can be obtained with water and a little bit of natural fiber, or solidified natural fat. Major world civilizations kept clean that way for millennia. What is advertised is *whiteness,* a value beyond cleanliness; *sterility,* the avoidance of all germs; *sudsiness,* a cosmetic factor; and *brand,* a surrogate community loyalty.

There is need for tranquility and a sense of contentment. But these are the last qualities drug advertisers would like you to obtain; not on your own anyway.

A drug ad denies your ability to cope with internal processes: feelings, moods, anxieties. It encourages the belief that personal or traditional ways of dealing with these matters —friends, family, community, or patiently awaiting the next turn in life's cycle—will not succeed in your case. It suggests that a chemical solution is better so that you will choose the chemical rather than your own resources. The result is that you become further separated from yourself and less able to cope. Your ability dies for lack of practice and faith in its efficacy.

A deodorant ad never speaks about the inherent value of applying imitation-lemon fragrance to your body; it has no inherent value. Mainly the ad wishes to intervene in any notion you may have that there is something pleasant or positive in your own human odor. Once the intervention takes place, and self-doubt and anxiety are created, the situation can be satisfied with artificial smells. Only through this process of intervention and substitution is there the prospect of value added and commercial profit.

The goal of all advertising is discontent or, to put it another way, an internal scarcity of contentment. This must be continually created, even at the moment when one has finally bought something. In that event, advertising has the task of *creating* discontent with what has just been bought, since once that act is completed, the purchase has no further benefit to

128

the market system. The newly purchased commodity must be gotten rid of and replaced by the "need" for a new commodity as soon as possible. The ideal world for advertisers would be one in which whatever is bought is used only once and then tossed aside. Many new products have been designed to fit such a world.

Buying Ourselves Back

The necessity for ever-growing markets, the need to create new need, the search for nuances of artificial discontent within previous artificial discontent have required delving ever more deeply inside the human psyche to root out more subtle aspects of experience. Thousands of psychologists, behavioral scientists, perceptual researchers, sociologists and others have found extremely high salaries and steady, interesting work aiding advertisers. Like miners seeking new deposits of coal in the mountains, these social scientists attempt to mine the internal wilderness of human beings.

Once the most obvious feelings have been catalogued, reshaped and developed, these people advance inward to the more subtle veins.

This delving can be amazingly thorough. Stanford Research Institute, one of the larger employers of social scientists doing marketing and advertising research, recently listed *eighteen* inner feelings of "an outdoor sportsman." They ranged from "love of nature" to "a desire to put down one's stay-at-home friends."

In its monthly publication, *Investments in Tomorrow*, Stanford Research Institute literally catalogs new areas where human feeling can be converted into needs. In the July 1975 issue, for example, it presents new opportunities to reach people who have pets, who do home handicrafts, or who seek the wilderness experience. These are all interesting categories because they commercialize aspects of human experience which became packageable only when humans were separated from any direct experience of them. Handicrafts, animals and wilderness became advertisable at the time when they became scarce. Not too long ago they were the stuff of daily life. The fact that most of us are uncomfortable in nature, frightened of it, makes the sale of commodities to mediate the experience —chemicals to keep the bugs off, glasses for fifteen varieties of sunlight, shoes for one kind of walking and boots for another kind—far easier to accomplish than before. Fear is one of the most desirable emotions for advertisers. Loneliness and self-doubt are good ones. So is competition.

One SRI category of market opportunity was particularly poignant: "self-discovery and inner exploration." SRI lists some market opportunities and appropriate appeals for bio-feedback machines, courses in self-improvement, books, work-shops, gurus and meditation systems. These are all marketable now that humans have been separated from their inner experiences. In an earlier world, the idea that inner experience was separable from "outer" experience was unknown. There was no such difference. The outer and the inner were one; there was not even the possibility of survival if one did not take that attitude. Now, however, we are so outwardly focused that inner experience has itself entered the realm of scarcity, making it packageable and capable of being sold back to us as commodity. Our inner lives are now promotable as products. We get to buy back what we already had.

There is an obscure movement of European intellectuals who call themselves "Situationists" and who have developed a comprehensive analysis of the process of removing inner life, in fact all human feeling, from one's immediate experience of it and then reprocessing it and selling it back. Writers like Guy Debord depict capitalist society as consisting of creatures who are redesigned to live life as a representation of itself. He compares this society with others, which lack the profit motive and, therefore, don't need or find desirable the expropriation of inner experience.

The role of advertising, the Situationists say, is to create a world of mirrors in which people can obtain new images of themselves that fit the purposes of the overall system. Through this mirror function and by its expropriation of inner experience, advertising makes the human into a spectator of his or her own life. It is alienation to the tenth power. Life itself becomes a spectacle.

By entering the human being's inner sanctum, our inner wilderness, advertising effectively pulls our feelings up out of ourselves, displays them and sells them back to us like iron from the ground. Our inner feelings are transmogrified into a new form—commodities. We desperately seek to get them back, and pay high prices for the privilege.

The Situationists are correct. Whenever we buy a product we are paying for the recovery of our own feelings. We have thereby turned into creatures who are the commodities we buy. We are the product we pay for and all life is reduced to serving this cycle. Life and commodity achieve absolute merger; the ultimate stage in the inexorable drive of the system to convert all raw material into "valuable" commercial form. Advertising is the internal delivery system for this bizarre process.

The Delivery System's Delivery System

There is one additional factor, however. Advertising itself requires a delivery system. This has been the role of the mass media. All the media have done an excellent job of placing advertising inside people's heads, but some are better at it than others. Television is by far the best, because it has nine natural advantages.

1) Television is itself a commodity, and an expensive

one too. Therefore it is physically consistent with the prevalent reality. Its purchase gives the commodity system a boost.

2) Television changes the nature of artificial environments from passive to active. Unlike buildings and machines, television literally enters inside human beings; inside our homes, our minds, our bodies, making possible the reordering of human processes from the inside.

3) Television is an experience that can be had by virtually everyone at the same time. By substituting for a greater diversity of experiences and unifying everyone with it, it aids commercial efficiency. With all people confined to the same mental and physical condition, a single advertising or political voice appropriate to the common mood can influence everyone.

4) Once diversity of experience is reduced to television, a relative handful of people can control everyone's awareness. Luckily for advertisers, in a capitalist system, whoever is in a position to pay for the technology has primary access to it.

5) Television is unique in that it smooths out any furrows in the commodity system. Dormant anxieties can be dulled by the television experience. Beyond being a delivery system for commodity life, it is the solder to hold that life together, the drug to ease the pain of confined and channeled existence.

6) Though television passes for experience, it is really more like "time out," as we shall see later. It is antiexperience. Its interaction with the human body and mind fixes people to itself, dulls human sensibility and dims awareness of the world. This enhances the commodity life by reducing knowledge of any other.

7) By focusing people on events well outside their lives, television encourages passivity and inaction, discourages self-awareness and the ability to cope personally, both of which are dangerous for advertising.

8) By speaking in images, television adds a dimension to the mirror-image process. Unlike radio or print media, advertising can now implant internal movies, forever available for self-comparison.

9) Television encourages separation: people from community, people from each other, people from themselves, creating more buying units and discouraging organized opposition to the system. It creates a surrogate community: itself. It becomes everyone's intimate advisor, teacher and guide to appropriate behavior and awareness. Thereby, it becomes its own feedback system, furthering its own growth and accelerating the transformation of everything and everyone into artificial form. This enables a handful of people to obtain a unique degree of power.

VII

THE CENTRALIZATION OF CONTROL

A LTHOUGH television was invented in the 1920s, it did not exist for any practical purposes until after World War II. It is easy to forget that advertising, at least on the scale we have come to know it, barely existed before then either.

In 1946, advertisers spent about $3 billion. For the previous two decades, advertising expenditures had been fairly constant at about that level. By 1975, however, the national advertising budget had grown by 1,000 percent to $30 billion.

Most of the increase went into television advertising. Within only ten years of its effective inauguration, television was absorbing 60 percent of all advertising spending and driving hundreds of newspapers, magazines and radio stations out of the market.

A symbiotic relationship developed. Advertising financed television's growth. Television was the greatest delivery system for advertising that had ever been invented. We could call it love at first sight, except in this case, the match may have been prearranged.

If you are old enough, think back to the days immediately after World War II. Although I was only ten in 1945, I remember the expectant and uncertain feeling of the times very well. Everyone was relieved that the war was over and was expecting things to get back to normal, but what was normal? Memories of the Depression loomed. I remember listening to my parents talk with their friends on those backyard summer evenings of 1945, and I could feel the fear.

Like most ordinary people, my parents knew that the war had alleviated the Depression. During the war, American industrial capacity, lying fallow only a few years before, had actually expanded to build the military machine. My father's own business was an example. Now there were no more uniforms to make, and no more tanks. The war had given men jobs as soldiers and women jobs as factory workers. Full employment had practically become a reality. Now Johnny was marching home again, jobless.

If this was the talk among ordinary people, one can only imagine what was said in industrial boardrooms and at the Department of Commerce. With industrial capacity and capital investment expanded as they were, the consequences of a drop in production could make the 1930s look like golden years. A long-standing criticism of capitalism—that it can stave off cyclic depression only through war—seemed about to be confirmed.

Economic Growth and Patriotic Consumption

Suddenly in 1946, government and industry started making identical pronouncements about regearing American life to consume commodities at a level never before contemplated. It wasn't that military production was about to be abandoned. Even now it remains the single most important factor in the

United States economy. However, in 1946 with the war just over, it was not clear that the decline in military spending would be as temporary as it turned out to be. Some new off-setting factor was needed.

Thus, a new vision was born that equated the good life with consumer goods. An accelerated economy, continuing the booming expansion of wartime, added to a new consumer ideology achieved the greatest economic growth rate in this country's history from 1946 to 1970.

To make such growth possible, both ends of the transformation process described in the last chapter had to be hyped up. First, we needed to insure an abundant supply of raw materials to convert into commodities. This led to a burst of American investment overseas as well as to enormous aid programs for sympathetic "underdeveloped" countries. Often we secured our supply by the creation of client governments propped up with military aid. Raising anticommunism to the status of a holy war in the 1940s and 1950s formed the political foundation for these military and economic programs and underlay the assertion of the patriotic virtues of foreign investment.

At the other end of the transformation equation, an accelerated movement of commodities into consumers' homes was critical. People had to be convinced that life without all these products was undesirable and unpatriotic. It was time to forget the rationing of the war years and consume for your country.

Advertising and television were the dynamic duo that would rededicate the consuming American. Advertising's ability to create a passionate need for what is not needed was already well established. Since economic growth and a consumer economy had to be based upon selling far more commodities than were needed to meet actual needs, economic growth depended upon advertising. Television, which had been lying around in mothballs since the 1920s, was dusted off and enlisted as the means to deliver the advertising life-style fast, right into people's homes and heads.

Quick to spot any new technology that could aid their urgent cause, big advertisers immediately invested hundreds of millions of dollars in developing this idle sales tool. And so advertising gave birth to television, and television gave advertising a whole new world to conquer. Together they made possible an enormous, though temporary, economic bonanza.

Can you recall the TV advertising of the 1940s and 1950s? Smiling, happy people. Scrubbed children. Housewives showing their impossibly clean wash. Smiling junior-executive husbands emerging from their new cars, greeted at the picket fence by their clean, cheerful families? The happy mowing of the lawn. The happy faces reflected off the polished toasters?

The nuclear family was idealized to a greater extent than ever before, because the family was the ideal consumption unit. Women had to get out of those factories and overalls and back into little pink dresses in the kitchen. Those returning soldiers needed jobs. Rosie the Riveter gave way to June Allyson. Separate family units maximized production potential. Private homes. Private cars. Two cars. Private washing machines. Private television sets.

Within a few years, the world started changing. The battery-operated lawn mower I saw on television one day appeared on my lawn the next week. So did the car. The whole neighborhood started looking like a television commercial. The woods near my house disappeared and were replaced by hundreds of identical versions of my house. Neighborhoods everywhere started looking like each other. Freeways replaced country roads. Shopping centers replaced corner markets. Pavements covered everything.

"Prosperity," "security," "happiness," studded ads and presidential speeches alike. This incredible outpouring of commodities, this entire revamping of landscape, this filling of houses with gadgets was supposed to constitute some kind of latter-day Nirvana. That's what everyone was thinking, saying, and believing. It was what made America America.

One of my high school teachers during the 1950s told my class that it was America's commitment to a consumption economy that made our country different and better than all others. He told us that by expanding our economy, we would soon make everyone wealthy. America was already the world's only classless society, he said. Workers and managers were equal partners in a glorious process benefiting everyone. In America everyone was equal. Our standard of living made it that way. Everyone could have a car. Everyone could have a television. Everyone could own a home. Everyone could have a business. We were not like Mexico and Nicaragua, dirty little countries, where there were a few rich people and everyone else was poor and all of them wished they had what we had.

A few years later at the Wharton School of Business at the University of Pennsylvania, I learned how and why this commodity life and the economic growth it produces was supposed to be so good for absolutely everyone. I learned what they had been talking about in those boardrooms and at the Department of Commerce. It was called the "trickle-down theory."

The Trickle-Down Theory

It goes more or less like this:
Industrial expansion, rapid economic growth and the consumption economy benefit everyone. The theory—which is the basis of Keynesian American economics—has it that when people buy more and more commodities, they produce more

profits for industry, enabling it to expand. When industry expands, more jobs result. This puts more money into circulation, enabling people to buy *more* commodities, expanding profits again, yielding more investments, more jobs and starting the cycle around on another turn.

I have oversimplified the process, leaving out such variables as savings, borrowing, and so on. The way I have presented it is more or less the way it is translated through the media and through our educational system into popular understanding: a beautiful circle of activity, everyone helping everyone else, labor and management rowing the boat together, all serving the common good and growing endlessly. It explained the patriotic urgency of people spending more and more on commodities. The benefits would "trickle down" to everyone in the country, including those at the bottom of the pyramid. Jobs, money, prosperity, happiness, security, democracy, equality were all lumped together as inevitable results of this cycle.

I believed in it. We all believed in it. Most people believe in it still. Presidents get elected based on whether they can convince the public that they will stimulate the beautiful cycle. Jimmy Carter was elected for saying he knew how to do it.

The trickle-down theory is the nice simple kind of economic model that can be sold to a mass population removed from any deeper understanding of how things really work. Trying to come to grips with economic nuance is for most of us no easier than trying to understand how much nuclear radiation is "safe." Who knows? The "experts" know.

Like every other organizing model in our society, economic processes have been removed from personal participation, appropriated into a nether world of flow charts, financial analyses and circle graphs. Like scientific and technological systems, once economic systems reach a certain size and complexity, they can be controlled only by forces far outside the grasp of the individual and community. One explanation of them sounds as plausible as another. In the absence of a really thorough training in economics—a training which itself supports many arbitrary and fantastic theories—this trickle-down model of the benefits of a consumer society sounds perfectly valid.

It certainly seemed valid for a little while. People had jobs, the economy was growing, and homes were filling up with ever more intricate gadgets.

Only now, thirty years after the trip was launched, can we see the process from the vantage point of joblessness, inflation, bankruptcy and default, and realize that something was terribly wrong somewhere.

In fact, it was a fantasy. It was packaged and sold to us like the seven-piece matching living-room sets on the television screen. Buy now, pay later when you are richer than you are now. But when later came, very few of us were richer.

It turned out that the pursuit of all those happy goodies didn't produce happy people; it produced isolated, frustrated, alienated people. More important, the economic benefits did not trickle down to create some egalitarian democracy. The benefits trickled *up*.

Beneficiaries of the Advertising Fantasy

The period of rapid growth from 1946 to 1970, which coincided with the emergence of television and electronic advertising, concentrated wealth and power in this country to an unheard-of degree. It put effective control of the economy in the hands of a few corporate entities. It concentrated immense wealth among a handful of people. Meanwhile, the working classes, and the more disadvantaged nonworking people, to whom the commodity life had promised dazzling benefits, ended up in a far worse, more desperate and more dependent position than ever before.

A New York advertising man, Lawrence G. Chait, was

the first person to articulate clearly the economic concentration made inevitable by economic growth. In a now-famous speech he gave in Detroit in 1968, Chait said, "The factor of overwhelming significance in our business and financial life for some years now has been the trend toward concentration of economic power."

Pointing out that in 1965 this country had 412,000 business units, he added, "The fifty largest controlled 35.2 percent of the total manufacturing assets."

As for profits, "The twenty largest manufacturing corporations, [who hold] 25 percent of total corporate assets, had 32 percent of [the nation's] profits after taxes." That means that only .005 percent of the corporations in this country enjoyed one-third of all corporate profits.

Chait went on: "Assets and profits are, of course, important measures of concentration in national economic life, but there are other very interesting indices. In 1963, for example, there were 112 industries in which 4 companies accounted for more than 50 percent of production. In 29 of these 112 industries, the top 4 companies accounted for more than 75 percent of production. By 1963, 30 percent of the volume of production of consumer goods came from industries in which the top 4 firms accounted for over 50 percent of production."

Chait quoted economics professor Corwin Edwards to explain why the larger corporations *inevitably* get larger during periods of economic growth, absorbing or driving out smaller ones: "In encounters with small enterprises it [the corporate conglomerate] can buy scarce materials and attractive sites, inventions and facilities; pre-empt the services of the most expensive technicians and executives; and acquire reserves of materials for the future. It can absorb losses that would consume the entire capital of a smaller rival. . . . Moment by moment the big company can outbid, out-spend in advertising, technology or talent, or out-lose the smaller ones; and from the series of such momentary advantages it derives an advantage in attaining its larger aggregate results.

"The sociologists may very well take exception to this trend," Chait said, "but as pragmatists, we must recognize that this in fact is the direction in which the economic organization of our country is moving." Finally, he quoted Dr. Edwin G. Nourse, who believes, "There are no discernible limits at which such concentrations of economic power, once fully underway, would automatically cease."

A moving example of the way the process works is offered in *The American Farm* by Maisie and Richard Conrat. The authors point out that only two hundred years ago, 95 percent of the population of this country lived on farm land; now less than 5 percent do. The family farm is a creature of the past, and so is the moderately large farm. The economics of technological scale nourish only the hugest agribusinesses and their machines. The critical period in this change came immediately after World War II: "With astonishing rapidity, the 60 horsepower general purpose tractor was replaced by a new 140 horsepower model, then by a towering 235 horsepower machine with a $40,000 price tag. The single-row corn harvester gave place to machines that could handle four rows simultaneously, then eight rows. The cost of such new equipment made it economically imperative for farmers to take on more acreage. Between 1950 and 1975, the acreage of the average American farm doubled and the value of farm machinery trebled . . . those who could not keep up with the frenzied pace were shoved aside and forced to drop out. In the new agriculture there was no room for the man who simply wished to live on the land and work in the soil and sell enough to pay his bills. The dairyman with twenty cows was notified by his milk company that they would not be making pick-ups at his place anymore. From now on the company trucks were stopping only at the farms of the large operators. Small scale vegetable producers, orchardists, and general farmers found themselves underpriced and cut out of the market by supermarket chains and agribusiness corporations."

What was true for farmers was true for all business as the rapid-growth phenomenon gave automatic advantage to the larger, better-financed, more technologically advanced elements of the system.

Smaller competitors were driven from competition by the mere scale of the expenditure required at every level, from the cost of automation to the salaries of executives to the availability of bank loans. Banks, recognizing very early that large companies are better loan risks than small ones, actively aided the advancing juggernaut. Smaller companies were wise to face the fact that it was usually better to sell out before things got worse.

Nowhere were the advantages of size more evident than in advertising. *Only* the largest corporations in the world have access to network television time because it can cost $120,000 per minute while reaching 30 million people. Television is the media counterpart to the eight-row corn harvester.

The Effect on Individuals

It was not only abstract entities like corporations that benefited disproportionately during the commodity boom. So did the people who owned the corporations.

Dr. Lester C. Thurow, professor of economics and management at MIT and former member of the Council of Economic Advisors, published some enlightening figures in the *Public Interest Economics Newsletter* of December 1975.

By 1962, says Thurow, during the final spurt of the greatest economic growth of any industrial nation in history: "The top 18 percent of all families owned 76.2 percent of all privately held wealth in the U.S., while the bottom 25 percent, roughly 50 million people, had no assets at all. . . . recent estimates suggest no significant change . . ."

Thurow continues: "The top 5 percent of the families own more wealth than the bottom 81 percent. The top .008 percent hold as many assets as the bottom half of the population."

Thurow goes on to say that "wealth and power are even more concentrated than are indicated in these data, because of the inter-relationships among the wealthiest individuals and the large corporations they control."

In other words, this .008 percent can, through their stock ownership and interlocking directorships, effectively dominate the few corporations that in turn dominate the economy.

I believe Thurow is suggesting conspiracy, or at least a startling degree of collaboration among these few. Perhaps his academic standing prevents him from putting it that way. Since I don't have any academic standing, I am willing to draw the obvious conclusions.

Thurow goes on to talk about income: "The income gap between the bottom 5 percent [of the families] and the top 5 percent is 45 to 1, and the income gap between the bottom 1 percent and top 1 percent is 525 to 1. The top 1 percent received nearly three times as much income annually as the bottom 20 percent of the American population. The fact that only the government transfer payments [social security, welfare, food stamps] have kept the position of the lowest income groups from declining, indicates that the distribution of earnings by the private sector is becoming more and more unequal. . . . The lowest fifth of the population receives only 1.7 percent of the earnings as distributed by the market [private industry], *down from the already miserable 2.6 percent in 1943*. The top fifth receives through the market 28 times as much in wages and salaries as the lowest fifth."

Thurow's point is that if the government, that is, the taxpayer, didn't pick up the slack which industrial growth has created, the widening gap between the rich and poor would be perfectly obvious. In the false belief that industrial growth will provide benefits to the poor and unemployed, we provide tax breaks to aid industrial growth. Meanwhile, with our own taxes, we feed the growing number of hungry and poor, who are blamed for the rising taxes. We pay for what is being taken away from us. At each turn of the cycle, the situation becomes more desperate.

What these figures reveal is that America is every bit as dominated and directed by a tiny minority of wealthy people as the Mexico and Nicaragua of my high school teacher's fantasy. Looking at the past thirty years through our new reality of unemployment lines, bankrupted small businesses, and the immense profits of a handful of corporate giants, we can see that we are now much further away from an egalitarian society than we were a generation ago. The American Dream was a dream.

Flaws in the Fantasy

Since the dream was packaged and sold by advertising people, it ought to be no surprise that the flaws in it were never mentioned. It is inherent in the advertising process to tell only those parts of the story that encourage the desired belief.

Two major flaws were covered over. The first was that commodity consumption and economic growth, even if beneficial, could not go on forever. The second was that economic flow in a private enterprise economy, during periods of rapid growth, is inexorably distorted to favor the rich.

Unlimited economic growth is a planetary impossibility. It could only have been conceived by minds out of touch with natural limits. It is dependent upon a suicidal overuse of resources and an impossible rate of commodity consumption. It depends upon all elements of the resource-production-consumption cycle operating at an accelerated rate that cannot be maintained in the long run.

At the initial signs of raw materials shortages, of which oil and copper were only the first, production began to decline, jobs were lost, buying power decreased, while, contrary to the textbook laws of supply and demand, prices went up. The handful of corporations that totally dominate supply were able to raise prices, getting more money from the ever-shrinking number of people who could afford to pay.

In addition, many of our client governments abroad, which had been paving our way to *their* resources, began to fall to revolutionary movements. This was particularly true in African, Asian, and Middle Eastern nations, bringing into view the bottom of the bottomless pit of goodies.

Meanwhile the limits of commodity consumption were appearing. People cannot buy two new cars every year forever. Nor can road builders keep building roads once the landscape is mostly covered. People cannot replace their living-room furnishings, microwave ovens or television sets annually, no matter how much advertising they see. Eventually, purchase rates slow down. There is an end to the consumption process. Markets *can* be overexploited.

While many Americans do not realize that this is what has happened, the largest corporations have known it for some time. Many of them, seeing a burned-out market, have been dismantling their American operations and reestablishing themselves as transnational entities. The United States, with its ravaged cities and exploited landscapes, faces the prospect of becoming a sort of gigantic boomtown, exploited and abandoned.

With operations geared to nations that are just emerging as markets, the multinational corporations are taking television into places in Asia, Africa and South America where there are often no telephones or paved roads. Satellite television systems have been installed in many countries ahead of modern transportation or sanitation systems. TV provides pretraining for the commodity life that is coming up fast.

People in villages where electricity has just arrived are watching ads filled with ecstatically happy people using artificial milk, Coca-Cola and electric shavers.

Even if economic growth could go on forever, it does not benefit all people. It benefits only the owners of businesses, not the working people, and it surely has nothing to offer the jobless. It doesn't take a Marxist economist to explain why.

Such distinguished corporate experts as Louis Kelso have been predicting our present malaise for decades. In his brilliant *How to Turn Eighty Million Workers into Capitalists on Borrowed Money,* Kelso argues that as capitalist enterprise grows, the rich must get richer and the poor poorer because owners of businesses have more kinds of incomes. They have wage income, which is many times higher than that of the average wage earner, and they also have dividend income. Then, they have another advantage: In periods of economic growth, they enjoy large profits that may be used for further capital investment, which will provide additional profits at a later time.

Workers, whether blue- or white-collar, have only one income source: wages. There may be occasional wage hikes, but the rate of wage increases can never match the threefold opportunities of the business owners. The workers, therefore, fall further behind as time passes.

During the postwar period, while most of us were singing the praises of our expanding economy and buying toasters, washing machines, cars and gas-powered lawn mowers, all of which were designed to break down after a certain period, some people were able to use their double or triple incomes to build new plants and buy up small companies, labor-saving technology and raw materials such as Chilean mines, oil rights or Brazilian forests.

This is ignored by trickle-down theorists, who keep saying

that the owners of the businesses use their extra wealth in reinvestments which expand job markets, suggesting that it is actually desirable that some people have more money than others. But investment in labor-saving technology *reduces* jobs. Expansion of overseas facilities reduces *American* jobs. The purchase of small companies means the merging or elimination of some production facilities, further reducing jobs.

Aside from this, much of the surplus wealth is not spent on capital investment. It is plowed into inflation hedges such as gems, art and land, driving the prices of those items further out of the reach of wage earners.

As often as not, the disparity in incomes increases while the total number of jobs is reduced. In an economic climate where a few large businesses control supply and prices, as the number of jobs declines any employee who becomes too uppity or too demanding can easily be ousted. Where unions are strong, whole businesses can be packed up and moved, for example, to South Korea or Hong Kong, where workers tolerate fourteen-hour days at forty cents an hour. American wage earners are left with their single incomes, their shrinking power, and a widening gap between them and the people who control their lives.

The Depression Never Ended

As we slowly begin to understand that the American Dream was not merely a dream but a hoax, and that far from bene-fiting economic democracy, it produced a terrifying concentration of wealth and power, we can also grasp the quality of our new dependency. It is similar to the old company-store syndrome. These few huge enterprises control the jobs, and as job competition increases, they also control the salaries. As Tennessee Ernie Ford sang: We work for the company, we beg to keep our jobs, we don't make trouble, and we buy at the company store.

In retrospect we can see what should have been obvious all along. The Great Depression of the 1930s never ended. It went underground, covered over by a war which created jobs and expanded industrial capacity, and then, when the war was over, by an advertising fantasy, a pipe dream sold to us with a purpose.

The new American life-style based on commodity consumption, emphasizing credit buying on the never-never plan, and economic growth with its inevitable concentration of economic power, only produced a more virulent version of the older Depression. In the 1930s, as the number of jobs went down, at least prices did too. Now, because economic concentration has advanced to the point where price competition is passé, as jobs disappear, prices go up.

This new phenomenon was summarized in *Mother Jones* (February 1977) by economists David Olson and Richard Parker, reporting on a study by Dr. Howard Wachtel and Peter Adelsheim for the Joint Economic Committee of Congress:

"They found that corporations in food, utilities, rubber, tobacco, computers, aircraft, to name a few, had all raised their prices at times the textbooks say they should have rolled them back. How can corporations raise prices when the economy is stagnant, demand is falling, factories are operating well below full capacity and more and more people are out of work? The answer, Wachtel says, is economic concentration—entire industries increasingly dominated by a small number of ever-larger firms . . . fewer and fewer big businesses need to compete through pricing. This creates a situation in which prices can be increased and inflation kept rising even during periods of recession."

Meanwhile, the government of this country, like the governments of other Western countries, has been losing the power to control these actions. Existing outside the boundaries of the country, the multinational companies, in concert with banks, are capable of the economic domination of entire nations. Governments slip slowly into a new role subordinate to and supportive of them.

Dr. Lester Thurow concluded his paper in the *Public Interest Economics Newsletter,* "There is no satisfactory answer to the question of why the American people have been content to leave untouched the enormous concentration of wealth that characterizes this economy."

It is possible that Thurow was being coy when he made that statement, because there certainly is an obvious explanation. Too few people have ever heard of the figures listed here, and many of those that have heard them may have been too indoctrinated with accepted economic theory to grasp their true meaning. All of our cultural institutions teach us that Keynesian economics and the trickle-down theory of economic growth have a certain effect when they actually have an effect which is opposite to what is claimed.

Since the overwhelming majority of Americans are removed from any personal participation in economic processes, we have come to believe in an artificial economic construct propagated by the people who benefit from it and who control the media that explain it to us.

Domination of the Influencing Machine

In 1960, at the moment when our economic growth rate was near its highest point and the nation had been totally wired in to television, the trade publication *Advertising Age* commented, "Network television, particularly, is largely the creature of the 100 largest companies in the country."

150

In that year, the one hundred largest advertisers in the country accounted for 83 percent of all network television advertising. The top twenty-five of these accounted for 65 percent of the 83 percent. Since that time, the ratio has scarcely altered.

The domination of the one hundred largest is most apparent in network television, but it applies in other media. In 1974, for example, the top one hundred accounted for 55 percent of *all* advertising in all media, 59 percent of all network radio advertising, and 76 percent of network television ads. Since virtually all media in this country depend upon advertising for survival, it ought to be obvious that these one hundred corporations, themselves dominated by a handful of wealthy people, can largely determine which magazines, newspapers, radio stations and television stations can continue to exist and which cannot.

Public television also fits the mold. During 1975, more than 40 percent of all public-television programming was paid for by these same one hundred companies: mainly oil, chemical and drug companies. This is not quite the same level of domination that is found at the commercial networks, but the effect is the same. Survival depends upon them.

For both commercial television and public television then it is absolutely necessary to create programs that these one hundred advertisers will support. They are where the action is. Given the costs of television, they are the *only* action.

We are speaking of control by 100 corporations out of 400,000. The interest of the other 399,900 are irrelevant as far as television is concerned. As for the thoughts, wishes and feelings of the noncorporate segments of American society—nearly 250 million human beings whose perspectives are as varied as the Indian, the artistic, the humanistic, the ecological, the socialistic, to name a very few—these are not of the slightest importance.

Broadcast television, like other monolithic technologies,

from eight-row corn threshers and agribusiness to supertankers, nuclear power plants, computer networks, hundred-story office buildings, satellite communications, genetic engineering, international pipelines and SSTs, is available only to monstrous corporate powers. What we get to see on television is what suits the mentality and purposes of one hundred corporations.

While purporting to be a mass technology available to everyone, because everyone can *experience* it, television is little more than the tool of these companies. If four out of five dollars of television income derive from them, then obviously, without currying their favor the networks would cease to exist.

The corollary is also true. Without such a single, monolithic instrument as television, the effective power and control of these huge corporations could not be harnessed as it presently is. Monolithic economic enterprise needs monolithic media to purvey its philosophy and to influence rapid change in consumption patterns. Without an instrument like television, capable of reaching everyone in the country at the same time and narrowing human needs to match the redesigned environment, the corporations themselves could not exist.

The spread of television unified a whole people within a system of conceptions and living patterns that made possible the expansion of huge economic enterprise. Because of it, our whole culture and the physical shape of the environment, no more or less than our minds and feelings, have been computerized, linearized, suburbanized, freewayized, and packaged for sale.

It is a moot point whether those who control television knew what the outcome would be when they dusted it off after the war and sent it out to sell. Whether they invented television for that purpose or it invented them, the relationship was symbiotic. Its use was predetermined by the evolution of economic and technological patterns that led up to it and that have since continued on their inevitable path. As we shall see, its use and effects were also determined by the nature and limits of television technology itself.

ARGUMENT THREE

EFFECTS OF TELEVISION ON THE HUMAN BEING

Television technology produces neuro-physiological responses in the people who watch it. It may create illness, it certainly produces confusion and submission to external imagery. Taken together, the effects amount to conditioning for autocratic control.

VIII

ANECDOTAL REPORTS: SICK, CRAZY, MESMERIZED

DURING the years I was preparing this book, occasional pieces of publicity appeared about it. With each exposure mail would arrive in my home. From one article alone I received more than two hundred fifty letters. Most were passionate and troubled. It became clear that watching TV was an experience that an amazing number of people were eager to describe.

I also kept an informal record of the terms people used in ordinary conversation to describe how they felt about television. In all, I recorded about two thousand conversational and written descriptions.

While I make no claims about this amounting to any kind of bona fide scientific sampling, the phrases people chose had a definite consistency. To give you an idea, I'm going to list the fifteen phrases most frequently used.

If you could somehow drop all preconception of television and read this list as though people were describing some instrument you'd never seen yourself, I think the picture you would obtain is of a machine that invades, controls and deadens the people who view it. It is not unlike the alien-operated "influencing machine" of the psychopathic fantasy.

1) "I feel hypnotized when I watch television."

2) "Television sucks my energy."

3) "I feel like it's brainwashing me."

4) "I feel like a vegetable when I'm stuck there at the tube."

5) "Television spaces me out."

6) "Television is an addiction and I'm an addict."

7) "My kids look like zombies when they're watching."

8) "TV is destroying my mind."

9) "My kids walk around like they're in a dream because of it."

10) "Television is making people stupid."

11) "Television is turning my mind to mush."

12) "If a television is on, I just can't keep my eyes off it."

13) "I feel mesmerized by it."

14) "TV is colonizing my brain."

15) "How can I get my kids off it and back into life?"

At one point I heard my son Kai say: "I don't want to watch television as much as I do but I can't help it. It makes me watch it."

I don't mean to suggest that there weren't many favorable reports. Often the people who described themselves as "spaced out" *liked* that experience. They said it helped them forget about their otherwise too busy lives.

Many added the word "meditative"; others found it "relaxing," saying that it helped them "forget about the world." Some who used terms like "brainwashed" or "addicted" nonetheless felt that television provided them with good information or entertainment, although there was no one who felt television lived up to its "potential."

In all the time I collected responses, only eight people suggested they watched too little.

I also kept track of my own reactions. Though I now watch very little television—perhaps two or three hours per month, just to keep my hand in, as it were—I used to watch more. My reactions to the experience invariably reduced to one or two constants. Even if the program I'd been watching had been of some particular interest, the experience felt "antilife," as though I'd been drained in some way, or I'd been used. I came away feeling a kind of internal deadening, as if my whole physical being had gone dormant, the victim of a vague soft assault. The longer I watched, the worse I'd feel. Afterward, there was nearly always the desire to go outdoors or go to sleep, to recover my strength and my feelings. Another thing. After watching television, I'd always be aware of a kind of glowing inside my head: the images! They'd remain in there even after the set was off, like an aftertaste. Against my will, I'd find them returning to my awareness hours later.

My objective in keeping all these records was not so much to catalog how many people liked television and how many did not, or how many felt guilty about their habit, but rather to gather descriptions of the experience in the terms people chose to describe it.

After a while, I came to realize that people were describing concrete physical symptoms that neither they nor anyone else actually believed were real. The people who would tell me that television was controlling their minds would then laugh about it. Or they would say they were addicted to it, or felt like vegetables while watching, and then they'd laugh at that.

People were saying they were being hypnotized, controlled, drugged, deadened, but they would not assign validity to their own experience. Yet if there is any truth in these descriptions, we are dealing with a force that is far more powerful and subtle than Huxley's hypnopaedic machines. If television "hypnotizes," "brainwashes," "controls minds," "makes people stupid," "turns everyone into zombies," then you would think it would be an appropriate area of scientific inquiry. In fact, someone should call the police.

Science has a name for such collections of descriptions. They are called "anecdotal evidence" or "experiential reports." Such reports are not totally ignored by researchers, although they are not exactly taken seriously either. In the case of television, there is the problem that the symptoms are not fatal, they are subtle. Few people go to doctors complaining about them. They therefore remain below the threshold of visibility for scientific inquiry. Even when such reports are noticed, science does not accept them as valid unless they have been put through the grinder of scientific proof. Since it is beyond science to validate exactly what is meant by "zombie" or "brainwash" or even "addiction" or, as we will see, even "hypnosis," these symptoms inevitably remain *un*proved, leaving people who need external validation at a loss.

I have already stated my opinion that one major result of modern science has been to make people doubt what they would otherwise accept as true from their own observation and experience. Science, medicine, psychology and economics all deeply depend on people being mystified by their own experience and blind to the strict limits of scientific method.

In this country, where intervention between humans and their inner selves is so very advanced, the mystification is virtually total.

If the National Institutes of Health funded a $5 million study over a three-year period which gathered together all the "experts" to determine the effects of television on the body and mind, and then reported its findings to the president of the United States, who, frightened by the results, then appointed a commission of scholars and other experts to do it over again, one of whom smuggled a copy of the original "findings" to *The New York Times,* which then carried it on page one: SUPPRESSED STUDY SUGGESTS TELEVISION IS ADDICTIVE, HYP-NOTIC, STOPS THOUGHT: SIMILAR TO BRAINWASHING: OTHER PHYSICAL EFFECTS NOTED, *then* people would say, "You know, I always thought that might be true."

In my opinion, if people are watching television for four hours every day and they say they can't stop it, and also say that it seems to be programming them in some way, and they are seeing their kids go dead, then really, I deeply feel there is no need to study television. This evidence is what lawyers call "prima facie" proof. The only question is how to deal with it. I am satisfied that most people are already perfectly aware of what television is doing to them, but they remain tranquilized by the general wisdom that: the programming is the problem, and it is useless to attempt to change it anyway. Television is here to stay.

In the end, however, perhaps because this mystification also lurks in me, I decided to ask around in the scientific community to see who, if anyone, was concerned about the nature of the television experience.

Invisible Phenomenon

I contacted the Brain Information Service of the Bio-Medical Library of UCLA and spoke with Dr. Doris Dunn there. I asked her if that was an appropriate place to seek any published materials, including doctoral dissertations, which could relate television to a variety of medical and physiological syndromes.

She told me that the computer there could scan as many as

a half million items covering the neuroscience literature published since 1969. She said it was probably as thorough a scanning service as existed for this kind of material.

I told her that I was interested in anything that made any relationship between television and the following: Hypnosis, addiction, hyperactivity, the neurophysiology of light reception, brainwashing, dreaming, thinking, brainwave activity.

I told her that I was also interested in anything that could be uncovered concerning *any* neurophysiological responses to television and that I'd appreciate her adding her own creative good judgment.

I asked her if she thought much would turn up; she said she doubted it.

Later I called her back to tell her that, thinking it over, I realized she'd probably turn up quite a lot on X-radiation from television sets and that I didn't need it. A lot had already been published on that.

To get a sense of comparison, I asked her how many items she would expect to turn up in some *other* area of inquiry. I anticipated being able to make the point that science has failed to look at television as an instrument that produces biological reactions and that this in itself reveals an almost blind acceptance of the medium.

Two weeks later, I received a bibliography of seventy-eight items, covering the period 1969–1975. Dr. Dunn's covering letter said I could get a sense of comparison from the fact that for a subject like sleep and dreaming about one thousand items would be filed every year. On EEG brainwave activity "several thousand" are filed every year. However, not one of the dreaming articles contained significant reference to television, and only one article on brainwave activity referred to a relationship with television.

Of the seventy-eight references, there were twenty articles concerning a condition called "television epilepsy"—in which otherwise nonepileptic people go into fits while watching television—and several on eye damage, heart rate changes according to the program content, and some on X-radiation, which I'd anticipated.

Of the half million articles scanned by the computer, only two spoke of any relationship between television and hypnosis. There was one about television causing headaches, several on the effects of television on perceptions of scale and distance, and about a dozen on the effects of television on young people. (These latter articles turned out to be "behavioral," not physiological, articles which slipped through the gates.)

It is clear that the neurophysiological effect of television is no hot subject for scientific research.

To augment and also double-check the Brain Information Service, I asked San Francisco journalist and researcher Mickey Friedman if she would do some digging through the *Psychological Abstracts,* which contain virtually the same listings as the computer, but carry the subject categories back for several more decades. Friedman went all the way back to 1940 and found only nine additional references, including one on addiction, the first one, and one on hypnosis.

Then, in the spring of 1977, an extremely interesting book appeared, the first to argue that the experience of television— the act of watching it—is more significant than the content of the programs being watched. *The Plug-In Drug* by Marie Winn caused a sensation among worried parents, psychologists and educators. It asserted that television viewing by children was addictive, that it was turning a generation of children into passive, incommunicative "zombies" who couldn't play, couldn't create, and couldn't even think very clearly.

I read through the book seeking the sources of Marie Winn's research only to discover that she had run up against the same dearth of research that was already apparent to me. This did not stop her, to her credit, as she strung together long interviews of parents, children, and educators. She gave validity to a series of experiential reports that were parallel to those I'd collected. She combined these with whatever could be gathered from non-television-related research on cognition, on reading patterns, on verbal and nonverbal thinking, and on the observations of other writers, and what she could gather from her own observance of the television experience.

She drew a horrifying picture of a generation of children who were growing up without the basic skills that most earlier generations had used to get through life, children who could not even solve the problem of dealing with free time. She also described the disassembling effects television has upon family life, in which communication and even direct affection and participation in each other's lives were being processed through television experience, to the extreme detriment of everyone.

Having gone as far as she went, however, Marie Winn didn't apply her findings to adults and didn't relate any of the effects of television to the power drives of the wider society.

I decided to continue digging and soon found myself creating my own horrifying picture of television's effect and how it fits the needs of the juggernaut. The nature of the viewing experience itself, the technology of fixation (which I already knew from advertising), new research on biological effects, together with discoveries about the power of implanted imagery, combine to create a pattern in which the newly diminished role of the human being is more and more apparent.

Dimming Out the Human

Television is watched in darkened rooms. Some people leave on small lights, or daylight filters in, but it is a requirement of television viewing that the set be the brightest image in the environment or it cannot be seen well.

To increase the effect, background sounds are dimmed out just as the light is. An effort is made to eliminate household noises. The point, of course, is to further the focus on the television set. Awareness of the outer environment gets in the way.

Many people watch television alone a substantial amount of the time. This eliminates yet another aspect of outer awareness. Even while watching with others, a premium is placed upon quiet. Talking interferes with attention to the set. If you like to look at people while talking, turning your head actually breaks attention. So other people are dimmed out like the light, the sounds, and the rest of the world.

Dimming out your own body is another part of the process. People choose a position for viewing that allows the maximum comfort and least motion, that is, the least awareness of the body because like awareness of external light, sound or other stimuli, awareness of your own body can detract from the focus on the television. Positions are chosen in which arms and legs will not have to be moved. One may shift weight from time to time, or go for a snack, but for most of the experience, the body is quiet.

This dimming out is also true of the internal organs. The heartbeat slows to idle, the pulse rate tends to even out, the brainwave patterns go into a smooth and steady rhythm. The consequences of all this will be examined a little later. For now, let's just say that thinking processes also dim.

Overall, while we are watching television, our bodies are in a quieter condition over a longer period of time than in any other of life's nonsleeping experiences. This is true even for the eyes, which are widely presumed to be active during television viewing. In fact, the eyes move *less* while watching television than in any other experience of daily life. This is particularly so if you sit at a distance from the set or if your set is small. In such cases you take in the entire image without scanning. Even with huge television screens, the eyes do not move as much as they do when seeing a movie, where the very size of the theater screen requires eye and even head movement.

Even when you are working in an office, or reading a book, the eyes move more than they do while watching television. In offices there are always interruptions. While reading, you vary the speed at which you read, go over material and raise your eyes off the page from time to time.

In the wider world outside of the media, the eyes almost never stop moving, searching and scanning. For humans, the eyes are "feelers"; they are one of our major contacts with the world and are forever reaching and studying.

While you are watching television, in addition to the non-movement of the eyeball, there is a parallel freezing of the focusing mechanism. The eye remains at a fixed distance from the object observed for a longer period of time than in any other human experience.

Ordinarily, the process of focusing, defocusing and refocusing engages the eye nonstop all day long, even during sleeping and dreaming. But while you are watching television, no matter what is happening on the screen, however far away the action of the story is supposed to be inside the set, the set itself remains at a fixed distance and requires only an infinitesimal change in focus. As we shall see, the result is to flatten all information into one dimension and to put the viewer in a condition akin to unconscious staring.

However idle the eyes are during television watching, they are positively lively compared to the other senses. Sound is reduced to the extremely narrow ranges of television audio, while smell, taste and touch are eliminated altogether.

Artificial Touch and Hyperactivity

McLuhan made the case that television stimulates the sense of touch. He calls TV "tactile." I don't know if he intended that as one of his personal jokes, which got taken too seriously, or if he actually meant it, but it is one of the most dangerous of the many misleading statements he made.

He suggests that light playing against the skin is itself stimulating. The silliness of that statement can be gathered by merely comparing *that* low-level stimulation with the sort of stimulation the skin would receive from just about any minor body movement. Reaching for a grape involves more body-wide skin stimulation: clothes against skin, stretching, cool grapes bursting sour in the mouth.

Worse, McLuhan implies that in seeing images on a screen, the human is inclined to act on them, thereby inciting the sense of touch for action. This is a really irresponsible remark.

Images on television are not real. They are not events taking place where the person who views them is sitting. The images are taking place in the television set, which then projects them into the brain of the viewer. Direct response to them would therefore be more than absurd. So whatever stimulation is felt is instantly repressed. While McLuhan may be correct that seeing the images stimulates the impulse to move, the impulse is cut off. The effect is a kind of sensory tease, to put the case generously. The human starts a process and then stops it, then starts it again, then stops it, vibrating back and forth between those two poles of action and repression, all of it without a purpose in real life.

There is mounting evidence that this back-and-forth action is a major casue of hyperactivity; fast movement without purpose, as though stimulated by electricity. The physical energy which is created by the images, but not used, is physically stored. Then when the set is off, it comes bursting outward in aimless, random, speedy activity. I have seen it over and over again with children. They are quiet while watching. Then afterwards they become overactive, irritable and frustrated.

Marie Winn quotes Dr. Matthew Dumont, who says that television causes hyperactive response. But Australian psychologists Merrelyn and Fred Emery, in their study of television, from which I will be quoting at length later on, have gone so far as to absolutely predict that as television advances in Australia there will be a directly proportionate increase in hyperactivity. I believe that in extreme cases the frustration inherent in the TV experience can lead to violent activity, whatever the content of the program. Artificially teased senses require resolution. It is bizarre and frightening, therefore, that many parents use television as a means of calming hyperactive children. It would be far better to calm them with physical exercise, sports, wrestling, hugging, bathing and a lot of direct attention that gives them wide-ranging sensory and intellectual stimulation. Changes in diet would also help. The worst thing one can do for a hyperactive child is to put him or her in front of a television set. Television activates the child at the same time that it cuts the child (or adult) off from real sensory stimulation and the opportunity for resolution.

Television Is Sensory Deprivation

I have previously drawn a parallel between modern life and conditions of sensory deprivation. Artificial environments themselves reduce and narrow sensory experience to fit their own new confined reality. The effect and purpose of this narrowing is to increase awareness and focus upon the work, commodities, entertainments, spectacles and other drugs that society uses to keep us within its boundaries.

We can consider television to be an advance on that already prevalent condition. Sitting in darkened rooms, with the natural environment obscured, other humans dimmed out, only two senses operating, both within a very narrow range, the eyes and other body functions stilled, staring at light for hours and hours, the experience adds up to something nearer to sense deprivation than anything that has come before it.

Television isolates people from the environment, from each other, and from their own senses. In such a condition, the two semioperative senses cannot benefit from the usual mix of information that humans employ to deduce meaning from their surroundings. All meaning comes from this very narrowed information field.

We know that it is an accepted truth about sensory-deprivation conditions that subjects have no recourse but to focus on the images in their brain. And we know that in sensory-deprivation conditions, having no resources aside from mental images, the subject is unusually susceptible to suggestion.

When you are watching TV, you are experiencing mental images. As distinguished from most sense-deprivation experiments these mental images are not yours. They are someone else's. Because the rest of your capacities have been subdued, and the rest of the world dimmed, these images are likely to have an extraordinary degree of influence. Am I saying this *is* brainwashing or hypnosis or mind-zapping or something like it? Well, there is no question but that someone is speaking into your mind and wants you to do something.

First, keep watching.

Second, carry the images around in your head.

Third, buy something.

Fourth, tune in tomorrow.

IX

THE INGESTION OF ARTIFICIAL LIGHT

WHEN you are watching television the major thing you are doing is looking at light. The philosopher John Brockman was the first person to put it that way to me, remarking that this in itself represents an enormous change in human experience. For four hours a day, human beings sit in dark rooms, their bodies stilled, gazing at light. Nothing like this has ever happened before.

Previous generations, millions of them, looked at starlight, firelight and moonlight, and there is no doubt that these experiences stir important feelings. There are cultures that spent time gazing at the sun, but there is no culture in all of history that has spent such enormous blocks of time, all of the people together, every day, sitting in dark rooms looking at artificial light.

Anne Waldman, the poet, has suggested that television might itself represent a surrogate moon; a substitute for the original experience for which we, somewhere, continue to long.

If true, this might be merely poignant if it weren't for some important distinctions between looking at the moon or a fire and looking at television.

Television light is purposeful and directed rather than ambient. It is projected into our eyes from behind the screen by cathode-ray guns which are literally aimed at us. These guns are powered by 25,000 volts in the case of color television, and about 15,000 volts in black-and-white sets.

The guns shoot electron streams at phosphors on the screen. This makes the phosphors glow, and their light projects from the screen into our eyes. It is not quite accurate to say that when we watch television we are looking at light; it is more accurate to say that light is projected into us. We are *receiving* light through our eyes into our bodies, far enough in to affect our endocrine system, as we shall see. Some physicists say that the eye does not distinguish between ambient light, which has reflected off other surfaces, and directed light, which comes straight at the eye, undeterred, but others think the difference is important.

There is another hot debate in physics on the question of whether light is particulate matter or wave energy. For our purposes, however, what needs to be appreciated is that whether light is matter or energy it is a *thing* which is entering us. When you are watching television, you are experiencing something like lines of energy passing from cathode gun to phosphor through your eyes into your body. You are as connected to the television set as your arm would be to the electrical current in the wall—about which there is the same question of wave versus particle—if you had stuck a knife into the socket.

These are not metaphors. There is a concentrated passage of energy from machine to you, and none in the reverse. In this sense, the machine is literally dominant, and you are passive.

Health and Light

As I began to look around for an explanation to account for the physical symptoms people were describing, particularly those related to "deadness," "zombielike feeling," "irritation," and so on—symptoms ordinarily explained as psychologically induced—Stewart Brand sent me a copy of a book called *Health and Light* by Dr. John Ott, a former banker who quit to become a time-lapse photographer and then founded the Environmental Health and Light Research Institute in Sarasota, Florida. Now in his seventies, Ott presides over a board of directors of doctors and medical researchers who do pioneering work on the effects of light on the human body.

I had heard of Ott as a major source for government agencies seeking evidence of the effects of X-radiation emanating from television sets. He had been instrumental in convincing lawmakers to reduce the allowable limits of TV X rays. Over the past twenty years these limits have been reduced more than twenty times. There was a time when fifty millirems per hour was permissible, but now the limit is one one-hundredth of that, one half a millirem per hour. Ott has argued that even that is too high. In one celebrated series of studies, the roots of bean plants he placed in front of color television sets grew *up*ward out of the soil. Another set of plants became monstrously large and distorted. Mice which were similarly placed developed cancerous lesions. Ott argues that any amount of X ray emanation from television—most sets still produce some— is likely to be harmful to humans.

In *Health and Light,* Ott devotes himself less to discussing X rays than he does to discussing a more subtle danger in our environment, artificial light, particularly fluorescent. In this case, his research is not directed specifically at television light. But since television *is* fluorescent, the work is directly applicable.

172

While doing his time-lapse photographic work on plants, Ott made his first discoveries concerning interactions between the plants and the lights he was using for the photography. He noticed that when he changed from incandescent lighting to fluorescent, for example, plants would suddenly cease to grow in one pattern and grew in another. His time-lapse photography was able to record the change.

Also, as he changed from one fluorescent to another, similar peculiarities would appear on the film. Differences also occurred when the plants were moved from all artificial light sources into natural light.

Ott became interested less in the photography than in these changes. He began to change the lights deliberately to see what would happen. Then he undertook microscopic photography of the plant cells, to learn if it was possible to *see* the changes in cellular activity.

The cellular action of plants is called "the streaming of the chloroplasts." Through a microscope one can see the millions of cells moving about in an orderly pattern, resembling in some ways a traffic flow.

Ott discovered that when plants were kept in sunlight, the chloroplasts would continue in their regular pattern. When the light had to pass through ordinary window glass, groups of chloroplasts would begin to "fall off the streaming pattern." Under artificial lighting, the behavior of the chloroplasts altered markedly. As Ott changed the light from incandescent to fluorescent, or from one color of fluorescent to another, the chloroplasts might move faster or more slowly, group sluggishly, or they might leap about crazily, completely out of synchrony with the prior pattern.

The results were so marked that Ott began to wonder if similar cell changes could be found among laboratory animals when they were switched from one light source to another. The new science of photobiology has begun to discover that humans and animals, which are made up of virtually the same chemical mixture as plants (save for chlorophyll), *also* react to light in various ways. We receive light through the cells of our skin, but more remarkably, we receive light through our eyes and absorb it into our cell structure. Ott was interested in determining what effect changes in light might have on a particular strain of cancer-sensitive laboratory rat; he wanted to know if differences in cancer rates resulted from differences in light sources.

They did. Pink fluorescent produced the highest rates of cancer in rats; natural daylight the lowest. In one experiment involving three hundred cancer-sensitive mice, these were the results:

LIGHT SOURCE	SURVIVAL RATE
ordinary daylight	97%
all fluorescents	88%
white fluorescent	94%
pink fluorescent	61%

In another experiment involving two thousand mice, he found that those kept under pink fluorescent developed tumors and died, on the average, within seven and a half months. Those kept under other light sources had an average life span double that of the first group.

Cancer wasn't the only reaction to artificial light. When mice were kept under one particular pink fluorescent for long periods of time, their tails would literally wither and fall off.

Under a certain dark blue fluorescent, the cholesterol level in the blood of the mice rose sharply; male mice became obese, although the females did not.

Ott worked with other animals as well.

A red filter placed over ordinary incandescent light was found to weaken and rupture the heart cells of chick embryos. A blue incandescent light placed over the cages of chinchillas increased the number of females in the litter; a similar light increased the female population of some fish in a tank.

Other light changes caused aggressiveness, hyperactive behavior, aimlessness and disorientation, as well as changes in sexual patterns among mice, rats and other animals.

In his book, and in a later three-part article in the medical journal *Eye, Ear, Nose and Throat Monthly* (July 1974), Ott spelled out how he believes light affects us.

He first explains the connection between the light we receive in our eyes and our cell structure. This is the chain of events: Light passes through the eye to contact the retina. The retina has what Ott calls a "dual function." The first is the obvious one: translating the light into images by way of channels to the brain. The second, equally important function is for the light rays, *aside* from their role as image creators, to pass via neurochemical channels into and through the pineal and pituitary glands and therefore into the animal *and* human endocrine systems.

Identifying this series of connections is not original with Ott. Many researchers, some of whom I shall cite later, have found that this interaction affects hormonal structures, sexuality, fertility, growth and many other aspects of animal and human cell structure.

Ott says the *kind* of light that passes through the eyes determines the reactions of human cells. His experiments on plants and animals were attempts to demonstrate that even minute changes in *wavelength spectra* (what we call "color")—say, between one kind of artificial light and another, or between natural light and artificial light—cause important biochemical alterations.

Critical to understanding all of this is the term "light," which does not apply to a single, monolithic element. When we speak of "light" we ordinarily do not make distinctions between natural light or artificial light; nor do we make the distinction between kinds of artificial light. We tend to lump all of them together. One flips the switch to "on" and what one gets is "light." When it is "on" one can see. But there is where the similarity ends.

Natural sunlight is made up of all the radiant wavelengths of energy (spectra) that fit within what we call "light." What's more, it contains them in a specific mixture. So much of this and so much of that.

Artificial light from any source—whether incandescent or fluorescent—leaves out many segments of the spectral range contained in natural light, and it delivers an entirely different mix of spectral ingredients. Incandescent light, for example, emphasizes the portion of the spectrum near the infrared while minimizing or leaving out others. Artificial light is quite literally *not* the same element as natural light. To use the same term for both is to destroy understanding.

We learned in high school that plants ingest light and then convert it to energy for growth. The process is called photosynthesis.

The plant literally takes light into its cells and converts it into nourishment. For a plant, light is a form of food. Ott has shown that changing the light source so that a plant ingests one set of spectral ingredients rather than another changes the nourishment and therefore the cellular and growth patterns of the plant. If you grow your own plants at home, you also know this to be true. You may not have a microscope with which to watch it, but if you move a plant nearer to the window (or farther away), it changes. Plant stores now sell special bulbs which help plants grow. When you move the plant or buy the bulb, what you are doing is changing the amount and the spectral character of the light the plant receives. You are changing its diet.

Through photobiology we are finally beginning to grasp that what is true for plants seems also to be true for animals and humans. For all, light is a kind of food. Humans take the light in through the eyes; and via the retinal-pituitary-endocrine system, it passes into the cells.

Ott's particular contribution to photobiology is that thirty years ago he began saying that the exact mix of spectral ingredients that we ingest affects many aspects of human health and vitality. As you change the light, you change the spectra; as you change the spectra, you change the light-nourishment that finds its way to the cells; as you alter the cells, you alter the human body.

Outdoors to Indoors

To determine what mix of spectral ingredients is likely to produce the most vital humans, a logical place to start is with natural light, since this is the *only* light that humans ingested for millions of years.

During all of that time, the only human experience of light was of natural light: sun, moon, stars and, more recently, fire. Therefore, whatever light-receptive capacities exist in humans, and whatever cellular reactions humans have to light, they must have evolved to be attuned to the particular spectra emitted by those light sources.

Four generations ago, representing one one-fifty-thousandth of the human experience, we invented artificial light. It has been only two generations since artificial light became so widespread that we moved into artificially lighted environments. Now, most of the light we ingest through our skin and eyes is artificial. Meanwhile, we no longer receive the light we formerly received, because we are no longer outdoors. It is a kind of madness to think that this change would not affect us, another sign of our removal from any understanding of our interaction with the environment.

Ott has coined the term "malillumination" to describe the results on the body. We are "starved" for some natural light spectra, he says, and we have "overdosed" on those spectra that come from artificial lights: incandescent, fluorescent, mercury vapor, sodium, television and others.

Imagine that you suddenly gave up eating all fruits, vegetables, grains, nuts and meats, and began eating pasta, candy and sugary cereals only. All these groupings are "food," but the nutrients within each are substantially different. Where they are the same—there is *some* protein, for example in candy, and there is starch in some vegetables—they are of entirely different proportions. Eating pasta, candy and cereal will keep you alive, but eventually it will affect your health. And so it is with alterations in light-diet from the "natural" mix of spectral ingredients to the artificial mix.

Ott suspects that malillumination causes disorders ranging from lack of vitality to lowered resistance to disease, and hyperactivity. He believes it can also lead to aggressive behavior, heart disease and even cancer. He argues that the body cannot handle this intervention in a natural human relationship with the environment any more than it can handle food additives or chemicals in the air. The body breaks down on the cellular level.

As our life-style removes us further from full-spectrum natural light and into artificial environments, our condition becomes worse. Even when we are outdoors, Ott points out, we filter the light that we receive in our eyes with sunglasses (which eliminate certain spectra, while allowing others to pass through) as well as eyeglasses and window glass. Smog also has a role, he says, quoting a Smithsonian report indicating that during the last sixty years there has been a 14 percent decrease in sunlight reaching the surface of the planet.

My interest in the effects of light on humans was rooted in my investigation of television. Considering that human beings had not only moved away from natural light into artificial light, but that now our experience of artificial light is confined for four hours daily to television light, it began to seem obvious to me that a new level of distortion was underway. Human beings are soaking up far more television light, directed straight into their eyes, than any kind of artificial light that preceded it.

It seemed to me that if variations in kind and volume of artificial light can affect humans, then there might be specific effects to be discovered from the enormous amount of television light most people absorb.

If you will inspect your color television screen closely—I suggest you use a magnifying glass—you will find that your picture emanates from a collection of red, blue and green dots, or lines. As you move away from the screen the colors merge in your eyes to seem like other colors, but the television is emitting *only* red, blue and green light. These dots are made of phosphorescent metal placed inside the glass. The phosphors glow when the cathode gun shoots electrons at them. This process is barely different from that used in fluorescent lighting. Television is fluorescent.

I pored through Ott's books and papers trying to learn if he had thought to look into the effects of television phosphorescence while studying other fluorescents. I couldn't find any references and so I sought him out personally.

I asked Ott if he had studied the effects of the particular spectral emanations of color television: the red, blue and green phosphors. If so, what had he learned? If not, would he care to conjecture.

He said he hadn't done such research, although recently he had begun to think he should, but he added:

"We *have* studied the greens, reds, and blues that come from fluorescent lights, which of course would be very similar since both involve the excitation of mineral phosphors. It may not be precisely the same, but I've already proved what can happen with certain phosphorescences, particularly pink.

"In any event, I am sure they [TV phosphors] have three very narrow wavelength peaks, just as in fluorescent, but how broad the bands are, I just don't know." (A narrow wavelength peak would indicate a very high concentration within one spectral range; this would be suspect because it would more seriously concentrate and distort what the human ingests.)

Ott told me that color television was probably less harmful than black and white because color sets produce wider spectra, although seriously distorting the natural range of sunlight. On the other hand, color sets produce more X rays.

Ott volunteered another concern. He said that lately he had been thinking there might be a relationship between the light emanations from color television and other fluorescent lights and chemical food additives, causing hyperactivity in children.

"All those artificial colorings have a certain wavelength resonance. Dr. Ben Feingold of Kaiser Hospital has found that eliminating some of these artificial colorings and flavorings from children's diets will reduce their hyperactivity and also their allergic responses. What I'd like to do is take his findings and tie them to wavelength peaks of mercury-vapor lights, fluorescent lights and television light, because the heart of the matter could lie in an interaction of wavelength resonances between the chemicals and the light the body takes in. In television it could depend upon what the spectral peaks are. If they correspond to the wavelength absorption of some of these synthetic materials, then you can get tremendous reactions.

"It's the same with food. Different pigments have different wavelength resonances, so different food ingredients may resonate with different light ingredients. Let's say you eat a lot of spinach and raisins, both of which contain iron. Iron has a certain wavelength resonance, as do all metals. In fact, all matter interacts with other matter which may be similarly resonating. This is why soldiers will break rank when they walk across a bridge. Too many of them walking in step sets up a wavelength pattern which has been known to resonate with that of the materials of the bridge and the whole thing can collapse. It's the same with food and light. If you eat a little bit of iron or calcium in your food and that wavelength is lacking in the light you get, then you're not going to get any benefit. On the other hand if you find yourself in a peak of light, whether it's television light or any other that reacts to iron, then you would have to watch your quantities, because if you get too much, you get an overreaction. [Allergy, hyperactivity.] It could be too much of one or not enough of the other. Now with sunlight, you don't have those kinds of peaks. I'm sure that one way or the other your diet of both food and light is responsible for a lot of different physical reactions that we haven't been able to measure yet."

Seeking the Light

There was a time while I was working on this book that I became thrilled about the implications of the human ingestion of light. As I began to understand for the first time that there is a concrete relationship between our bodies and light, and that light is a kind of thing that we ingest for nourishment and growth, like food, I began to feel that humans probably hungered for and sought light the way plants do.

We know that humans seek food. A lot of life is spent in this process. We can say that seeking food is instinctive in all humans. Even babies know how to do it, within their limits.

If light is also food, then might we not seek it, as plants do? Is this why we look at the moon? Is this why we gaze at fire? Is there an innate longing for light, like a kind of cellular hunger? If so, then I suppose Anne Waldman could be right. With natural light gone, we seek a surrogate light: television.

Well, I couldn't possibly say any of that in a book. But I did write it in a letter to an anthropologist friend of mine,

Neal Daniels, who is acquainted with both "primitive" and "esoteric" religions. He wrote back:

"If photobiologists are correct, and I don't see why they shouldn't be, then they may be onto the biological foundation for the fact that every culture and religion in history has placed light at the center of its cosmology. 'Receive the light.' 'Seek enlightenment.' 'The mind of light.' 'The luminescent soul.'

"The Hopi Indians speak of light entering them through the tops of their heads. It's a goal of theirs to keep the tops of their heads open for the light. Of course they are speaking in spiritual terms. I know you are speaking more in health terms, as with food. But why couldn't the two be the same? It's very efficient and sensible to develop religions around natural processes which are the bases of survival. Most indigenous cultures do that. Only ours doesn't.

"Do you remember that film we saw on those Bolivian Indians? They had a meditational routine every day at the same time, sitting high on a cliff facing the sun. They called it 'taking light.' They give it the same kind of meaning as 'taking waters.' They claimed it had medicinal value, as well as stimulating spontaneous insight.

"As I think about it, except for Western medicine, there's hardly a medicine/healing system in the world where light is not used for health purposes . . . physical, mental, spiritual."

Anne Kent Rush, the author of *Moon, Moon* and a professional polarity therapist—a massage system that uses much of the knowledge of Chinese acupuncture medicine—gave me a compendium of data in this area. She told me that Chinese healing systems coordinate treatments of various organs with foods of specific color. For example, for lung disorders, white foods like turnips and onions will be prescribed. Heart disorders are aided by eating red foods such as beets and pomegranates. These might be combined with meditational practices in which the patient is asked to keep a certain color in mind. A spleen problem is considered to be caused partly by the body's insufficient absorption of nutrients found in green vegetables. Intestinal problems may be caused by an insufficiency or an overabundance of foods containing pink light. (Ott told me the reason vegetables are green or blue is because of their interaction with selected light spectra. When I asked him if he'd read about any of these color healing systems, he told me he had not.)

In Mahayana Buddhism, each *chakra* (energy center) of the body is described as processing certain parts of the color spectrum, while also intermixing the colors processed by other energy centers.

In acupuncture, the two principal light-reception glands, the pineal and the pituitary, are the subject of specific light treatments, designed to keep them in balance.

Rush told me that many cultures consider the body's experience of color, which is to say spectra, as a prime factor in health. However, when faced with this kind of evidence, *this* culture places it all in a "primitive" category. We consider it superstition or mythology rather than knowledge or science.

It is only when a James Reston submits to acupuncture while having his appendix out in China, and then writes an article about it in the *Times*, that most of us are willing to have another look.

Serious Research

Not feeling that I could rely upon esoteric religion, primitive medical practice, or the work of John Ott as my only evidence that television light might be harming our bodies, I made a telephone call to the head medical researcher at a well-known nonprofit organization which, like Ott's organization, has done some excellent work in exposing the danger of

X-radiation from television. (He declined to be named.) I asked him what, if anything, had been done on television light. Had he looked into the possible effects of the red, blue and green emanations?

"Where the hell do you get that crap?" he said. "I'm sick and tired of kooks not acquainted with serious research who go around spreading that stuff!"

I told him about some of the research, particularly Ott's.

"I know about that guy," he said. "He's no scientist, and people are paying far too much attention to him. He doesn't even have a biology degree."

I asked him if he'd read any of Ott's books or papers, which, after all, had been published in "serious" medical journals and had been supported by medical schools all over the country. I pointed out that Ott's board of medical people was highly respected.

"Listen," he said, "I'm really too busy to waste time on conjecture. There's a difference between careful research and pseudoscience."

I answered by reminding him that the work of *his* organization was usually called "pseudoscience" by corporate and government scientists, whose conceptions he himself usually attacked. Could he now be falling into the same trap? I asked him again if he'd read any of Ott's work.

"Listen," he said again, loudly, "we are now discovering that artificial light might be terrific for you. It's good for people, not bad. If you want to read something really serious, go get a copy of *Scientific American* and read the article by Dr. Richard J. Wurtman on how artificial light is curing all kinds of diseases."

"Well," I asked, "are you saying that some artificial light has beneficial effects? If so, could not some other artificial light made up of other spectra have negative effects? Have you read Ott?"

"No I haven't," he shouted. "I don't read quacks. Nor

do I talk to quacks!" and he hung up. I went out and bought *Scientific American* (July 1975).

I was astonished at Wurtman's article because it completely contradicted the views my irascible interviewee had ascribed to it. Wurtman, who is a professor of endocrinology and metabolism at MIT, was arguing that the body can be seriously affected by changes in light spectra. This is the same argument Ott makes. Wurtman's descriptions are very similar to Ott's.

"Since life evolved under the influence of sunlight, it is not surprising that many animals, including man, have developed a variety of physiological responses to the spectral characteristics of solar radiation. The findings already in hand suggest that light has an important influence on human health, and that our exposure to artificial light may have harmful effects of which we are not aware. The solar spectrum is essentially continuous, lacking only certain wavelengths absorbed by elements in the sun's atmosphere, and at midday it has a peak intensity in the blue-green region from 450 to 500 nanometers . . .

"The most familiar type of artificial light is the incandescent lamp . . . [which] is strongly shifted to the red, or long-wave length end of the spectrum. Indeed about 90% of the total emission of an incandescent lamp lies in the infrared.

"Since the [human] photoreceptors are most sensitive to the yellow-green light of 555 nanometers, most fluorescent lamps are designed to concentrate much of their output in that wavelength region . . . since fluorescent lamps are the most widely used light sources in offices, factories, and schools, most people in industrial societies spend many of their waking hours bathed in light whose spectral characteristics differ markedly from those of sunlight."

Wurtman offered a chart that traced the path of light

through the eye showing graphically what Ott had called the "dual function." The light passes through the eye and creates chemical interactions in the pineal gland, the pituitary gland, the hypothalamus, the spinal cord, various nerve systems as well as the ovaries and the gonads, thereby affecting sexuality and fertility.

"When young rats are kept continuously under light, photo-receptive cells in their retina release neurotransmitters that activate brain neurons; these neurons in turn transmit signals over complex neuroendocrine pathways that reach the anterior pituitary gland where they stimulate the secretion of the gonadic hormones that accelerate the maturation of the ovaries."

Wurtman indicated that among rats that had had their eyes or their pituitary gland removed, ovarian growth was no longer affected by light. He suggests that no one has yet identified *which* light spectra are the catalysts for ovarian action.

Louise Lacey, in her book *Lunaception,* makes the argument that women's menstrual cycles in pretechnological times were attuned to moonlight. Wurtman, who perhaps had not read the book, was effectively presenting evidence for how this could happen. (Dr. Wurtman: I suggest a spectral analysis of moonlight.)

Wurtman indicated there are some diseases that are known to be affected by specific light spectra.

A skin disease, erythropoietic protoporphyria, is caused by an imbalanced reaction to wavelengths in the region of 400 nanometers, the region of the color violet.

Herpes infections and psoriasis represent imbalances within a similar range: 365 nanometers, ultraviolet. (The treatment for these now combines light-therapy with the ingestion of certain herbs and foods. The light apparently interacts with the food, just as Ott said it would.)

With respect to infant jaundice Wurtman reports:

"Perhaps 25,000 premature American infants were successfully treated with light last year as the sole therapy for neonatal jaundice . . . blue light is the most effective in decomposing pure solutions of bilirubin, an imbalance of which causes the problem . . . however full spectrum white light in almost any reasonable dosage has proved effective in lowering plasma-bilirubin levels. . . . The observation that ordinary sunlight or artificial light sources can drastically alter the plasma level of even one body compound opens a Pandora's box for the student of human biology. It represents the strong possibility that the plasma or tissue levels of many additional compounds are similarly affected by light. Some such responses must be physiologically advantageous, but some may not be."

Wurtman also considers the periodicity of light and the mammalian relationship to the light-dark cycle. He says that as we make our days longer with artificial light, there are major changes in the body. He reports relationships between time of day or night and contents of the blood, temperature of the body, sleep and wakefulness, the production of catecholamines, magnesium, sodium, potassium, phosphates and other minerals.

"In our laboratory at MIT we have investigated the daily rhythmicity in the body temperature of rats to see what colors of light are most effective in inducing a change in rhythms to a new light-dark cycle and what intensities are needed. The body temperature of rats normally rises by one or two degrees centigrade at the onset of darkness and falls again at daybreak. We found that green light is the most potent in changing the phase of the temperature cycle and that ultraviolet and red wavelengths are the least potent."

Wurtman concludes:

"Both government and industry have been satisfied to allow people who buy electric lamps—first the incandescent ones and now the fluorescent—to serve as the unwitting subjects in a long-term experiment on the effects of artificial lighting environment on human health. We have been lucky, perhaps, in that so far the experiment has had no demonstrably baneful effects."

While he supports the idea that variations in artificial light affect our health, Wurtman never once mentions television light, which by now is a primary artificial light for most Americans.

Frustrated, I decided upon one more interview, with Dr. Kendric C. Smith, professor of radiobiology in the Department of Radiology, Stanford University Medical School, and former president of the American Society for Photobiology. I had read a paper by Smith in *BioScience* (January 1974) which seemed promising.

He said, "Sunlight is probably the most important single element of our environment, yet it has been largely ignored by the scientific community . . .

"Visible light has the ability to exert measurable biological effects. Medical uses of the visible spectrum have been virtually ignored by physicians for the past ninety years . . .

"Light intensity as well as wavelength specificity may alter productivity and mood. In the infant, sensory overload by prolonged exposure to highly intense illumination may produce undesirable effects on development. Indeed the manipulation of the light-environment of adults as well as of infants can have consequences of which we may be quite unaware."

(One wonders, for example, about the effects on a newborn child of emerging from darkness into the dazzling bright fluorescent light of delivery rooms. Most primitive cultures deliver infants in *darkened* environments.)

When I went to see Smith, I asked him what is known about the effects of television light.

His answer? Nobody knows.

"We know less about the effects of light on humans than

almost any other thing. We know, however, that ultraviolet light is essential to man for the synthesis of Vitamin D, and visible light is essential for vision. We know that we need light to survive, but too much can be dangerous. Somewhere there's a balance."

I asked him where to start determining the balance.

"The first step has been to copy the sun, but we may not need all parts of the solar spectrum. For example, some plants use some parts, some plants use other parts of the spectrum. If we knew which wavelengths were best for each type of plant, we could design lamps that were optimal for each plant's growth and well-being.

"Except for vision and Vitamin D synthesis we have very little information on what part of the solar spectrum man uses and what part he doesn't."

Although he believes that you have to start with the characteristics of sunlight, Smith denounced what he called believers in "Godslight": people who believe that what is natural is automatically good.

I didn't tell Smith that I was one of those myself. In the end, I expect science to conclude that since "natural" was all we had for virtually the entire course of human evolution, that is what our bodies are attuned to. *Anything* that intervenes in this arrangement is potentially dangerous. Smith, on the other hand, has more faith in human intervention, believing that it will eventually be possible to find just which spectrum humans need for which growth characteristic, and that we can then plan our lighting environments accordingly. Visions of totally artificial underground environments and/or space stations, celebrated as offering everything humans need, flew through my mind. So many trees, so much light, so much recreation. Suburbs in the sky. I brought the subject back to television.

"What I'm really here for today," I said, "is to try to get at one narrow issue. If red, blue and green phosphorescent light is being projected at 25,000 volts directly into human eyes and from there to the endocrine system, and if humans are receiving light in that way for four hours a day on the average, while depriving themselves of natural light, what can be said about the possible effects of this?"

"There's been no data on that," he repeated.

I told him that I was alarmed at the fact that nobody was looking into such questions.

"I'm alarmed too," he answered. "I'm amazed at the lack of intellectual grasp of the situation. There has been a tremendous amount of research on the effects of temperature and pressure on man. Yet it has not been fashionable to study the effects of light on man, and light is probably the most important single element in our environment.

"What does it mean, for example, that people who are pre-disposed to motion sickness immediately become sick when they walk into a room illuminated with blue light? Why does this happen? What is the effect of blue light? These are the kind of data that are needed before we can even approach your question.

"We know that blue light will reduce the concentration of bilirubin in the blood of infants and now jaundiced infants are put under banks of light to treat them, but we don't know yet what the *other* wavelengths of light in the lamps might be doing to the infants.

"In another area, we know that our bodies are relatively transparent to red wavelengths of light. You can tell that by putting a flashlight inside your mouth. What you can see from the outside is not blood; it's the red rays passing through you. People are now beginning to be interested in the effects of red light on man."

Smith told me one last story which resonated with the Hopi Indian practice, mentioned earlier, of "keeping the top of the head open," and which was the highlight of my visit. It threw me back to my instinctive feeling that for knowledge about the effects of light, pretechnological medicines and practices may be as reliable as our own.

"There is research now underway," Smith said, "to gain further knowledge about the effects of light entering the body through the skull. It is known, for example, that light affects the testicular growth of sparrows and it's the light that comes in through the top of the head, not the eyes. We need to know if light entering the bodies of higher mammals by other routes than through the eyes has biological effects on them, and if so, what wavelengths are the active ones. We need to do this kind of research on the higher mammals, and we need to do it now."

I could quote from a few more interviewees of varying credentials and authoritativeness, but they all say the same thing. There is not the slightest doubt that light taken through the eyes affects the cells; there is no doubt that variations in light spectra cause variations in cellular activity; there is no doubt that sitting and looking at television light affects our cells in some way. But no one can say how, and not many are asking.

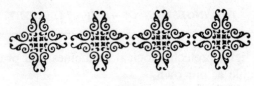

X

HOW TELEVISION DIMS THE MIND

WHEN you are watching television and believe you are looking at pictures, you are actually looking at the phosphorescent glow of three hundred thousand tiny dots. There is no picture there.

These dots seem to be lit constantly, but in fact they are not. All the dots go off thirty times per second, creating what is called the flicker effect of television, which is similar to strobe or ordinary fluorescent light.

For many years conventional wisdom held that since this flickering happens at a rate beyond the so-called flicker-fusion rate of the human eye, we do not consciously note it, and we presumably are not affected by it. However, recent discoveries about the biological effects of very minor stimuli by W. Ross Adey and others, and the growing incidence of television epilepsy among those particularly sensitive to flicker, have shown that whether we consciously note the flicker or not, our bodies react to it.

A second factor is that even when the dots go "on," not all of them are lit simultaneously. Which dots are on determines the picture. In a sense, the television screen is like a newspaper photograph or the images on a film, which are also comprised of dots, except that the television dots are lighted one at a time according to a scanning system that starts behind the screen. Proceeding along a line from the upper-right-hand portion of your screen across the top to the left, the scan lights some dots and skips others, depending upon the image to be conveyed. Then the scan goes down another line, starts at the right again and goes across to the left and so on.

What you perceive as a picture is actually an image that never exists in any given moment but rather is constructed over time. Your perception of it as an image depends upon your brain's ability to gather in all the lit dots, collect the image they make on your retina in sequence, and form a picture. The picture itself, however, never existed. Unlike ordinary life, in which whatever you see actually exists outside you before you let it in through your eyes, a television image gains its existence *only* once you've put it together inside your head.

As you watch television you do not "see" any of this fancy construction work happening. It is taking place at a rate faster than the nerve pathways between your retina and the portion of your brain that "sees" can process them. You can only see things that happen within a range of speeds. This is because four million years of human evolution developed our eyes to process only that data which were concretely useful. Until this generation, there was no need to see anything that moved at electronic speed. Everything that we humans can actually do anything about moves slowly enough for us to see.

Even though you don't see every dot go on and off in sequence, these events are happening. Your retina receives the light continuously and your brain cells record their reception. The only thing that doesn't happen continuously is the translation of the energy into images inside your head. That happens only at about ten times per second. Television is sending its sequential images at thirty times per second.

A few years ago there was a big fuss about advertisers exploiting the differential in these rates. A technique called subliminal advertising places images within the dot-scan sequence at a speed which is faster than sight. You get hit with the ad, but you can't process this fast enough, so you don't know the ad is registering. Your seeing processes are plodding along at nonelectronic speed while the advertisers have access to electronic speed. Your brain gets the message, but your conscious mind doesn't. According to those who have used the technique, it communicates well enough to affect sales.

For the entire four hours or more per day that the average person is watching television, the repetitive process of constructing images out of dots, following scans, and vibrating with the beats of the set and the exigencies of electronic rhythm goes on. It was this repetitive, nonstop requirement to reconstruct images that are consciously usable that caused McLuhan to call television "participatory," another unfortunate choice of words. It suggests exactly the opposite of what is going on.

I wish he had said "overpowering." The word "participatory" has been passed around at thousands of cocktail parties, misleading people to assume that if only they could have managed to get through McLuhan's books, they'd have discovered that their innate feeling (anecdotal evidence) that the experience is passive and that it "deadens my mind" was somehow wrong. In fact, watching television is participatory only in the way the assembly line or a hypnotist's blinking flashlight is. Eventually, the conscious mind gives up noting the process and merges with the experience. The body vibrates with the beat and the mind gives itself over, opening up to whatever imagery is offered.

194

Hypnosis

As the largest category of terms that people use to describe their television viewing relates to its hypnotic effect, I asked three prominent psychologists, famous partly for their work with hypnotism, if they could define the TV experience as hypnotic and, if so, what that meant.

I described to each the concrete details of what goes on between viewer and television set: dark room, eyes still, body quiet, looking at light that is flickering in various ways, sound contained to narrow ranges and so on.

Dr. Freda Morris said, "It sounds like you're giving a course outline in hypnotic trance induction."

Morris, who is a former professor of medical psychology at UCLA and author of several books on hypnosis, told me that inducing trances was really very easy. The main method is to keep the subject "quiet, still, cut down all diversions and outside focuses," she said, and then to "create a new focus, keep their attention and at a certain point get them to follow your mind."

"There are a great variety of trance states. However, common to all is that the subject becomes inattentive to the environment, and yet very focused on a particular thing, like a bird watching a snake."

"So you mean," I said, "that the goal of the hypnotist is to create a totally clear channel, unencumbered by anything from the outside world, so that the patient can be sort of unified with the hypnotist?"

She agreed with this way of putting it, adding that hypnotism has power implications which she loathes. As a result she uses her first session with patients to teach them how to self-hypnotize, reducing her power over them. "I don't use tricky signals to set them off anymore, or get them to look into my eyes. That encourages their giving power to me; however, I'm sorry to say that most doctors don't encourage self-hypnosis. I guess they want the power."

Dr. Ernest Hilgard, who directs Stanford University's research program in hypnosis and is the author of the most widely used texts in the field, agreed that television could easily put people into a hypnotic state if they were ready for it.

He said that, in his opinion, the condition of sitting still in a dark room, passively looking at light over a period of time, would be the prime component in the induction. "Sitting quietly, with no sensory inputs aside from the screen, no orienting outside the television set is itself capable of getting people to set aside ordinary reality, allowing the substitution of some other reality that the set may offer. You can get so imaginatively involved that alternatives temporarily fade away.

"A hypnotist doesn't have to be interesting. He can use an ordinary voice, and if the effect is to quiet the person, he can invite them into a situation where they can follow his words or actions and then release their imagination along the lines he suggests. Then they drift into hypnosis."

Dr. Charles Tart, professor of psychology at the University of California at Davis, author of several best-selling books on altered states of consciousness, told me, "Hypnosis is probably the closest metaphor as a state but I don't know if I could equate it [with television watching]. Hypnosis is a state where you destabilize the ordinary state and then eventually get people into an altered state where they will follow a particular stimulus input much more strongly and with much less critical reflection than they would normally; there is certainly a lot of comparability there."

Tart explained that the way you induce *any* altered state of consciousness is by: disrupting the pattern of ordinary awareness, and then substituting a new patterning system to reassemble the disassembled pieces. He said this applied to any altered state of mind, from drug-induced alteration to Sufi dancing or repetitive mantras, and, he said, it could also apply to television.

Morris said that since television images move more quickly than a viewer can react, one has to chase after them with the mind. This leaves no way of breaking the contact and therefore no way to comment upon the information as it passes in. It stops the critical mind. She told me about an induction technique called "confusion," which was developed by a pioneer in hypnotism, Dr. Milton Erickson. "You give the person so much to deal with that you don't give him a chance to do anything on his own. It's fast, continuous, requiring that he try to deal with one thing after another, switching around from focus to focus. The hypnotist might call the patient's attention to any particular thing, it hardly matters what. Eventually, something like overload is reached, the patient shows signs of breaking and *then* the hypnotist comes in with some clear relief, some simple instruction, and the patient goes immediately into trance."

The more I talked with these people, the more I realized how very obvious the process was. Every advertiser, for example, knows that before you can convince anyone of anything, you shatter their existing mental set and then restructure an awareness along lines which are useful to you. You do this with a few very simple techniques like fast-moving images, jumping among attention focuses, and switching moods. There's nothing to it.

Morris described a formula she learned in medical school in which the hypnotist builds "attention, involvement, emotion and expectation," which are at last relieved when the hypnotist's instruction comes through. I then told her about a formula I learned in the Wharton School of Business which reduced to the easily memorizable AIDS. Attention. Interest. Desire. Sell. The first two are disassembling, the third is reassembling. The "sell" is tantamount to the hypnotist's instruction. Repetition over time reinforces the instruction, like the hypnotist's posthypnotic suggestion.

Jacques Ellul, in his classic book *Propaganda,* describes the process of influencing a large number of people at once by using virtually the same formula of dissociation and restructuring, especially through the media, which automatically confines reality to itself.

Some version of this same method appears in all power relationships where one person attempts to dominate the awareness of others. A preacher shatters your ordinary reality and then, in the midst of dismay and confusion, substitutes another, previously organized system of perceptions. A political leader attempts to do the same. To the degree that the audience or congregation or patient is separated from prior connections or grounding, the task is made easier.

I have described how Werner Erhard systematically disassembles all connections to increase focus on his version of reality.

Reverend Moon requires all followers to give up every worldly connection and all possessions, turning them over to him. Then he replaces the "Moonie's" life-style with a new one that consists of virtually nothing but repetitive sayings, repetitive games and repetitive foods until all of life assumes the condition of mantra. This clears the mind for Moon's instructions, and if you have ever met a "Moonie," the word "trance" is a mild way of describing his or her condition. People who have left the Moonfold invariably describe leaving as "waking up," "breaking the power" and so on.

The hypnotic method can work not only in the intimacy of dark rooms with flashing lights where a voice is speaking soft instructions; it can operate wherever the ingredients are appropriate. It is simpler to hypnotize someone in a confined space where external reality is removed.

It is also simpler when the wider context is already disassembled, leaving the subject in confusion.

One explanation that I've heard for the Hitler phenomenon is that with the social and economic conditions in post-Weimar Germany so out of control, the singularity of his voice, amplified by radio and microphones and supported by the rising cheers at rallies under klieg lights turned upon forty-foot swastikas, itself became a nationwide resolution of disorder. A clear channel of clarity out of confusion. Reassembly out of disassembly.

One can draw parallels with the U.S. today. In a confusing society, with grounding lost and expectations sinking, we have the television itself as the guru-hypnotist-leader, opening a clear channel into surrogate clarity. Always constant. Whatever the changing images on the screen, there is always the light, flickering upon our retinas. Whatever the changing words, there is always the even tone. Whatever he says, the voice of Walter Cronkite remains constant, reassuring, unconcerned. Whatever the action, the gestalt continues, program after program, one program merging into the next, images following images, the wider world a distant shadow. There is no need to do more than follow the images, hear the voices, watch the cycle of realities building and then resolving, program after program.

But if I had hoped for some way of proving from my interviews that TV is hypnotic, I could not.

"About the only way you can tell if someone is hypnotized," said Morris, "is if they can do some of the things hypnotized people do . . . if they get lost within the hypnotist's imagery, then we say they're hypnotized. There are no physiological measurements for it."

I came away from these interviews realizing that hypnosis is nothing special. It happens in many of life's experiences—from lullabies in the crib to theatrical productions to television. Hypnotism functions wherever circumstances produce that singular, clear channel of communication. To the degree that it exists with television, it is a one-way channel—the set speaking into the mind of the viewer.

Television Bypasses Consciousness

I do not think of myself as hypnotized while watching television.

I prefer another frequently used phrase. "When I put on the television, after a while there's the feeling that images are just pouring into me and there's nothing I'm able to do about them."

This liquid quality of television imagery derives from the simple fact that television sets its own visual pace. One image is always evolving into the next, arriving in a stream of light and proceeding inward to the brain at its own electronic speed. The viewer has no way to slow the flow, except to turn off the set altogether. If you decide to watch television, then there's no choice but to accept the stream of electronic images as it comes.

The first effect of this is to create a passive mental attitude. Since there is no way to stop the images, one merely gives over to them. More than this, one has to clear all channels of reception to allow them in more cleanly. Thinking only gets in the way.

There is a second difficulty. Television information seems to be received more in the unconscious than the conscious regions of the mind where it would be possible to think about it. I first felt this was true based on my own television viewing. I noticed how difficult it was to keep mentally alert while watching television. Even so the images kept flowing into me. I have since received many similar descriptions from correspondents.

One friend, Jack Edelson, described his feeling that "the

images seem to pass right through me, they go way inside, past my consciousness into a deeper level of my mind, as if they were dreams."

As we study how the TV images are formed, it is possible to understand how Edelson's description might be keenly accurate.

I have described the way the retina collects impressions emanating from dots. The picture is formed only after it is well inside your brain. The image doesn't exist in the world, and so cannot be observed as you would observe another person, or a car, or a fight. The images pass through your eyes in a dematerialized form, invisible. They are reconstituted only after they are already inside your head.

Perhaps this quality of nonexistence, at least in concrete worldly form, disqualifies this image information from being subject to conscious processes: thinking, discernment, analysis. You may think about the sound but not the images.

Television viewing may then qualify as a kind of wakeful dreaming, except that it's a stranger's dream, from a faraway place, though it plays against the screen of your mind.

The stillness required of the eyes while watching the small television screen is surely an important contributor to this feeling of being bypassed by the images as they proceed merrily into our unconscious minds. There are hundreds of studies to show that eye movement and thinking are directly connected. The act of seeking information with the eyes requires and also *causes* the seeker/viewer to be alert, active, not passively accepting whatever comes. There are corollary studies which show that when the eyes are not moving, but instead are staring zombielike, thinking is diminished.

Television images are not sought, they just arrive in a direct channel, all on their own, from cathode to brain. If indeed this means that television imagery does bypass thinking and discernment, then it would certainly be more difficult to make use of whatever information was delivered into your head that way. If you see a person standing in your living room, you can say, "There is a person; how do I feel about this?" If, however, the person is not perceived until she is constructed inside your unconscious mind, you'd have to bring the image up and out again, as it were, in order to think about it. The process is similar to the way we struggle to keep our dream images after waking.

If television images have any similarity to dream imagery, then this would surely help explain a growing confusion between the concrete and the imaginary. Television is becoming real to many people while their lives take on the quality of a dream. It would also help explain recent studies, quoted by Marie Winn and many others, that children are showing a decline in recallable memory and in the ability to learn in such a way that articulation and the written word are usable forms of expression. We may have entered an era when information is fed directly into the mass subconscious. If so, then television is every bit Huxley's hypnopaedic machine and Tausk's influencing machine.

Have you ever kept a journal or a diary? At various times in my life I have done both. Sometimes I've recorded dreams, sometimes waking experiences. I have found the process very educational.

The act of recording a dream or the events or feelings of the day is an act of transferring internal information from the unconscious mind, where it is stored, into the conscious mind, where you can think about it. In this way patterns can be seen, understanding developed, and perhaps personal change stimulated.

Whether or not you have kept a journal, I am sure you are aware of the difference between a dream which you are able to describe in words, and one that you can't quite get at. In the former case, the more you talk, the more of it comes into your awareness. The talking seems to drag it up from the unconscious space where it seeks to return.

Once you have described a dream to a friend, or written it down in a journal, you have literally moved it out of one mental territory, where it was inaccessible, into another territory (consciousness), where it is accessible. At that point you can think about it.

The same is true with a review of the day's activities. At the end of the day, most of us feel that the day has been a blur of activity. If you review it, however, either out loud to a friend or in writing, the day takes on patterns that you would otherwise miss. The events become concrete, integrated with your conscious mind, available.

Entire cultures are based on this process of transferring information from the unconscious to the conscious mind. The most widely studied are the Senoi people of Malaysia, who begin each day by describing the details of their dreams to each other. The Balinese do this unconscious-conscious transfer process via shadow theater, in which people's behavior is "played back" so it can be consciously noted and discussed. Other cultures talk a lot, describing the details of life's intimate experiences all day long. Describing the details helps one "see" them and understand them.

In America, where people are less in the habit of intimate conversation, the feedback role has been given to therapists, particularly those who work with groups. The therapy is in the talking and in the response of group members bringing the unsaid into awareness.

In some ways, reading a book also has a feedback role because reading is a kind of interactive process, similar to conversation or writing in journals. Unlike images, words that you read do *not* pour into you. The reader, not the book, sets the pace. All people read at different speeds and rhythms. When you are reading you have the choice of rereading, stopping to think or underlining. All of these acts further conscious awareness of the material being read. You effectively create the information you wish to place in your conscious mind.

We have all had the experience of reading a paragraph only to realize that we had not absorbed any of it. This requires going over the paragraph a second time, deliberately giving it conscious effort. It is *only* with conscious effort and direct participation at one's own speed that words gain any meaning to a reader.

Images require nothing of the sort. They only require that your eyes be open. The images enter you and are recorded in memory whether you think about them or not. They pour into you like fluid into a container. You are the container. The television is the pourer.

In the end, the viewer is little more than a vessel of reception, and television itself is less a communications or educational medium, as we have wished to think of it, than an instrument that plants images in the unconscious realms of the mind. We become affixed to the changing images, but as it is impossible to do anything about them as they enter us, we merely give ourselves over to them. It is total involvement on the one hand—complete immersion in the image stream—and total unconscious detachment on the other hand—no cognition, no discernment, no notations upon the experience one is having.

It is my hypothesis that these effects are unavoidable, given the nonstop nature of television imagery, the process of dot construction inside the head, and some outrageous technical trickery invented by advertisers that will be described later. However, in keeping with my intention to seek proof for my own observations, I decided to seek scientific evidence.

I talked with the three most widely published dream researchers in the country. I wanted to know how they might compare television imagery with dreams, or if television imagery itself might not qualify as a kind of dream. None had thought to investigate this, and each assured me that no one else had either, though it surely sounded to them like an interesting hypothesis. I suggested that they should get cracking.

Then I came across an astonishing study from Australia.

Television Is Sleep Teaching

In Chapter Eight I referred to a fascinating study of television completed in 1975 by a team of researchers headed by psychologists Merrelyn and Fred Emery at the Center for Continuing Education, Australian National University at Canberra. It caused a sensation in Australia but was barely noted in America.

The Emery report acknowledges, with a certain degree of rage, that its findings are not based on great amounts of evidence. The authors remark that it is tantamount to scandal that there has been so little research on the neurophysiology of television viewing.

Nonetheless, they were satisfied in the end that when we watch television, our usual processes of thinking and discernment are semifunctional at best. They conclude that while television appears to have the potential to provide useful information to viewers—and is celebrated for its educational function—the technology of television and the inherent nature of the viewing experience actually inhibit learning as we usually think of it. Very little cognitive, recallable, analyzable, thought-based learning takes place while watching TV.

The report says: "The evidence is that television not only destroys the capacity of the viewer to attend, it also, by taking over a complex of direct and indirect neural pathways, decreases vigilance—the general state of arousal which prepares the organism for action should its attention be drawn to specific stimulus.

"The individual therefore may be looking at the unexpected or interesting but cannot act upon it in such a way as to complete the purposeful processing gestalt.

"The continuous trance-like fixation of the TV viewer is then not attention but distraction—a form akin to daydreaming or time out."

The report explains that since television information is taking place where the viewer is not, it cannot be acted upon. The viewer must deliberately inhibit the neural pathways between visual data and the autonomic nervous system, which stimulates movement and mental attention. To do otherwise than inhibit the process would be ridiculous. The viewer is left in a passive but also frustrated state.

The authors present a forty-page technical treatise summarizing relevant brain research to trace the effects on the mind of a "simple, constant, repetitive and ambiguous visual stimulus," particularly upon the left side of the brain, the area where language, communicative abilities, cognitive thought—comprehension—are organized.

"The nature of the processes carried out in the left cortex and particularly area thirty-nine [the common integrative area] are those unique to human as opposed to other mammalian life. It is the centre of logic, logical human communication and analysis, integration of sensory components and memory, the basis of man's conscious, purposeful, and time-free abilities and actions. It is the critical function of man that makes him distinctively human."

The Emerys say that the evidence shows that human beings "habituate" to repetitive light-stimuli (flickering light, dot patterns, limited eye movement). If habituation occurs, then the brain has essentially decided that there is nothing of interest going on—at least nothing that anything can be done about—and virtually quits processing the information that goes in. In particular, they report, the left-brain "common integrative area" goes into a kind of holding pattern. "Viewing is at the conscious level of somnambulism," they assert.

The right half of the brain, which deals with more subjective cognitive processes—dream images, fantasy, intuition—continues to receive the television images. But because the bridge between the right and left brains has been effectively shattered, all cross-processing, the making conscious of the unconscious data and bringing it into usability, is eliminated. The information goes in, but it cannot be easily recalled or thought about.

If the Emerys are correct, then their findings support the idea that television information enters unfiltered and whole, directly into the memory banks, but it is not available for conscious analysis, understanding or learning. It *is* sleep teaching.

All of this helps explain recent findings that children, after watching television, have difficulty recalling what they have just seen. Whatever "knowledge" they gain is the sort that passes through the conscious regions where it would be available for recall and use.

Television as sleep teaching would also help explain my own observations, from political work, that the more that public issues are confined to television, the *less* knowledgeable the public seems to be about them. The voter cannot process information he or she is apparently receiving. When Carter and Ford made their implicit agreement to avoid content and concentrate on style, they were right on the mark.

The Emerys report at length upon one study that measured brainwave activity during television viewing. It established that no matter what the program is, human brainwave activity enters a "characteristic" pattern. The response is to the medium, rather than to any of its content. Once the set goes on, the brain waves slow down until a preponderance of alpha and delta brain waves become the habitual pattern. The longer the set is on, the slower the brainwave activity.

The Emerys explain that slow, synchronous brainwave activity is ordinarily associated with "lack of eye movement, fixation, lack of definition, idleness, inactivity, overall body inertness." They quote from A. R. Luria, who writes in *The Psychophysiology of the Frontal Lobes*: "No organized thought is possible in these phasic states and selective associations are replaced by non-selective association, deprived of their purposeful character."

Alpha is the mental state most commonly associated with meditation, but before anyone equates meditation with television, it's important to make a critical distinction. In the former, you produce your own material and in the latter it comes from outside; it is not internally generated. Dr. Freda Morris, the psychologist-hypnotist quoted earlier, told me that people who are good at meditation are among the most difficult to hypnotize. "They start going into hypnotic trance, but at a certain point they begin producing their own material and cannot be influenced by outside instruction unless they choose to be. They've got their own thing going." She told me that she doubted that good meditators watch much television and added that meditation might be an excellent ability to develop in people who are bothered by television addiction. In fact, she said, television addiction might itself be symptomatic of an inability to produce one's own mental imagery.

Herbert Krugman, a Florida researcher whose brainwave work the Emerys drew upon, compared brainwave activity while watching television with brainwave activity while reading magazines.

"It appears that the mode of response to television is . . . very different from the responses to print . . . the basic electrical response of the brain is clearly to the medium and not to the content differences," said Krugman. "The response to print may be fairly described as active . . . while the response to television may be fairly described as passive . . . television is not communication as we have known it. Our subject was trying to learn something from a print ad, but was passive about television. . . . *Television is a communication medium that effortlessly transmits huge quantities of information not thought about at the time of exposure.*" (My italics.)

I took the Krugman report and the Australian study to Dr. Erik Peper, a widely published researcher on electroencephalographic (brainwave) testing, formerly associated with MIT, currently a professor of Interdisciplinary Sciences at San Francisco State University.

It turned out that Peper had worked with Dr. Thomas Mulholland on a study similar to Krugman's.

"Krugman's statement is correct," Peper told me. "You get a decrease in beta [fast waves] and an increase in slow activity with a large percentage of alpha."

I asked Peper to explain the meaning of this.

"Alpha wave patterns, recorded over the occipital areas of the scalp, disappear at the moment when a person gives visual commands (focuses, accommodates, and verges), when he takes charge of the process of seeking information. Any orienting outward to the world increases your brainwave frequencies and blocks [halts] alpha wave activity. Alpha occurs when you don't orient *to*. You can sit back and have pictures in your head, but you are in a totally passive condition and unaware of the world outside of your pictures. The right phrase for alpha is really 'spaced-out.' Not orienting. When a person focuses visually, or orients to anything, notices something outside himself, then she or he gets an immediate increase in faster wave activity and alpha will block [disappear]. Many meditators are in alpha but in meditation you are learning self-control and how to call upon your own internal processes. There is no such discipline with television. You are not training your mind to control itself, which biofeedback, and also meditation, accomplish; television trains people only for being zombies. Instead of training active attention, television seems to suppress it."

209

I asked Peper to describe the Mulholland experiment.

"As far as I know, this study is the only one that has been made, aside from Krugman's. Ten kids were asked to watch their favorite television programs. Our assumption was that since these programs were their favorite shows, the kids would be involved in them and we'd find there'd be an oscillation between alpha slow-wave activity and beta. The prediction was that they would go back and forth. But they didn't do that. They just sat back. They stayed almost all the time in alpha. This meant that while they were watching they were not reacting, not orienting, not focusing, just spaced-out."

I told Peper about a study which showed that children who were watching television were far slower to react to an emergency than children who were doing something else.

"That's predictable," Peper said. "When they are watching television they're being trained not to react."

He then volunteered his own thoughts about television as an educational medium: "To really learn anything, you have to interact with the source of the data. With television you don't really think. I know that speaking for myself, I can only really learn if I get engaged, as in the Socratic method of teaching. The best teaching is an interactive form. Some people learn best, for example, by writing notes because the notes are a feedback system." (Like a journal or a diary.)

"Television watching is only receiving," he went on, "no longer reacting. It can't do anything but hold your attention; you are receiving, not looking. The key for why they're in alpha is that when they're watching they're not looking *at*, not orienting. This is all by way of totally agreeing with Krugman. If you have a light which is not really being attended to, you can get an infinite amount of alpha. Perhaps it's that the TV target is so far away, the screen so small that your eyes needn't move; you're looking at infinity, in a way, like looking at the hypnotist's flashlight. If you look at moving targets, you have at least a little active interaction;

210

that would tend to put you into beta. But with television though there seems to be movement, you stay all the time in alpha."

I asked Peper if he agreed with Krugman that reading was a more active learning process. "Definitely," he said. "Reading produces a much higher amount of beta activity. You would expect abnormality in anyone who produces alpha while reading. The horror of television," he added, "is that the information goes in, but we don't react to it. It goes right into our memory pool and perhaps we react to it later but we don't know what we're reacting to. When you watch television you are training yourself not to react and so later on, you're doing things without knowing why you're doing them or where they came from."

Television Is Not Relaxing

If television puts our minds in a passive-receptive mode, if it inhibits thinking processes as the preceding remarks certainly suggest, can this be seen as positive? As mentioned in Chapter Eight, many of my correspondents seem to like what happens to them. People say "it relaxes my mind," others use the term "spaced-out," some call it "meditative." The evidence that television produces alpha brain waves, commonly associated with meditation states, encourages the idea that something beneficial can result, especially for our mentally obsessed culture.

In many ways, we are a people isolated in our heads. Nature is absent. Our senses are deprived.

The business person lives in the mental world of offices: paper work and forward-focused, driven-thinking processes. The suburban person lives in predefined mental and physical movement patterns: freeways, mechanical kitchens, repetitive routines. The child sits in schools, fixed in chairs, focused on mental work, attempting to channel thoughts in a way that will help later in this world.

As the environment has been reconstructed into linear monolithic patterns, and as our days have been reconstructed to function within those patterns, our minds have had to adjust.

We drive them forward into obsessive work. We push our thoughts into line, marching with military precision, objectified, analytical, isolated from our senses, our feelings and any alternate patterns of mind. We need to do this. The creative free-roaming mind would help neither the child get through school nor the adult pay rent.

We have celebrated "the life of the mind," but is this the mind we wanted?

When we speak of relaxing our minds nowadays, it is not as though we have been working them at anything like their capacity. If our minds are strained, it is from confinement within one pattern of thinking. Most of our mental capacities have gone fat and soft, or dead from atrophy. It may be that our minds are not tired from overwork, but underwork.

If you have ever done physical exercise on a regular basis, you know the result is not exhaustion, but stimulation. The more of it you do, the more you wish to do, and the more you can do. It is only after extraordinarily long effort that one becomes depleted and needs to rest. And then the relaxation is sweet.

In our culture, the chronically exhausted person is the one who sits all day, or the one whose physical work is chained to fixed patterns: assembly line, store counter, waiting on tables.

I believe it is the same with our minds. Confined to one mental process, they are exhausted by underuse and repetition. After a day of paper work, turned off in so many realms of experience, compulsive and obsessive in those that remain, we dearly seek to escape mentally.

212

Psychiatrists report that an increasing number of people these days complain they cannot quiet their minds. One cannot *will* the mind to cease its fixations and rumination. Even when it comes to sleep or sex or play, experiences that require shifting out of focused thought, the mind continues to churn.

It is little wonder, therefore, that we have seen the sudden growth of Eastern religious disciplines, yogic practices, martial arts, diverse exercise regimens and many forms of meditation. They help relieve the agonies of uncalm minds pacing their narrow cages. They stop obsessive thinking and open alternative mental awareness. They allow for the reception of new experiences. They encourage yielding as opposed to always driving forward. They teach people to take in rather than put out.

While many people use these ancient disciplines to achieve freedom from the driving of their minds, most people do not, choosing drugs instead. Alcohol is good. Valium is better. Some sleeping potions work. And there's television.

They all succeed. Drugs provide escape while passing for experience and relaxation. Television does as well.

All help break obsessive thinking, but this is where their similarity with meditation and other disciplines comes to an end.

I have quoted from Dr. Morris and Dr. Peper to the effect that in meditation one produces one's own internally generated imagery. Both contrast meditation with television viewing in which the images are imposed.

This difference between internally generated and imposed imagery is at the heart of whether it is accurate to say that television relaxes the mind.

Relaxation implies renewal. One runs hard, then rests. While resting, the muscles first experience calm and then, as new oxygen enters them, renewal.

213

Similarly, one thinks and thinks, driving one's mind forward. To relax the mind, one needs to cease thinking, to calm the mind. In Zen meditation, for example, something called "empty mind" is desirable because once achieved, renewal begins. When the mind is quiet, one produces one's own new imagery, or experiences a new sense of one's place in the world.

There are other forms of meditation, however, that are less interested in *self*-renewal and discovery. These are the forms imposed by the "right wing" of the religious disciplines, those with autocratic leadership: Erhard, Moon, Maharaj Ji, L. Ron Hubbard. These leaders are not interested in "empty mind," but in minds which are empty only long enough to be refilled by them.

Whether you are doing Zen meditation or the specific mantras of Reverend Moon, your mind may go into alpha. But one condition is not similar to the other. With the latter, your mind is not renewed, it is occupied.

And so it is with television. When you are watching, absorbing techno-guru, your mind may be in alpha, but it is certainly not "empty mind." Images are pouring into it. Your mind is not quiet or calm or empty. It may be nearer to dead, or zombie-ized. It is occupied. No renewal can come from this condition. For renewal, the mind would have to be at rest, or once rested, it would have to be seeking new kinds of stimulation, new exercise. Television offers neither rest nor stimulation.

Television inhibits your ability to think, but it does not lead to freedom of mind, relaxation or renewal. It leads to a more exhausted mind. You may have time out from prior obsessive thought patterns, but that's as far as television goes. The mind is never empty, the mind is filled. What's worse, it is filled with someone else's obsessive thoughts and images.

In this way, television serves to continue the same channeled mental processes from which one is seeking relief. The mind is as weary after watching as before. No invention or creation can result, only sleep, if you are lucky, as with the aftermath of alcohol and Valium.

XI

HOW WE
TURN
INTO OUR IMAGES

MORE than any other single effect, television places images in our brains. It is a melancholy fact that most of us give little importance to this implantation, perhaps because we have lost touch with our own image-creating abilities, how we use them and the critical functions they serve in our lives. Not being in touch, we don't grasp the significance of other people's images replacing or gaining equality with our own. And yet there are no more terrifying facts about television than that it intervenes between humans and our own image-creating abilities and intervenes between humans and our images of the concrete world outside of our minds.

In this chapter, we will look at how images, *any* images, directly affect human beings and how we humans slowly turn into whatever images we carry in our minds. Then in the next chapter, we will concentrate on television images.

What makes these matters most serious is that human beings have not yet been equipped by evolution to distinguish in our minds between natural images and those which are artificially created and implanted. Neither are we equipped to defend ourselves against the implantation. Until the invention of moving-image media, there was never a need to make any distinction or defense.

And so the final effect, as we will see, is that the two kinds of image—artificial and natural—merge in the mind and we are driven into a nether world of confusion. Like the Solaris astronauts, we cannot differentiate between the present and the past, the concrete and the imaginary. Like the schizophrenic, we cannot tell which image is the product of our own minds, which is representative of a real world, and which has been put inside us by a machine.

Humans Are Image Factories

I have heard people say they can't visualize; they can't make pictures in their heads.

It's true that some people do it more easily than others, but everyone does it.

If you believe yourself to be among those who can't, please simply bring your mother to mind. Or your best friend. Have you done that? Can you see them in your head? It's quite easy.

If I ask you to recall your childhood bedroom, you can probably do that as well. Many people can find enormous detail in that image.

If you have managed to make a picture in your head of any of these, it is definite proof that you can do it and that the phenomenon exists.

I would like to recommend a book called *Seeing With the Mind's Eye* by Nancy Samuels and Mike Samuels. It is the most thoroughgoing popular work on imagery that I've come across. The authors list ten categories of natural human imagery:

1)   Memory. You can remember people's faces. You can visualize the place you work in.

2)   Eidetic images. (Photographic memory.) You can remember the details of your room. You have "photographed" them.

3)   Imagination. You can make up images. You can also create images in your own mind.

4)   Daydreams or fantasy. A kind of imagination that occurs while you are doing other things. You are working in your office, but your mind is creating images of . . . what? The time you hit a home run? The last sexual experience? These are pictures.

5) * Hypnagogic images. The images that come in that half-awake space just before sleep.

6)   Hypnopompic images. The images that come in that half-awake space just before you are fully awake.

7)   Dreams. You may not remember them, but virtually everyone has them. They are pictures.

8)   Hallucinations/visions. An image that takes place inside the head but that is confused with something that is taking place outside. Usually associated with psychosis. Under stress conditions everyone has them. Drugs can cause them; meditation can produce them; so can sleep deprivation and high fever. Truck drivers complain of them after long hours on the freeway.

9)   After-image. The movie is over, but the image remains in the head.

10)   Recurrent image. The *experience* is over—you are home from work—but the face of the boss looms in your mind. You can't clear it out.

The authors acknowledge that this list is incomplete and one category overlaps another. The point is merely to show that a wide variety of natural imagery exists and that everyone experiences some of it. Humans are veritable image factories. We are constantly producing images ourselves and we are absorbing and storing images from the world outside ourselves.

The Concrete Power of Images

The Samuelses argue that images carried within human beings have a definite evolutionary and biological role. Like light, of which they are constructed, images are concrete. Images are things. We see something in the world, a river, and this river image enters our bodies through our eyes, becoming ingrained in our brain cells. The proof that the river is ingrained is that we can remember it. The image held in our mind, say the Samuelses, produces physiological as well as psychological reactions. We slowly evolve into the images we carry, we become what we see, in this case, more riverlike.

Today we are still recovering from the work of such men as behavioral psychologist John Watson. He achieved prominence early in this century by pioneering and popularizing the notion that if you couldn't test a phenomenon and measure it, then it didn't exist. Psychology, in those days, was eager to gain the admiration of the more respectable sciences and thus confined itself to measuring whatever could be quantified, duplicated and predicted. "In the U.S., psychology became so overwhelmingly behaviorist-oriented," say the Samuelses, "that virtually no works were published on mental imagery for fifty years." Even today there are schools of psychological thought which hold that imagery itself is fictional.

In a way this point of view represents the ultimate denial of human experience. All humans carry images in their heads, yet some scientists can say these images have no power or don't exist. In turn, this denial of human imagery laid the groundwork for the common notion, held even today, that surrogate images, implanted from television, have little or no effect.

Many earlier cultures recognized the enormous power of images that are held in the mind. The Samuelses present an exhaustive history of these prior views and then present voluminous physiological evidence (measurements!) which at last fit the scientific model of proof that the images we carry have something important to do with who we individually become.

I cannot, of course, do justice to their very long work here, nor is it my purpose to repeat it. But some excerpts may be useful.

"Hermes Trismegistres believed that thoughts have characteristics similar to the physical world, that thoughts have vibrational levels and energy levels which bring about changes in the physical universe. . . . From a Hermetic point of view, the person who holds a sacred image in his mind experiences the effects produced by the specific energy of that image."

Before Hermes, similar notions were expressed among the Sumerians, the Assyrians and the Babylonians, dating as far back as 4000 B.C. Included among these notions were that there are concrete powers inherent in color and form. If a thing was shaped a certain way, its image was ingested in that form and was retained in the body as a system of energies. (A merger with modern photobiology is coming up.) Sculptures were thought of essentially as energy organizers. The very sight of them was believed to create states of mind and systems of beliefs.

The Samuelses imply that specific sculptural forms were chosen for the benefit that would accrue from seeing them, or ingesting their image. This would explain the wide variety of what we have since called "gods" or "goddesses" in the form of animals, supernatural creatures, heavenly bodies. These offered a way of integrating nature into oneself, similar to what Indians did by imitating animals. The sculptures encouraged knowledge of natural processes. Now we say that these images were worshiped. This is probably wrong. They were not worshiped any more than the Eskimo today worships the sculpture of the walrus. In making the sculpture the sculptor experiences walrus-ness, and so does the viewer.

The Samuelses indicate that the Hebrews, emerging between 3000 and 2000 B.C., won an important political victory by denouncing what they called the "worship of graven images." By destroying the power of the sculptures of the Sumerians and others who preceded them, they effectively destroyed nature-based religion and the veracity of images. This made possible the substitution of an abstract, single, male, human all-powerful God. Because it was a sin to create any sculpture of it, it maintained its abstract nature. Although they absorbed God, the Christians somewhat overcame this problem. They created images of Jesus, a step backward (or forward) toward paganism.

Many Western religions, and all non-Western religions, were unaffected by the Judeo-Christian slaughter of diverse, nature-based imagery. They continued to inform their universal understanding through images representing virtually every natural form and tendency. This continues to apply to the great majority of people in the world today. It even applies, of course, to those Hebrews who followed the teachings of the Cabbala, which represented a kind of underground among Hebrews for centuries.

Today's yogic disciples are rooted in the belief that focusing one's mind upon objects, either outside the body or inside it, affects one's entire physical nature. *Samadhi,* a much-sought yogic state, is the union that one experiences with an object or image that one looks upon—the form of an egg, or a mandala, for example. Union in this case means that the image itself is a concrete energy which travels between the object and the brain of the viewer. The image becomes a kind of solder that merges the three previously separated entities: sculpture (or form), person, image. Unlike solder, the image—made up of a thing we call light—can enter all the way into the cells.

When you or I look at a sculpture or painting or, for that matter, an igloo or high-rise building, the image enters us in the form of light rays. This is concrete, not metaphoric.

The form of the sculpture, artwork or structure determines the quality of the experience, what you can learn from it, what feelings you derive from it, and what image you retain inside your body/mind/cells.

The image becomes part of your image vocabulary. It remains in your mind. That is, it remains in the *cells* of your brain. It has physical character.

Sculptures of the Buddha are created to instill in the person who views them the attitude of the Buddha figure, its mood, its way of being. This is its information content—shape, color, weight, attitude, relation to gravity. The person who contemplates the Buddha figure for long hours becomes more like the Buddha figure. It is just a question of time. No thought is necessary. The image goes in and does its thing.

The person who observes the square form of the high-rise literally ingests this image, slowly absorbing it, remembering it, becoming it; adopting its character. The person who observes the pyramid ingests this image; its shape has power.

The person who ingests the tree image, becomes treelike. The viewing of a river produces riverlike people. The viewing of Christ on the cross instills the Christ experience. The viewing of birds in flight creates bird-flight in the mind of the viewer.

Viewing Kojak means absorbing his character and his way of being.

As one reviews non-Western cultures and their religious expressions, certain forms keep repeating themselves. They are said to represent universal energy formations. I have already mentioned the egg and the mandala.

Consider Tantric art, for example. You find the egg form reproduced in thousands of ways. It is claimed that the image of the egg enters the mind and body of the viewer. Its smoothness, curvature, pattern of reflecting light, its "calmness," "centeredness," and "perfection" instill themselves in the observer, if the observer permits it. The egg is also the seed of life. From it, everything else follows. As a result, the egg image is at the heart of many meditation practices which employ imagery.

Modern physics is now finding that the mandala form is quite literally a reproduction of an essential organizing shape in the universe. The nucleus of the atom is a perfect mandala. If we could view it from space, our solar system would form a mandala—the bursting universe with stars fleeing outward from the center forms a mandala.

The contemplation of the mandala form—whether via Tibetan thankas, Hebrew Stars of David, Indian sand paintings, Tantric visualization, Hopi sun images—exists in virtually every culture of the world. Is this an accident? Or is everyone onto something?

By now, the power of images seems transparent and obvious to me. I am furious at the unconscious years I spent considering such beliefs, whenever I heard of them, as freaky, weird, unscientific or superstitious. Now, sensitized largely through my own research and what I have discovered of other people's, such as the Samuelses', as I walk around I literally feel assaulted by the images that are offered by the artificial world we live in whether they are buildings or signs or fire hydrants or television.

I was talking about this to a young woman friend who told me about a time when, nearing a nervous collapse, she was confined to a mental institution.

"It was the most awful experience of my life," she told me. "I was placed in an empty room with padded walls and a steel door. I had felt troubled and confused until that point, but right then and there I really cracked. I went nuts. Seeing that, the doctors fed me with drug after drug. I couldn't keep track of what they were giving me. I went from one wild state into another, just trying to get on top of the drugs. I begged them not to drug me. I tried to escape. It seemed that they were trying to drive me insane. I felt like I'd been put into a sensory-deprivation chamber, locked up without anything to touch or smell or see or feel.

"The thing that got me out of there was this one woman, a nurse, sixty years old or so, big and fat, shaped like a house. She would come visit me, ostensibly to check me, but what she would do is get me to visualize beaches, the moon, nature. She would describe sunsets in really intimate detail. I would get all the way into these descriptions and though it sort of tore me up to be locked in this steel room, drugged, often bound up, she was able to take me out of that space and bring visions into my mind. It re-created old feelings in me. My heart felt like bursting at the sight of these imagined sunsets, but most of all these visions created a calm that allowed me to beat those drugs. I learned how to let them by, and then I figured out that what those doctors wanted was for me to submit, so I faked submission. I stopped fighting and struggling and they let me out. It was the images of the sunsets, and the calm they created in me, which were my secret weapon. By holding those images, I could hold onto my sanity."

Can you remember your childhood well enough to recall that you had certain favorite objects? Lately, in watching my own children, seeing that there are certain objects they seem to love for reasons which are totally beyond my ken, I have begun to remember similar objects from my own life.

There was a particular stone, for example, very dark in color with a few yellowish lines running through it. I kept it under my pillow, and when I was alone, I would look at it for amazingly long periods of time. I would caress it. Even now as I put it into writing, a flood of feeling invades me. I realize now that I had a physical relationship with that stone; I literally *loved* it. I loved its shape, its color, the way it felt. It also stimulated me, and does even now as I remember it. It made me think. And yet this is nonsensical.

There was also a small furry ball, and a kind of silly drawing of a bear on the wall. I don't remember where it came from, but even now I can picture it in my mind. I remember it had voluptuous shapes, a round head, a large ovalish body. There was something profoundly comforting in that image. How could that be so?

Metaphysics to Physics

By all accounts, the great majority of the people of the world agree that image, color, form and symbol are concrete, physical and real, capable of affecting the viewer of them. It is only among Western technological cultures, an extreme minority of the world, that this notion is suppressed and ridiculed. But now, as with so many previousy rejected areas of knowledge, Western science is slowly beginning to catch up.

In *Seeing With the Mind's Eye,* the Samuelses present some evidence that neurophysiologists are able to trace the pathways of images from the brain into the cells.

"It has been found that mental images have many of the same physical components as open-eyed perceptions. . . . Our bodies react to mental images in ways similar to how they react to images from the external world. The American physiologist Edmund Jacobson has done studies which show that when a person imagines running, small but measurable amounts of contraction actually take place in the muscles associated with running. The same neurological pathways are excited by imagined running as by actual running. . . . But anatomists have also been aware of pathways between the cerebral cortex, where images are stored, and the autonomic nervous system which controls the so-called involuntary muscles. The autonomic nervous system controls sweating, blood vessels, expansion and contraction, blood pressure, blushing and goose-pimpling, the rate and force of heart contractions, respiratory rate, dryness of mouth, bowel motility and smooth muscle tension. There are also pathways between the autonomic nervous system and the pituitary and adrenal cortex. The pituitary gland secretes hormones which regulate the rate of secretion of other glands; especially the thyroid, sex and adrenal glands. The adrenal glands secrete steroids, which regulate metabolic processes, and epinephrine, which causes the 'fight or flight' reaction. *Through these pathways, an image held in the mind can literally affect every cell in the body* . . . [My italics]

"The nervous innervation of voluntary and involuntary muscles is also associated with the physical expression of emotion. When an image or thought is held in the mind, there is neuronal activity in both hemispheres of the brain. Nerve fibers lead from the cerebral hemisphere to the hypothalamus, which has connections with the autonomic nervous system and the pituitary gland. When a person holds a strong fearful image in the mind's eye, the body responds, via the autonomic nervous system, with a feeling of 'butterflies in the stomach,' a quickened pulse, elevated blood pressure, sweating, goose-bumps and dryness of the mouth. Likewise, when a person holds a strong relaxing image in the mind, the body responds with lowered heart rate, decreased blood pressure and, obviously, all the muscles tend to relax."

So the image you carry in your mind *can* affect your actual physical body and your emotional state.

The Samuelses describe research done with yogic practitioners who can voluntarily control many of their autonomic (involuntary) body processes, from breathing rate to body temperature to heartbeat. It is not unusual for a trained yogi to be able to fluctuate heartbeats voluntarily from eighty beats per minute to three hundred beats. The research showed that "the techniques by which they were able to do these things were found to be made of detailed visualizations."

The Samuelses provide nearly one hundred fifty pages of examples of the physical uses of images, ranging from athletes who use visualization to increase their performance to the dramatic growth in medical uses of visualization by doctors in aiding cancer victims to gain control of their own disease and by psychologists in easing the agonies of upcoming stressful situations.

The classic article on the effects of mental rehearsal is by Australian psychologist Alan Richardson, reporting on changes in performance among three groups of basketball players. Between test sessions, the first group physically practiced foul shooting, the second group practiced mentally, the third group didn't practice at all. The results showed that between the initial test and the final test, the first two groups improved their performance by virtually the same percentage. The third group did not improve. "Similar studies involving dart throwing and other athletic activities show the same kinds of results," say the Samuelses.

The image in the mind sends the autonomic nervous system through a rehearsal of impulses. When the real event comes along, it has been practiced. The image stimulating the autonomic nervous system is itself the practice.

Similar descriptions appear in an article by Dr. Richard Suinn in *Psychology Today*, July 1976. Suinn was asked to help some skiers who were training for the Olympics.

"I instructed the skiers to practice their athletic skills by using mental imagery. The technique has been used before. Jean-Claude Killy, a three-gold-medal skier, has reported that his only preparation for one race was to ski it mentally. He was recovering from an injury at the time and couldn't practice on the slopes. Killy says the race turned out to be one of his best. . . . Without fail, athletes feel their muscles in action as they [mentally] rehearse their sport. . . . The imagery of visuo-motor behavior rehearsal apparently is more than sheer imagination. It is a well-controlled copy of experience, a sort of body-thinking similar to the powerful illusion of certain dreams at night."

Suinn describes incidents where athletes in sports ranging from swimming and skiing to pistol shooting use mental imagery to rehearse the actual competition. It proved better training, in many instances, than practice runs in noncompetitive conditions. With imagery, the competitive conditions were more nearly simulated in the nervous system. So the imagery was more valuable rehearsal than actual physical practice.

"During one recent experiment, I recorded the electromyography responses of an Alpine ski racer as he summoned up a moment-by-moment imagery of a downhill race. . . . Muscle bursts appeared as the skier hit jumps. Further muscle bursts duplicated the effort of a rough section of the course, and the needles settled during the easy sections . . . his EMG recordings almost mirrored the course itself. There was even a final burst of muscle activity after he had passed the finish line, a mystery to me until I remembered how hard it is to come to a skidding stop after racing downhill at more than 40 miles an hour."

The image held in the mind produced measurable physiological responses. The involuntary nervous system is activated by the image. The image is itself training.

Modern psychology is making much of these techniques, but a sensible person will automatically evoke images in order to rehearse an event, without any therapist's instructions. It could just be called "thinking through" an event beforehand, whether it is a speech or a difficult encounter. Every lawyer that I've ever met does it before every court appearance. Most business people do it. By giving time to the planning of the events, you are taking charge of them, preprogramming your body and mind.

Even more interesting perhaps are the increasing uses of visualization in modern medicine, techniques very similar to those used by "primitive" healers and medicine people. The idea is taking hold that, like the yogis, patients can control their own internal chemistry, the functions of the organs, the flow of the blood and so forth by way of the images held in the mind.

Prominent among the practitioners of medical visualization is a European neurologist, J. H. Shultz, who uses something called "autogenic therapy," taking people through imaginary tours of their bodies, visually discovering their organs, the cells, and eventually picturing them as functional and healthy.

The Samuelses report: "Autogenic therapy is widely used in Europe and has been extensively researched. . . . A seven-volume work cites 2400 studies. Researchers examining the effects of the standard autogenic exercises have demonstrated an increase (or decrease) in skin temperatures, changes in blood sugar, white blood cell counts, blood pressure, heart and breathing rates, thyroid secretion, and brain wave patterns. . . . Autogenic training has been used in coordination with standard drug and surgical procedures in Europe to treat a broad range of diseases including ulcers, gastritis, gall bladder attacks, irritative colon, hemorrhoids, constipation, obesity, heart attack, angina, high blood pressure, headaches, asthma, diabetes, thyroid disease, arthritis and low back pain, among others."

Dr. Carl Simonton, who is director of cancer therapy at

Gladman Memorial Hospital in Oakland, California, and his wife, Stephanie Simonton, have been receiving acclaim lately for their amazing results in inducing what have been called "spontaneous remissions" in cancer by using techniques of meditation and attitude adjustment based on visualization.

The patient is instructed to picture his or her cancer and to imagine the immune mechanism working the way it is supposed to, picking up the dead and dying cells.

"Patients are asked to visualize the army of white blood cells coming in, swarming over the cancer, and carrying off the malignant cells. . . . These white cells then break down the malignant cells, which are then flushed out of the body.

". . . The cancers may be imagined in the form of animals, snakes, armies, non-objective force-fields, whatever seems to have meaning in a particular patient." The Simontons also use photos of cells, photos of cancers, X ray photos of the person's own cancer to aid the process of imaging and at some point they ask patients to visualize themselves totally well.

Critics of the Simontons' success statistics like to argue that it is not the visualizations themselves which have produced the results, but rather the belief in them, the placebo effect. But, of course, this is an absurd criticism, because the belief in the cure is itself likely to come in the form of a visualization of the healthy body. In either event, it is the image that effects the cure.

The Samuelses' book is an amazing and fascinating work. They quote from virtually every religious discipline, every healing system in the history of the world about which any evidence exists. They quote from Sufis, Hindus, Gnostics, Rosicrucians, and Indians as well as from Christian and Hebrew texts. They quote from dozens of psychotherapies and nearly as many medical systems. They quote from artists about inspiration, scientists about "flashes of insight" (Einstein said that his relativity theory popped into his mind at a moment when he was imagining himself being carried along standing on a beam of light), but there are two notable absences from their work. They do not discuss the role of image emulation and they never once mention television.

Image Emulation: Are We All Taped Replays?

A few years ago, when my kids were six and seven respectively, they asked to see *The Towering Inferno*. I took them and a six-year-old friend of theirs, Veva Edelson, to see it. When we returned home, I heard the three of them playing in the next room and wrote down what they were saying. Here is a portion of it.

YARI: (*Shouting*) How're you doing there; are you holding onto the top of the building?

KAI: (*Also shouting*) Yeah, but my rope and my gun fell down. How are you doing?

YARI: I'm in the middle of a lot of fire here. Call Squad Thirty-eight.

VEVA: You have to come down because the whole first floor is burning.

YARI: I don't know how I can get down; the stairs are blocked and the elevators are burning.

VEVA: (*Interrupting the game*) Let's say our walkie-talkies ran out of batteries and we can't talk.

YARI: (*Continuing the interruption*) Let's say the wiring explodes (*Then he makes a hosing sound on Kai, who is lying under a chair, which is supposed to be the building.*)

VEVA: (*Still interrupting*) Let's say the fire went out. (*Then, back into the game*) Squad Fifty-one, I've got to talk to you. Right now there's about thirteen men dead and five women and two kids.

YARI: I'm not Squad Fifty-one, I'm Squad Thirty-eight, and I'm down here giving a five-dollar parking ticket.

Children's games are largely based on their experiences. If they live in the country, their games will involve animals. If they go to movies, their games will reflect that. If they watch television, you can see it in their games. In all cases, the characters and creatures they are imitating are based upon the pictures of them which they carry in their minds.

I have watched my kids after they have seen *Star Trek* on TV. Yari, the older, becomes Captain Kirk—efficient, "manly," determined, in charge, unafraid, coplike. Kai, the younger, is second in command. He plays Spock, affecting his behavior: wry, unsmiling, unfeeling, scientific, detached, cerebral.

The games continue for hours. Often they replay the same story a few times, as though they were rehearsing it or attempting to memorize it. This, of course, is exactly what they are doing—rehearsing it, to ingrain it in themselves.

Another day, I noticed that Yari was taking giant leaps around the garden and making a clicking sound with his tongue against the roof of his mouth. I realized that this noise was one he made frequently while doing something active and that it was an imitation of the electronic sound that accompanies all of the bionic acts of the Bionic Man. Later that week I watched the program with my kids.

During one sequence the Bionic Man is shown running at bionic speed across a field, to the accompaniment of the clicks. The movements are shown in slow motion, so they become especially vivid. I asked my kids about this:

JERRY: When you guys are running, do you sometimes imagine that you're the Bionic Man and try to run like him?

YARI: I always do.

JERRY: How about you, Kai?

KAI: I do too; is that bad?

How to answer that? Is it bad? Is it bad for kids to do a

natural thing—emulation, imitation—which is how children for millions of years have learned about the world? That is certainly not bad. But in this case, they were imitating a mechanical person. I can't tell him it's bad because I don't want him to doubt his own learning processes, and yet the more he practices and maintains his bionic images, the more he imitates them. Slowly, he assumes the role in real life. The Bionic Man slowly becomes real in the person of . . . my kid!

I told him it wasn't bad and changed the subject.

In Chapter Four I described how emulation is a method used by human beings to understand and integrate nature into themselves.

To get an idea of the naturalness of the process, just think of ways in which you are like your parents or your children are like you.

I believe that a parent may have less to do with the characteristics a child picks up from the parent than the kid does, because of simple evolutionary emulation processes that continue constantly. We attempt to train children in one area, only to discover that they've picked up parts of ourselves that we'd rather they hadn't noticed.

My son Kai has begun to walk with his toes spread slightly outward, ducklike, as I do, and also as my father does. I can remember the moment as a child when I *chose* to imitate my father's walk, out of a simple desire to be closer to him, to know how he is inside. Now, thirty-five years later, I walk exactly as he did at *this* age, even though it is not a desirable way of walking. One's balance is not ideal, physical spontaneity is limited and movement possibilities narrow. The manner of walking amplifies a certain static emotional condition that my father had to struggle with and which, finding it also in myself, I don't much like.

In retrospect, I can see that this way of walking is illustrative of an instinct to "hide" rather than "act," and perhaps its roots go all the way back to his childhood in the Warsaw ghetto. Who knows? It hardly matters by now. And yet the walk has passed through three generations and is beginning to reappear in Kai.

The point is that imitation from generation to generation is automatic. The tool used is the image of the person being imitated. As I walk, I imagine my father's walk. This makes it possible for me to repeat it. Without the image I could not repeat it. After many years, of course, the image has submerged though the walk remains.

We tend to speak of image emulation as applicable only to children, as though at some fixed age one ceases to learn in this way. This is absurd.

As there are ways in which my children imitate me, there are also ways in which I imitate them. Kai, for example, has a gentle and efficient way of speaking and moving, and I have often caught myself copying it. Yari has an energy and enthusiasm—a brightness—which I have learned to call upon myself. He teaches me how by merely being that way. I copy him as the Indian copies the panther and the Zen student copies the river. Slowly I become more like both of my children just as they also become more like me.

The same applies to husband and wife. It is a subject of *New Yorker* cartoons that husbands and wives (and even pets) begin to resemble each other after years together. I have seen countless examples of it, and I believe my wife and I are such an example. After living with someone over decades, one picks up her or his mannerisms, facial expressions, even lines on the face and body attitudes. There is no way to avoid doing this. It's automatic. Humans are hopeless emulators. We can't stop it if we wish to. We look around us, and whatever is there day after day becomes the environment for our ingestion whether it is the Bionic Man or one's own family. We absorb it, take it into ourselves, turn into it. We become each other's mirrors or buddhas or mandalas. Slowly we turn into what we see. It is a basic way of learning how to be. The process goes on for our whole lives.

San Francisco, unlike New York, achieves its primary cultural influence not from Europe but from Asia. An example of this occurs in many city parks from about six A.M. daily to eight A.M. I walk through one such park each day about seven-thirty A.M. The scene is this: about forty people, half of them Western, half Chinese, are facing an old Chinese man who is doing Tai Chi.

I have watched the way he teaches. He *never* speaks (he knows no English). He merely faces his "class" and moves. They copy his movements. If there is something particularly difficult, he does it several times. There is no discussion of theory; the movement itself is the theory. Once you have absorbed the movement inside yourself, the meaning of the movement invades your consciousness. So the teaching method is 100 percent imitation. After the class is over, the students practice with the image of him in their minds.

Imitating Media

Perhaps you have caught yourself kissing another person as you first saw kissing in the movies or on television. My children have a phrase to describe this: "television kiss." It is fortunate for them that they've noted that there are television kisses and other kinds, because it will help protect them from absorbing it, taking it into themselves where it will come back out ten years later, like a replay.

Most of us did not make that distinction as we sat in darkened rooms or theaters as children. Since we didn't see all that much *real* kissing, the media kiss became our image of kissing. We found ourselves producing that model of kiss later in life.

I was fourteen years old when I tried kissing for the first

235

time. I imitated Humphrey Bogart's kiss, but I didn't feel it. Only later did I realize that perhaps Bogart didn't feel it either; he was merely kissing the way the director said he should. So there I was imitating a kiss that was never real in the first place, worried that there might be something wrong with me for lacking the appropriate feelings and failing to obtain the appropriate response.

The journalist Jane Margold was driving home one night in Berkeley with her brother, Harlan. Suddenly a man crawled into the street right in front of them. They screeched to a stop and then, stunned, just sat there for a moment. They finally got out and cautiously went up to the man to find that he'd been stabbed several times in his upper body, was bleeding profusely and was in danger of dying right there. The man's assailant was nowhere to be seen.

In describing the event to me, Jane said that she instantly flipped into a media version of herself. She had never faced anything like it before and had no direct feelings. Instead, playing through her mind were images of similar events she'd seen on television or in films. The media images superseded her own responses, even to the point of removing her from the event. She was there, but she didn't experience herself as being there. She was seeing the event, but between her and it, floating in her mind, was an image of an implanted reality which would not get out of the way. She thought such thoughts as: "This is real; there's a wounded man lying here in front of me, bleeding to death, yet I have no feeling. It seems like a movie."

In fact, it was the very movielike quality that eventually got her into action. Without feeling, she performed mechanical acts. She and her brother comforted the man, directed traffic, dispatched people to summon police and an ambulance. She became extremely efficient, but throughout, she had the sense of performing a script.

In *Myth America,* Carol Wald and Judith Papachristou detail a history of the images of women from 1865 to 1945, as presented in print media. They argue that the images, created exclusively by men, formed the operative visual myths about women in America and that as the images spread and entered people's minds, they became mirrors of reality. Men wanted their women to be that way; women, seeing only those images, attempted to and eventually did become like the images. It was a kind of alchemy in which the image finally produced the reality.

"To the degree that pictures seem real, people were inclined to accept what the [male] artist saw in good faith. . . . Through such an arrangement, the myth becomes apparent. . . . Myths prevail. Here, all the expected roles of women are illustrated, from romantic elopement, blushing bride, and honeymoon to household drudge and nagging wife. . . . All are expressions of [male] feeling made visible through art . . ."

The authors are careful to point out that the images of women had little to do with the reality of women's lives, which were filled with hardship, and the need to solve problems against enormous odds, many times on their own. Nonetheless, because the images were everywhere, they began to dominate the reality, making women wish to be like men's images of women, encouraging men to perceive women in those terms and helping institute a power arrangement between the sexes that is only now being challenged.

The images became the mirror against which the whole society compared women's behavior, and because of their power they succeeded in becoming a personal and also a political and economical reality. Yet, those were print images, which are not nearly so powerful as the moving images that have since achieved an even greater presence in everyone's mind.

The women's movement of today, like all other movements that are interested in recovering self-definition—black, Oriental, Indian, worker, homosexual and others—has discovered that its struggle must be waged not only against the creators of the images—the people and media who purvey them—but also against the very mental images women already carry around in their own minds; stereotypes, which they emulate with their own behavior. Because of this, many political movements have taken on aspects of personal therapy movements. The goal is to rid oneself of what are often called "tapes." This phrase, heard equally from political people and people involved in many therapy systems—from "radical psychiatry" to, yes, *est*—is used quite literally. The tape is the image, the picture one carries in one's mind that is continually replicated, unconsciously, however useless, self-destructive, or idiotic it may be.

When women carry inside their heads the image of the idealized subservient housewife-mother-secretary, they automatically tend to imitate the image. This continues until the moment when they say, "Wait, I didn't create this person in my head; who did?"

When black people invented the image "Black is beautiful," its point was to destroy a previous image carried in the minds of whites and blacks alike that black was not beautiful. Only then could personal change be made, leading to political results.

The suppression of Indian people in this country, at first achieved with guns, was later accelerated and confirmed by the media images of the Indian as a savage who needed to be saved by white, Western education, morality and life-style. The critical ingredient in this was the implantation within young Indians themselves of the belief that this image was a correct one. With that came self-hatred.

Only by realizing that the image carried in the mind—the tape—is *real* and *implanted* is it possible to disconnect oneself from the cycle of taped replay and subvert an otherwise inevitable process whereby the image is translated into reality.

You may be among those who believe that the evolution of image into reality takes place via the mysterious processes implied by Hermes, the Tantras, the Cabbala or the Rosicrucians. Or you may be impressed with the biophysiological evidence that images are carried in the cells. Or you may believe that the emulation process is the primary way image becomes reality. Or you may believe, as I do, that the evolution of image into reality involves all these routes and others.

But whichever is most important, the result is the same. We evolve into the images we carry in our minds. We become what we see. And in today's America, what most of us see is one hell of a lot of television.

239

XII

THE REPLACEMENT OF HUMAN IMAGES BY TELEVISION

TELEVISION is the most important single source of images in the world today. If people are ingesting television images at the rate of four hours a day, then it is clear that whatever uses people have for the images they carry in their heads, television is now the source.

When you are watching television all categories of your own image-making capacities go dormant, submerged in the television image. TV effectively intervenes between you and your personal images, substituting itself.

When you are watching TV, you are not daydreaming, or reading, or looking out the window at the world. You have opened your mind, and someone else's daydreams have entered. The images come from distant places you have never been, depict events you can never experience, and are sent by people you don't know and have never met. Your mind is the screen for their microwave pictures. Once their images are inside you, they imprint upon your memory. They become yours.

What's more, the images remain in you permanently. I can easily prove this to you.

Please bring to mind any of the following: John F. Kennedy, Milton Berle, Howdy Doody, the Bionic Man, Captain Kangaroo, Archie Bunker, Johnny Carson, Captain Kirk, Henry Kissinger.

Did any of these images appear in your mind? Were you able to make a picture of them in your head? If so, that is proof that once they have entered your brain they remain in there. They live in there together with all the memories of your life. Yet you don't know these people. And many of them are fictional characters.

Now would you make the effort, please, to erase these TV people from your mind? Make them go away. Erase Johnny Carson or Henry Kissinger. Can you do that? If so, you are a most unusual person. Once television places an image inside your head, it is yours forever.

Suppression of Imagination

Try to remember a time when you *first* read a book or heard a radio show and then *later* saw a film or a television program of the same work.

If you read, say, *Gone With the Wind*, *Roots*, *Marjorie Morningstar* or *From Here to Eternity,* or heard any radio show such as "The Lone Ranger" first, you created your own internal image of the events described while you read or listened. You imagined the characters, the events and the ambience. You made pictures in your mind. These pictures were yours. Of course they were influenced by the author—what he or she told you—but the creation of the actual image was up to you.

Marjorie Morningstar was an image in your mind *before* you saw the film. Then you saw the film with Natalie Wood playing Marjorie. Once you had seen Natalie Wood in the role, could you recover the image you had made up?

Marjorie became Natalie Wood from that point on. So we can say that when your self-produced image was made concrete for you, your own image disappeared.

When you listened to the Lone Ranger on radio, you created a picture of him and Tonto. When you saw them later on television, could you retain your new image, or did you get stuck with the actors? It was almost certainly the latter. If you then heard the radio program again, what image of the characters were you left with?

In any competition between an internally generated image and one that is later solidified for you via moving-image media, your own image is superseded. Moses is Charlton Heston. The Sundance Kid is Robert Redford. Isis is a Saturday morning cartoon. Woodward and Bernstein are Redford and Hoffman. Buffalo Bill is Paul Newman. McMurphy is Jack Nicholson. (When Carlos Castaneda was offered an enormous sum of money to sell the screen rights to the Don Juan series, he refused saying, "I don't want to see Don Juan turn into Anthony Quinn.")

Let me ask the question in reverse. If you saw the movie version of *Gone With the Wind* before you read the book, could you develop your *own* image of Rhett Butler? Or did he remain Clark Gable? Did you see Natalie Wood in the part *before* you read *Marjorie Morningstar*? If so, could you erase Natalie and come up with your own Marjorie? I doubt it very much. Once the concrete image is in you, it stays.

The power that television images have to replace imaginary images that you created yourself operates in all realms of external-image information. All of our minds are filled with images of places and times and people and stories with which we've never had personal contact. In fact, when you receive information from any source that does not have pictures attached to it, you make up pictures to go with it. They are your images. You create the movie to go with the story. You hear the word "Africa" and a picture comes to mind.

These internal movies can be of historical events and periods, such as the signing of the Declaration of Independence or the age of dinosaurs. They may be of happenings to which we have no direct access, such as life in a primitive village, or of exotic places we have never been—Borneo, China, the moon.

The question is this: Once television provides an image of these places and times, what happens to your own image? Does it give way to the TV image or do you retain it?

Here is a list to check with. Please attempt to bring these to mind:

I have already mentioned China, Africa, Borneo and the moon. How about life under the sea? Life in an Eskimo village? A police shoot-out. An argument among homosexuals. A mugging. Dope smugglers. A Russian village. A preoperation conference of doctors. An American farm family. The war room of the Pentagon. Ben Franklin. The Battle of Little Big Horn. The FBI. The Old South. The Crusades. The landing of the Pilgrims. The flight of Amelia Earhart. An emergency ambulance crew. A Stone Age tribe. The raid on Entebbe Airport. Ancient Greece. Ancient Rome. The Old West.

Were you able to come up with images for any or all of these? It is extremely unlikely that you have experienced more than one or two of them personally. Obviously the images were either out of your own imagination or else they were from the media.

Can you identify which was which?

Most of the people in America right now would probably say that the images they carry in their minds of the Old South are from one of two television presentations: *Gone With the*

Wind and *Roots*. These were, after all, the two most popular television shows in history, witnessed by more than 130 million people each. And none of the 130 million was actually in the Old South.

Historical periods like the Crusades or the Old West are frequently pictured on television and in films. I have little doubt that most people would call upon their film or TV images if I asked them to bring those periods to mind. How could it be otherwise?

The same applies to the depictions of life-styles. What images do you use to understand the quality of life for lesbians? Or artists? Or farm laborers? Or members of the American Nazi Party? What images do you carry of Eskimo villagers or nomads in the Sahara or Indians in the Amazon?

Like historical periods, or groups of people with whom you are not in personal contact, most current events are also removed from your direct participation. You watch news reports in which Harry Reasoner tells you what is happening politically in China. You watch a congressman explain events in Chile, and then you see a street in Santiago. You see pictures of grounded oil tankers or fighting in Angola or elections in Sweden or scientific testimony on nuclear power.

You don't participate in these things and you can't see them for yourself. The images you have of them are derived from the media, and this becomes the totality of your image bank.

Now let's go a step further.

Please bring to mind a baseball game or a football game. Have you got one? Hold it for a moment.

If you are like most Americans, you *have* actually been to a game. You have seen one directly and probably participated in one personally. You have probably also watched at least one of them on television. Here's the question: Which one did you bring to mind? The television version or the one you experienced directly?

244

The answers vary on this point, but many people I have asked will report that the television image is the one which springs to mind first, if only because it was the most recent. Most will say the images rotate.

Once images are inside your head, the mind doesn't really distinguish between the image that was gathered directly and the one that derived from television.

Of course you *can* distinguish. When I asked you whether it was a television image or a firsthand image, you were certainly able to identify which was which. But until I asked you, you may not have thought to do that.

Have you ever met movie stars or famous television personalities? Whenever I have met them I have always remarked to myself upon the difference in the personal image they presented and the television or film image. I could recognize them when I saw them in person, I am only saying that it was different. The main point is this: When I think about them now, in retrospect, their television images are just as likely to spring into my mind as their real-life images. I can *decide* to bring up their *real* images if I wish to, but if their names are mentioned in passing conversation, or I read a review of a production they've been in, I am actually more likely to bring up a media image than one of the real person I have met.

Have you ever visited McDonald's? Which images dominate in your mind, those from your actual visit or those from television? They rotate, don't they? They take on a certain equality in your memory banks. You can make the distinction between the direct image and the advertising image, but do you? If for some reason the subject of McDonald's comes up in conversation, which image comes into your mind as you talk? Do you make the distinction? If you are like most people to whom I've asked this question, it is only with great effort that you are able to distinguish which one is the personal experience and which is the television experience. It takes a certain amount of effort to do so; one doesn't ordinarily bother. The television image can be as real in effect as the personally experienced image.

The mind doesn't automatically distinguish which image is from direct experience and which has been imposed by the media. If I should now ask you to erase the television image of McDonald's, leaving only the reality—the personally experienced direct contact—can you do that? Please make the effort and see if you can.

We are left with a very bizarre phenomenon. Television is capable of dominating personally derived imagery—from books or imagination—and it is also capable, at least some of the time, of causing confusion as to what is real experience and what is television experience. The mind is very democratic about its image banks, all are equally available for our recall and use. And so when we call on our images for whatever purposes we may have for them, we are as likely to produce an implanted image as one which was originally our own.

The root of this unfortunate problem lies with the fact that until very recently, human beings had no need to make distinctions between artificial images of distant events and life directly lived.

The Inherent Believability of All Images

Seeing is believing.

Like many an axiom, this one is literally true. Only since the ascendancy of the media has this been opened to question.

Throughout the hundreds of thousands of generations of human existence, whatever we saw with our eyes was concrete and reliable. Experience was directly between us and the natural environment. Nonmediated. Nonprocessed. Not altered by other humans.

If we saw a flock of birds flying southward, then these birds were definitely doing that. We could believe in it. We might interpret this concrete information in various ways, perhaps misinterpret it, but there could never have been a question as to whether it was happening. The information itself, the birds and their flight, could not be doubted.

This is the case with all sensory information. Whatever information the senses produce the brain trusts as *inherently* believable. If the sense could not be relied upon, then the world would have been an utterly confusing place. Humans would have been unable to make any sensible choices leading to survival. If there were no concretely true information, there could have been no sane functioning; the species could not have survived. This belief in sense perception is the foundation, the given, for human functioning.

This is not to say there is no illusion.

In a desert environment, as we know, mirage can cause some to believe they are seeing things that are not there. But the humans who are fooled in this way are the humans who are new to that environment. It's a problem of experience and interpretation. Their senses are not yet attuned to the new informational context. People who live for generations in such places learn to allow for illusions and don't actually "see" them in the way that visitors do. They learn to look at the edges of images, like the shadow spaces of Castaneda's Don Juan, and to perceive a reality which is different from the visitor's.

In jungle environments, and among certain creatures, there is camouflage. Animals use it to fool each other, including humans. Humans also use it, or devise image tricks, to fool animals and other humans. In this way images become pro-cessed images, deliberately altered, and may serve to fool an observer whose senses and interpretations are not sufficiently sharp.

These are the classical exceptions which prove the point,

because the basis of success for camouflage and illusion is that humans *will* believe what they see. In this sense, camouflage is a kind of sensory jujitsu that only confirms the original point; the senses are inherently believable.

In the modern world, information from the senses cannot be relied upon as before. We attempt to process artificial smells, tastes, sights and sounds as though they could reveal planetary reality, but we cannot make anything of them because we are no longer dealing directly with the planet. The environment itself has been reconstructed into an already abstracted, arbitrary form. Our senses are no longer reacting to information that comes directly from the source. They are reacting to processed information, the manifestation of human minds. Our information is confined in advance to the forms that other humans provide.

Now, with electronic media, our senses are removed a step further from the source. The very images that we see can be altered and are. They are framed, ripped out of context, edited, re-created, sped up, slowed down and interrupted by other images. They arrive from a variety of places on the planet where we are not and were filmed at times which are not the present. What's more, many of the images are totally fictional. The things that we see are not happening and never happened. That is, they happened, but it is only the acting that happened, not the event.

Obviously, in the present age, we ought not rely on images to the same degree that our ancestors relied on the image of flying birds.

Meanwhile, the images proceed inward as though they were the same as natural, unprocessed imagery. They move, walk, talk, and seem real. We assume they are real in the way images have always been real. We are unaware of any alteration. The change is difficult to absorb.

What is required is a doubting process, a sensory cynicism

248

that would have been profoundly inappropriate, even dangerous, for all previous human history. To assume that some sensory data could be eliminated totally and other sense information made unreliable would have left humans totally confused, lost in space, without knowledge of how to do anything, as though the sensory environment itself had somehow gone mad (*Solaris*). The synapse would be broken. Contact lost. That is the present situation.

We are only the second generation that has had to face the fact that huge proportions of the images we carry in our heads are not natural images which arrived as though they were connected to the planet. Like the Eskimo transplanted to the city, or the Indian from the jungle who must suddenly deal with metallic birds, we do not have the ability to cope. Evolution has not arranged for us to allow for varying degrees of absorption and reliance on visual and aural information. There is nothing in the history of the species which aids our basic senses in understanding that imagery can be altered in time, speed or sequence, or that an image can arrive from a distance. Without training in sensory cynicism, we cannot possibly learn to deal with this. It will take generations to let go of our genetically coded tendency to soak up all images as though they are 100 percent real. And think if we do manage to do that, what will we have? Creatures who cannot believe in their senses and who take everything as it comes, since nothing can be directly experienced (*1984*).

Without the human bias toward belief, the media could not exist. What's more, because the bias is so automatic and unnoticed, the media, *all* media, are in a position to exploit the belief, to encourage you to believe in their questionable sensory information. This bias to believe has commercial value for the media since it allows them to keep your attention, as though it were south-flying birds you were seeing. The media, all media but particularly moving-image media, which present data so nearly natural, effectively convert our naïve and automatic trust in the reliability of images into their own authority.

All Television Is Real

There is a widespread belief that some things on television are "real" and some things are not real. We believe the news is real. Fictional programs are not real. Sports events are real; when we see them happening on television, we can count on the fact that they happen as we see them. Talk shows are real, although it is true that they happen only for television and they sometimes happen some days before we see them. Situation comedies are not real; neither are police dramas, although they may be based on real events from time to time.

Are historical programs real? Well, no, not exactly. Most are re-created versions of events that happened a long time ago when cameras didn't even exist. The people we see in them are actors, playing real people, or at least people who used to be real but are now dead. The actors are speaking for them, but they are usually not saying the exact words that the real people said. Also, some of the events in the historical treatment are dropped out—for reasons of time, or because they don't fit the line of the story—and some others are left in. So is it real? Or is it semireal? Or not real?

Advertising is, of course, definitely not real. Well, on the other hand, those are real people in those ads—we see them walking and talking—but the situations they are portraying are not real, although of course they may be true to life. Does this make them more real? How about Captain Kangaroo? Sesame Street? Are they real? Again, they are real people dealing with real subjects: animals, kids, math, jokes . . . but what does "real" mean in that context?

Our society assumes that human beings *can* make the distinction between what is real and what is not real, even when the real and not-real are served up in the same way, intercut with one another, sent to us from many distant places and times and arriving one behind the other in our houses, shooting out of a box in our living rooms straight into our heads.

What we see in our heads are real-looking human beings, walking and talking as though they were real, even though much of the time they are not, or, that is, the parts they are playing are not, or the people they are playing are no longer alive.

❖　　❖

As I write these lines, my son Kai is seven years old. He still asks me if the Bionic Man, a definitely fictional character in a fictional story, is real or not. I remind him that the week before, he asked me the same question and I told him that the Bionic Man was not real, that he is an actor, that the story is made up, and so on.

"Isn't that a person on the screen?" he asks.

"Well, yes, but he leaps around, throws cars, and so on; humans can't do that."

"But couldn't somebody do that? Couldn't they invent something so people could do that?"

The line of inquiry goes like that. He asks me questions about other programs as well.

"Are the quiz shows real?"

"Yes."

"Are they happening now?"

"No."

"When did they happen?"

"I don't know, maybe a week ago."

"Do they really win those prizes?"

"Yes, I think so."

"Is Kotter real? Is that a real school?"

"No, Kotter is an actor. The kids are actors."

"You mean those kids don't go to that school?"

"There is no school. That's television. That's a studio."

"What's a studio?"

"It's a place where they make up scenes to look like they're real, but they're not really real. They're all playing parts."

There are loose ends in my explanations because these are images of real people on the screen, and they are often doing logical, amusing and interesting things. It is difficult to get at exactly what I'm talking about. After all, there it is. Those are real people. It's happening. It *is* real. When Kai is watching television, he is watching people doing things, and they *are* doing them. It is the same as the south-flying birds. He is right. The things that he sees are real. It's just that they are made-up real. That is what I am trying to tell him. But that is pretty subtle.

The question of what is real and unreal is itself a new one, abstract and impossible to understand. The natural evolutionary design is for humans to see *all* things as real, since the things that we see have always been real. *Seeing things on television as false and unreal is learned.* It goes against nature. Yet how is a child to understand that? When the child is watching a television program, he or she has no innate ability to make any distinction between real and not-real. Once an image is inside the box and then inside the child's mind, having never existed in any concrete form, there is no operable distinction. All such images are equally real and the child is correct to see it that way. Only after the image is ingested can it be noted as unreal, and by then it's too late. It doesn't work. The images are already stored in the brain, with all the other images. Whatever I as parent can say about the images being in a separate category called "unreal" has only superficial meaning. Images are images. They run through Kai's dreams the same way whether they're real or not. They occupy his mind, whether real or not. The Bionic Man's movements, his way of speaking, his attitudes, his way of relating to people, are in Kai's mind no matter what I tell him about reality and unreality.

252

By now, Kai has learned that although he still has questions on all this, he'd better not ask too many of them. Even parents get annoyed with them, and other adults may actually laugh. Slowly, as he gets older, he is becoming educated. He finally knows how to discern what adults in our modern world mean by real and not real and can remind himself of that as he watches. He is learning to repress millions of years of genetic programming to accept all images as real, and to interfere with his own instincts, substituting interpretation. In this way he becomes more adult, which is to say, alienated from himself. He learns, as we all have, that images from television cannot be relied upon automatically as true and believable and that they have to be evaluated in some way: separated, categorized, dealt with differently from other images. He is developing sensory cynicism.

He does this, as we all do, by placing his intellect above his senses, as a kind of judge, reporter, observer upon his own experience. He says to himself, "This is real to me but I have learned that there are things in this world which are not real, even though they look perfectly real; many of these things are on television. Somebody wrote this program and those are actors playing the parts so it isn't real, so I don't believe it."

But he does believe it.

Of course you and I can tell the difference between real and not real on television. Correct? Well, friend, maybe *we* can, but there is sure as hell a lot of evidence that everyone else is pretty confused.

Scientific Evidence

Now, this is an area that *has* been studied. There have been hundreds of reports showing that adults are having only a slightly less-hard time than children separating what is television from what is life.

Volume IV of *Television and Social Behavior*, prepared by

the National Institute of Mental Health for the Department of Health, Education and Welfare, reports that a majority of adults, nearly as high a percentage as children, use television to learn how to handle specific life problems: family routines; relationships with fellow workers; hierarchical values; how to deal with rebellious children; how to understand deviations from the social norm, sexually, politically, socially and interpersonally. The overall fare of television situation-comedies and dramatic programs is taken as valid, useful, informative, and, in the words of the report, "true to life."

Most viewers of television programming give the programming concrete validity, as though it were not fictional. When solving subsequent, similar problems in their own families, people report recalling how the problem was solved in a television version of that situation. They often make similar choices.

The report states:

". . . practical knowledge and methods of problem-solving lead the list of knowledge reported acquired through these programs. Furthermore, these dramatic programs are most often seen as realistic. . . . Many viewers then seem to be seeing the shows they value as directly relevant to their own lives . . . [they] evidently take the fictionalized content of dramatic programs more seriously and literally than most social thinkers and behavioral scientists have recognized."

In a society like ours, in which people have become increasingly isolated from each other in their offices, private cars, single-family living units and television-watching, sharing personal information has become a rarity. The extended family is gone and neighborhood community gatherings are increasingly the exception to the rule. There is less and less interpersonal sharing of intimate problems, few windows into other people's lives. Now our only windows are professional counselors, psychiatrists, and, least expensive and most available, television. It becomes the window for most people. That it looks into fictional lives is irrelevant.

Reports similar to the HEW report have been published many times. Recently, Dr. George Gerbner, dean of the Annenberg School of Communications at the University of Pennsylvania, and Dr. Larry Gross of the same institution completed a study for the National Institute of Mental Health, reported upon in *Psychology Today* (April 1975). Gerbner and Gross found that "Although critics complain about the stereotyped characters and plots of TV dramas, many viewers look on them as representatives of the real world. Anyone who questions that assertion should read the 250,000 letters, most containing requests for medical advice, sent by viewers to 'Marcus Welby, M.D.' during the first five years of his practice on television.

"Imagine a hermit," they suggest, "who lives in a cave linked to the outside world by a television set that functions only during prime time. His knowledge of the world would be built exclusively out of the images and facts he could glean from the fictional events, persons, objects and places that appear on television. His expectations and judgments about the ways of the world would follow the conventions of TV programs with their predictable plots and outcomes. His views of human nature would be shaped by the shallow psychology of TV characters."

Gerbner and Gross found definite distortions of reality in three areas that they measured:

Heavy viewers of television were more likely to overestimate the percentage of the world population that lives in America; they seriously overestimated the precentage of the population who have professional jobs; and they drastically overestimated the number of police in the U.S. and the amount of violence. In all these cases, the overestimate matched a distortion that exists in television programming. The more television people watched, the more their view of the world matched television reality.

Knowledge that the television programs were fictional— surely no one who watches them can *consciously* doubt that police dramas are fiction—does not prevent one from "believing" them anyway, or at least gaining important impressions which lead to beliefs.

If you need further proof of this, there is always advertising.

A recent study showed that a greater percentage of voters based their decisions concerning candidates and ballot propositions on information received from advertising than on information received in any other way. This may be partially due to the fact that, except for big electoral races which are widely reported in all news media, we are likely to receive a greater *quantity* of data from advertising than from news. This is certainly true of most congressional races, and is even more true of local assembly races and ballot issues.

Yet we all know that advertising cannot be considered truthful. In fact, it is by nature one-sided. Advertising always reflects only the facts and opinions of the people who pay for it. Why else would they pay for it? And yet, knowing that, people use advertising information as though it can be relied upon.

The situation is clearer still when it comes to product advertising. When you are watching an advertisement, you know for sure that the advertiser is trying to get you to do something: buy the product. You also know that the people in the ad are not "real," that is, they are actors who are speaking lines, in situations that do not represent their actual lives. Everyone knows this. We all know that the motive of the sponsors and the actors and the writers of the ads is that they are all trying to implant a feeling in us that will eventually get us to buy something.

We know they are doing this but we very often act on the ad. Advertisers don't care at all if you know the advertising is fictional. They make very little effort to fool you about that, because whether or not you know it is fictional, the image of the product goes into your head. From then on, you've got the image and there's no letting it go.

If you then walk through a supermarket and spot the tooth-paste that you've been carrying as an image, a little click goes off in your head. Familiarity. It doesn't mean you'll buy the toothpaste, but the click goes off anyway. *They* implanted the image, and *you* then carry it around inside you like some kind of neuronal billboard. There's nothing you can do about it if you're going to keep watching television at all. Your knowl-edge of real and not-real is useless. All images are real.

In a sense, the advertising images are *more* real than other television images because you get to see the image "live" right in your supermarket. First you ingest the image of the tooth-paste from television and file it. Then you see it in the store and you recognize it. (Have you heard your child say, "Hey, I saw that on television"? There's a real excitement being ex-pressed.) If you buy the toothpaste, it's then right there in your bathroom, so the image from the screen materializes in your home. Advertisers are the alchemists of our day.

It works the same way, albeit more subtly, with the *be-havioral* content of advertising and programs. You see Archie Bunker or the Waltons solve a family problem. You find yourself in a family situation which is not dissimilar. The image flashes past. You may reject it, but it flashes past none-theless. If that's the only imagined instance you have available to call upon for such a situation, you are somewhat more likely to be influenced by it. You don't interrupt your behavior to say, "Wait a minute; I've got to keep straight my bank of television imagery from my bank of real-world imagery." The mind doesn't work that way.

The Irresistibility of Images

Western society, biased toward the objective mental mode of experience, tends to be blind not only to the power of images but also to the fact that we are nearly defenseless against their effect. Since we are educated and thoughtful, as we like to think, we believe we can choose among the things that will influence us. We accept fact, we reject lies. We go to movies, we watch television, we see photographs, and as the images pour into us, we believe we can choose among those we wish to absorb and those we don't. We assume that our rational processes protect us from implantation, or brainwashing. What we fail to realize is the difference between fact and image. Our objective processes can help us resist only one kind of implantation. There is no rejection of images.

Raise your eyes from the page for a moment. Look about your room. Can you reject what you are seeing?

In Nicholas Roeg's *The Man Who Fell to Earth*, the main character is a visitor from another planet who arrives on Earth and is slowly transformed by what he sees. He becomes transfixed by television. At one point, in a fit of madness, he screams at the TV screen: "Stop it, get out of my mind, go back where you came from." But the images don't go back. They remain. He goes crazy.

You are watching Walter Cronkite. He is reporting the news. He apparently tells facts. It is impossible for you to judge the truth of most of what he tells you. He reports events from a thousand miles away. You take his information on faith, or you decide that he is wrong. Then he says the bank you work in was robbed today. "Not true," you shout, "wrong bank." You have rejected the news. You could reject it because it came as a fact that you could check. You could halt its entry into you.

Meanwhile, however, you have ingested Cronkite. His smile, his hand movements, his tone of voice, the way he holds his head. The image enters your cells. Style is also content.

If you are watching the Bionic Man, or the president explaining a policy, or the Fonz talking to his girl, or Dr. Marcus

258

Welby, or the spokesman for Bank of America, you are receiving several levels of information at the same time.

There is the verbal information and the ideas connected to this. Then there are the images, the way people behave, their movements, mannerisms, forcefulness or peacefulness, their style of emoting, their tone of voice, their way of relating to each other, the kind of people they are, their seriousness, grimness, lightness, joyfulness, heaviness and so on. We absorb these along with the objective news. They are all content as much as my walk is for Kai, or his gentle way is for me.

If you see Kissinger or Cronkite or Bionic people or slaps on the back or kisses or violence—the images of these are not in the realm of correct or incorrect. They just *are*. There's nothing to disagree with. There's no way to resist them. They flow inward, passing through all discernment processes. Even if you could keep your mind alive while watching—no mean feat—the images would still enter into your unconscious storage areas. You've got them. They're yours.

You may not believe Jimmy Carter when he speaks. But you've got Jimmy Carter inside you.

You may believe the Fonz is an actor, and your kids may believe this too. But they slowly become like the Fonz. They move and walk as he does.

You may believe the Bionic Man is fiction, but his image lives within you. You can bring it to mind if I ask. It is part of your image pool. You may draw on it forever.

You may watch television and "know" those are actors performing, but the image of one person stabbing another is in you. You've got it. It's yours. Thinking will not halt its entry into you or into thirty million others.

You may watch the actor playing doctor in the commercial, speaking seriously, professionally, authoritatively. You know this is an actor, but you ingest him nonetheless. His authoritativeness becomes yours.

We all become more like Cronkite, like Carter, like Bionic

people. We all become more violent or more Fonzlike, or display a TV-announcer authority.

Once they are in your mind and stored, all images are equally valid. They are real whether they are toothpaste, Walter Cronkite, Kojak, President Carter, Mary Hartman, Captain Kangaroo, Marcus Welby, Pete Rose, a Ford Cougar, a cougar, the Fonz, the Bionic Man, Alistair Cooke, Rhoda, or your mother and father. Once inside your head, they all become images that you continue to carry in memory. They become equally real and equally not-real.

Our thinking processes can't save us. To the degree that we are thinking as we watch television, a minute degree at most, the images pass right through anyway. They enter our brains. They remain permanently. We cannot tell, for sure, which images are ours and which came from distant places. Imagination and reality have merged. We have lost control of our images. We have lost control of our minds.

ARGUMENT FOUR

THE
INHERENT BIASES
OF
TELEVISION

Along with the venality of its controllers, the technology of television predetermines the boundaries of its content. Some information can be conveyed completely, some partially, some not at all. The most effective telecommunications are the gross, simplified linear messages and programs which conveniently fit the purposes of the medium's commercial controllers. Television's highest potential is advertising. This cannot be changed. The bias is inherent in the technology.

XIII

INFORMATION LOSS

A GOOD way to think about television—in fact all the media—is as a kind of telescope in the sky, flying around, constantly looking. Then from its perch in the sky, it zooms down to a single spot on the planet, a small group of people shooting each other. It takes this single event out of billions and billions of other little events and sends it zooming through space to television antennas, and then out through an electron gun into (on the average) 30 million people sitting at home in dark rooms with their eyes still. The event gets reconstructed in the brains of these people as an image. Recorded. All these 30 million people have recorded the same image from this single distant spot where they are not. This becomes their experience of that moment.

Bias against the Excluded

If the telescope has selected a shooting from an entire planet's worth of activities, in the next moment it may choose a Super Bowl game, or a threatening remark by a Middle Eastern leader, or a program of people trying to win prizes, or a movie about the Old West. All other subjects were not selected, at least in this moment. The telescope did not select views of the ocean as the tide comes in, or people sitting on front porches, or young people knocking on doors to tell a neighborhood about a zoning hearing.

The question to ask is if there is a logic in this selection. Are there reasons why the telescope selects one thing and not another?

There certainly are. Dozens of them.

The first and most obvious of these reasons is the one that most critics of television devote themselves to. The people who control television, businessmen, operate strictly out of considerations of budget and profit, in addition to bringing along their own political, perceptual, and social biases. It was to allay their influence that so many thousands of media reformers devoted years of effort to democratizing access to the medium and its content. And yet at present there are still no poor people running television, no Indians, no ecologists, no political radicals, no Zen Buddhists, no factory workers, no revolutionaries, no artists, no Communists, no Luddites, no hippies, no botanists, to name only a few excluded groups.

To have only businessmen in charge of the most powerful mind-implanting instrument in history naturally creates a boundary to what is selected for dissemination to nearly 250 million people. There can be little disagreement with the point that if other categories of people had control, then the choices would be different. If television is a medium of brainwash, then a more diverse brainwash would surely be an improvement over the sort we get at present.

The overriding bias of television, then, the bias which contains all the other biases, is that it offers preselected material, which excludes whatever is not selected.

Now, of course, this is utterly obvious. And, yes, it is true of all experiences. When you are doing one thing, you exclude everything else that you might be doing.

This only becomes significant concerning television when

264

we forget that: 1) someone has *selected* our experience for us, and 2) we have given up awareness, information and experience that is not part of television.

In the years I was researching and working on this book, I only ran into one person who works *in* television and was speaking publicly on points similar to this one. He was Robert Keeshan, the actor who plays Captain Kangaroo. At the 1974 Communications Seminar at San Francisco State College he said:

"When you are spending time in front of the television, you are not doing other things. The young child of three or four years old is in the stage of the greatest emotional development that human beings undergo. And we only develop when we experience things, real-life things: a conversation with Mother, touching Father, going places, doing things, relating to others. This kind of experience is critical to a young child, and when the child spends thirty-five hours per week in front of the TV set, it is impossible to have the full range of real-life experience that a young child must have. Even if we had an overabundance of good television programs, it wouldn't solve the problem."

The act of sitting in front of television is itself a replacement of other modes of experience and the awareness these would bring. In this way, television is an acceleration of a condition that began with our artificial environments. We are already separated from most experiences with an unmediated planet. We have given up our personal sensory informational systems. The artificial forms around us already limit our experience and awareness. Our knowledge of the outside world was confined to a narrower field even before television was invented.

With television, however, the artificial information-field is brought inside our darkened rooms, inside our stilled minds, and shot by cathode guns through our unmoving eyes into our brains, and recorded. We have no participatory role in gathering data. Our information is narrowed to only what the telescope provides. If we don't experience a wider information field, we lose knowledge of that field's existence. We become the hermit in the cave who knows only what the TV offers. We experience what is, not knowing what isn't.

The people who control television become the choreographers of our internal awareness. We give way to their process of choosing information. We live within their conceptual frameworks. We travel to places on the planet which they choose and to situations which they decide we should see. What we can know is narrowed to what they know, and then narrowed further to what they select to send us through this instrument of theirs.

The kind of people who control television is certainly a problem. But this is only the beginning. While our field of knowledge is constrained by their venality and arrogance, the people who run television are constrained by the instrument itself.

Television is no open window through which all perception may pass. Quite the opposite. There are many technological factors that conspire to limit what the medium can transmit. Some information fits and some doesn't. Some information can pass through, but only after being reshaped, redefined, packaged, and made duller and coarser than before. Some ways of mind can be conveyed and some cannot.

The wrinkle in the story is that what *can* be conveyed through television are the ways of thinking and the kinds of information that suit the people who are in control. This is why they like it so much. It is obviously efficient for them to concentrate their communications within a medium that is good at conveying their forms of mind, just as a person with a drive for power is more apt to express that in politics than in gardening. Conversely, it is logical that the medium will not respond well to people or attitudes that defy its limits.

It will throw them off, or distort their messages, as a computer would shun anyone who wishes to use it to express feelings of loving tenderness. It might program such a message, but only the words will come out on the tape; not the loving tenderness.

So we have a chicken-egg problem. It's difficult to tell which came first, the technology or its controllers. It may not be that the corporate mentality won the war to control television. As the rest of Argument Four will suggest, the technology itself picked its master, through the inexorable technological factors that confine its use.

Fuzzy Images: The Bias against Subtlety

As has been mentioned, the television screen produces its image by way of a grid of dots located along five hundred lines. This might seem to be sufficient for fairly detailed images, but it is not. Roughly speaking, the experience of looking at a TV picture is like looking at the world through a tea strainer. The picture is located along the grids. You fill in the blanks.

Compare the image of your television screen with any other image in your television room: the bookcase, the table, the rug. Obviously the actual object is vivid in comparison with the television image.

Television production people are exquisitely aware of this. There is an electronics term to describe it: "signal-to-noise ratio." Ordinarily applied to sound, the term can be applied to images as well.

The "signal" is the primary image that they are attempting to convey. The "noise" is the background, the fuzz, from which the signal has to stand out to be seen properly. A "clear" picture is one in which the signal and noise are well differentiated. In television, however, since the differentiation is difficult to achieve, program decisions and production styles have to be chosen to maximize what is possible. As a result, there is a tendency to concentrate on images which offer a large signal-to-noise distinction.

An enormous percentage of television images are close-ups of faces. This is not accidental. Faces in close-up are about the sharpest signal that television can produce while still conveying content. Even so, if the background behind the face is complex, filled with varieties of objects and color tones, the face merges with the background and it all becomes a confusing jumble. So even while showing faces, television producers must keep the background "clean," stark, unencumbered. Dramatic programs are constructed so that there are very few adornments and props. This avoids a cluttered image and increases the potential for the primary image to communicate something.

This limitation does not exist to the same extent with movies, where the signal-to-noise ratio is much greater, allowing for images filled with detail. However, when a movie is played on television, much detail is lost. If you will think back to a time when you first saw a film in a theater and then saw it on television, you will realize how much richness is lost in the translation from one medium to the other.

There is also a low signal-to-noise ratio in television sound. It is very low fidelity, although it *could* be greatly improved. High-fidelity sound, equal to recording sound, is possible with television speaker technology but too costly for mass markets.

An additional factor fuzzing up the sound is the high-pitched whistle that emanates from all television sets. Caused by the interaction of the audio and visual electron fields, this whistle is unavoidable with television technology, at least in marketable price ranges. And so both television picture and sound remain fuzzy.

This problem of indistinctness, rarely noted or discussed

268

by critics of television, cannot be overestimated. It is a major factor influencing all decisions made by television producers. It skews all programming—both choices of subject and treatment of the choices—toward those that offer the highest possible contrast between foreground and background, signal and noise, color and tone. This leads to images which tend to the larger as opposed to the smaller, to the broad as opposed to the detailed, to the simple as opposed to the complex, to the obvious rather than the subtle. Because of these tendencies, inexorably imposed by the technology itself, the communicable content of all programs is affected. Beyond confining the visual image and the choices of sound, these tendencies affect the emotional content. Because the images are indistinct, subtle feelings are more difficult to transmit through television than the larger emotions—the foreground emotions, as it were—that can be depicted efficiently by larger facial expressions, or even by noncloseup body movements.

Even with a reliance on facial close-ups, what television can convey is a reduced version of what is possible in real life or even in still photography or film. The human relationships which are shown on television, therefore, tend to be those that *can* be shown on television. These dwell on the grosser end of the human emotional spectrum. The more subtle expressions, those which express intimate, deeply personal feelings, are lost in the blur.

In recent years there has emerged a very vocal group of outraged psychologists, educators and parents who speak of the urgent need to show positive behavior, such as loving, caring, sharing, and warmth, in television programs. They deplore the emphasis on "antisocial" behavior that is common on TV. Unfortunately these reformers are doomed to fail in their efforts because the medium is far better suited technically to expressing hate, fear, jealousy, winning, wanting and violence. These emotions suffer very little information loss when pushed through the coarse imagery of television. Like other gross personal expressions—hysteria, or ebullience, or the kind of one-dimensional joyfulness usually associated with some objective victory—the facial expressions and bodily movements of antisocial behavior are highly visible. Hate, anger, competitiveness are obvious broad-band feelings with broad-band expressions. Most of them can be well communicated solely through body movement. No detail is needed to get the point, and neither is any special talent on the part of actor or director. They come through the filter of television with a minimum of information loss. The signal-to-noise ratio is relatively high.

For these technical reasons, among others we will get to later, there is an emphasis on sports and violence in television programming, and there is great viewer interest in them.

The popularity of such programming is not so much a sign that public tastes are vulgar, as they are assumed to be in many quarters ("People want that kind of programming"), as it is a sign that these programs are the ones which manage to communicate *something*, at least, through television. Rather than illustrating the limits of the public mentality or taste, they illustrate the limits of the medium itself. The public wisely chooses programs which work best in a medium in which anything of a more subtle nature loses so much in translation as to be noncommunicative.

This is not to say that the businessmen who are the television powers that be aren't predisposed to further the values of competition and social Darwinism which *they* understand best and which are inherent in sports and violence programs. But no matter what their inclination, the fact exists that the kind of programming in which the least information is lost is the grosser forms: sports, violence, police action, as well as quiz shows, game shows, soap opera, situation comedy and news about murder, conflict, war, power politics and charismatic leaders. All of these categories of programming communicate on television because they deliver clear, easily grasped visual and auditory signals, together with broad-band emotional content, all of which make them highly efficient in a low-definition medium.

On the other hand, the kinds of feelings and behavior which the reformers like to call prosocial cannot be conveyed through television by obvious facial expression or physical movement.

While it may be possible to show friendship in a dramatic context, it cannot be explored very far visually, because expression of such feelings exists in an inward rather than outward realm of experience. Love is simply not as easy to demonstrate through coarse imagery as anger or competition. The heights of intimate feeling—between lovers, or parents and children, or among children—are actually experienced in life's quietest moments. Ordinarily they do not involve any visually obvious action, unless it is the most subtle facial expression—peace, tranquility, satisfaction—not easily captured in any photography, but damned near impossible in the coarse imagery of television.

How would you show caring on television? You could present images of people who presumably care about each other doing things which express that feeling. Yet, the things people usually do to express real caring are very small, intimate things. The inner feeling may be strong but, unlike rage, the acts which express it are rarely sweeping.

What about warmth? Well, you could illustrate warmth with hugging or tender smiles. It's not that it can't be done, it's just not as easy to show on television as coldness is. The behavior of the Bionic Man, for example—coldness, determination, efficiency, domination—is easy to see because it can be demonstrated with nearly no facial expression at all. Therefore, this sort of behavior communicates more efficiently on TV.

Even if a given subtle emotion can be conveyed from time

to time, you could never build an entire program on it as you could on violent emotions. In signal-to-noise terms the entire program would become indistinct in comparison with the background of more aggressive, expressive and efficient action shows.

What I am discussing here are tendencies of the medium. These are biases, not absolute restrictions. Though extremely rare, there *are* occasional examples of television programs that overcome the bias. Bergman's *Scenes From A Marriage* was one such example. It succeeded only because of the rare skill and sensitivity of the director and the performers. Their deep understanding of the medium allowed them to use it efficiently. *Scenes* qualifies as the exception that proves the rule.

Many Americans saw this production in movie houses, but it was originally created for television. This is why Bergman devoted so much of the production to facial close-ups. In a theater two and one-half hours of facial close-up became oppressive. When one is sitting in a movie house, one wants something beyond closeup imagery. However, on television, nothing other than closeup imagery could convey the subtle themes of a plot that concerned the excruciating shifts of feeling within a disintegrating marriage.

Bergman had to convey tenderness, affection, caring, concern and intimacy, together with ambiguity, and then violence, rage, sorrow. These latter scenes, the violent ones, were among the very few in which he allowed the camera to pull back from the action, because the physical movement could convey the meaning.

In demonstrating the best that is possible on television if you honor the medium's limits absolutely, Bergman also illuminated the absoluteness of the limits. He took television as far as one could and succeeded well enough. There is the tendency to forget that one cannot go further.

Bergman is one of the rarest talents in the history of moving-image media, and given even his difficulty in communicating subtle feeling, the inherent resistance of television becomes clearer. Lesser talents, not daring to try what Bergman did, have to work *against* the medium, as it were, choosing more confined, easier-to-handle imagery, and emotional content that fits the narrowed scope of TV. Most directors will not even attempt to deal with subtle realms of information and they are wise not to. Producers and sponsors will also tend to avoid such subtlety because it is so unlikely to get high ratings.

Roots was *not* an exception to this rule. In fact, it proves the rule. In the book, the cultural nuances of relationships were emphasized and developed, while the TV production avoided them altogether. Nor was there much effort to present the subtle ambience of the African natural environment, which was also highly developed in the book. The television production wisely concentrated on the larger, more explicit, and therefore more reproducible elements of *conflict* in the story and the kinds of family attachment made familiar by soap operas. This is not to say that the production didn't have value. It is only to remark that the values which were conveyed were the simplest ones to convey. The more subtle values, which are at the heart of the African culture and, therefore, formed the basis for the quality of feeling that existed among the uprooted slaves, were necessarily dropped out. In the end, the viewer got some fairly good information and feeling about good guys and bad guys during a certain period of history, but virtually no understanding of the successful repression of an entire culture and way of mind.

So it goes in all dramatic programming. Nuance is being sacrificed to the larger and more visible elements of stories, and the cause of the sacrifice is a technical limitation of the medium.

Problems of subtlety don't present themselves in quiz

shows, sports events and sitcoms. These are confined to areas of human expression which are easy to capture, easy to communicate, and easy to understand, even with directors and writers of ordinary talent and in a medium as vague as television. As a result, there is a tendency to favor such productions.

The bias toward the coarse, the bold, and the obvious finds its way into all other categories of television programming, including even those that deal with so-called objective events in the world. Public affairs programs are seriously biased away from coverage of highly detailed, complex, and subtle information, and so are news shows. Ordinarily this bias is believed to result from time factors—it takes too long to explain complicated issues. However, certain kinds of visual information are harder to capture than others. News producers will always choose the more easily communicable image.

Edward Epstein, in his very important *News From Nowhere,* interviews television news producers, seeking to define an inherent bias in the news that is related to technical and other factors. He observes:

"The one ingredient most producers interviewed claimed was necessary for a good action story was visually identifiable opponents clashing violently. This, in turn, requires some form of stereotype: military troops fighting civilians, black versus white students, workers wearing hardhats manhandling bearded peace demonstrators, were cited by producers as examples of the components for such stories. Demonstrations or violence involving less clearly identifiable groups make less effective stories, since, as one CBS producer put it, 'It would be hard to tell the good guys from the bad guys.'

". . . since news stories tend to be constructed from those aspects of a happening that can be easily filmed and recorded, and not from the poorly lit, softly spoken or otherwise inaccessible moments, events tend to be explained in terms of what one producer called 'visual facts.' One correspondent pointed out, for example, that television coverage of riots or protests at night tends to focus on fires, even if they are insignificant trash can fires, since they provide adequate light for filming. Hence urban riots tend to be defined in terms of the 'visual facts' of fires, rather than more complicated factors. Visual facts, of course, cover only one range of phenomena, and thus tend to limit the power of networks to explain complex events."

The Bias away from the Sensory

Television cannot transmit information that comes in the form of smell, touch or taste.

Furthermore, as we have discussed, the information it can transmit through the visual and auditory senses is extremely narrow. The ranges of color, brightness, depth are confined by the technology. The aural range is confined within narrow amplitudes, pitches and tones, dictated by low-cost speaker systems. The sounds we hear are flattened by the speakers. Smaller or distant sounds are blotted out by the whistle of the electron fields.

Unfortunately, given the human tendency to accept the information of our senses as total and reliable, we are not aware of the aspects of the visual and aural information that are dropped out of this new information package. We assume that when we see and hear something, we are seeing and hearing everything that is being transmitted, as though we were actually observing the event directly. Or else we assume that what is lost is too minor to matter. We are inclined to believe the information as though it had not been processed, reduced and reshaped before we experienced it.

In addition to the elimination of three sensory systems and

275

the narrowing of two others, there is another sensory oddity in the television experience. Television disconnects the two operative sense modes—visual and aural.

You are sitting in a room watching an image from miles away. You see the place, but the image you see and the sounds which reportedly connect to the image are *not* really connected. The sounds are "nearer" to you than the images are.

Let's say you are watching two people walking on a far-away hillside. In real life, you could not make out what the characters are saying, but on television you can. The voices are amplified or dubbed in, so you can hear a conversation that would otherwise be inaudible. The natural informational balance between aural and visual has been shattered. Now, information that you take in with the visual sense cannot be used to modify or help process the information from the aural sense because they have each been isolated from each other and reconstructed.

Furthermore, while you are watching and listening with your disconnected aural and visual senses, you are smelling some chicken roasting in the kitchen and you are drinking a beer.

So television has attached two of your sensory modes to a distant spot, altered their natural arrangement to each other, but left other aspects of your sensory apparatus at home in present time. This is a very peculiar arrangement and in a way it's sort of funny, like playing a perceptual game in a technology museum. It takes on importance when we understand that the average person submits to this condition for four hours every day, and while in this state is receiving important information about life. All of the information is narrowed to fit the sensory transmission limits of the medium and distorted by the sensory disconnections in the human.

One can imagine the emergence of a new psychological syndrome: "sensory schizophrenia." The cure will involve exercises to resynchronize wildly confused senses with each other, with the mind, and with the world.

Because of all the preceding it ought to go without saying that any messages that are dependent upon sensory understanding and interaction are not going to work on television.

This is very unfortunate for the ecology movement.

It always surprises me whenever any attempts are made to show wilderness or wildlife on television. The fuzzy image previously described is the first problem: forests become blurs, ocean depths are impossibly foggy, the details of plants are impossible to see. So the viewer depends on the voice-over to know what's going on. Because of the blur naturalist programs focus on such objective behavior as playing, fighting, mating, eating, just as they do with human sitcoms and soap operas. There are more animal programs than plant programs because animals come through better on the fuzzy medium, and the larger and more rambunctious the animal the better.

But even if TV images were not as coarse as I have described them, there would still be no way to understand a forest or swamp or desert without all the senses fully operative, receiving information in all ranges, and freely interacting with each other.

An interesting recent illustration of the problem was a news feature concerned with a decision that a town council had to make. A land developer sought a permit to convert a large marsh area into a new community of homes. Should the permit be okayed?

It was quite a thoroughgoing, earnest report. Considering the subject, not ordinarily conceived as "good television" by producers, it was also an extraordinarily lengthy report, about eight minutes of an evening newscast.

The report presented interviews with the council members, interviews with the developer, and interviews with a local conservation group that opposed the project. It presented several minutes of images of the plants in the marshland, flocks of birds, nesting grounds, all with the appropriate wild-sounding calls.

Having worked as a publicist for many years, in fact, as a publicist for environmental groups, I knew how much work the environmentalists had put into this program and how important they felt it to be. In the end, though, I knew they had failed no matter how this particular vote came out, because if there is anything which cannot be conveyed on television it is a feeling for a marsh. I suspected that the result of the program would be to decrease concern for marshes.

The great majority of viewers watching that program had never visited this marsh or any marsh. These images and words about marshes were probably more than they had ever seen or heard before. Since the news report told them interesting things they did not know—how many varieties of creatures lived there, for example—they may have considered it quite a complete story. In terms of popular media, indeed it was. However, while the viewers knew more than before, they were not likely to be aware of what they did not know and were not getting. As the images of the marsh went hurtling into their brains, accompanied by a news reporter's description of an egret nesting ground, they probably assumed that most of the relevant data were in hand, that they had learned enough to make a judgment.

Images and words about a marsh do not convey what a marsh is. You must actually sense and feel what a strange, rich, unique and *un*human environment it is. The ground is very odd, soft, sticky, wet and smelly. It is not attractive to most humans. The odor emanates from an interaction between the sometimes-stagnant pools and the plants that live in the mud in varying stages of growth and decay. If the wind is hot and strong, there can be a nearly maddening mixture of sweet and rotting odors.

To grasp the logic and meaning of marsh life, the richest

biological system on Earth, one needs to put one's hand into the mud, overturn it, discover the tiny life forms that abound. One needs to sit for long hours in it, feeling the ebbs and flows of the waters, the creatures and the winds.

Television cannot capture very much of this. The attempt to push the information through television goes flat. It doesn't work. The viewer is left to evaluate aspects of the experience that television *can* capture, and these reduce to objective facts like the arguments among opposing viewpoints as to the best *use* of this area. People need homes. The developer has a right to profit. The tax base of the community is affected. Meanwhile, the ecologists speak of flyways and breeding grounds, endangered plants and nearly extinct creatures.

A whole world of sensory information has been abandoned, and yet it is in this world that real understanding of marshes exists. And without the understanding who can care about the marsh? Taxes become more important. Birds can be seen elsewhere. Images of mud and reeds do not inspire the mind, especially compared with the hard facts of our world. People need jobs building the houses. Nobody ever "uses" swamps anyway.

It is possible that viewers of that program had a greater feeling for swamps when the swamps resided totally in their imaginations, where, at least, they had the richness that fantasy can create. On television, the fantasy is destroyed and the perspective is flattened.

What was true for this news report is true for all television programs that concern nature. Seeing the forests of Borneo on television makes one believe that one knows something of these forests. What one knows, however, is what television is capable of delivering, a minute portion of what Borneo forests are. It cannot make you care very much about them. When Georgia-Pacific proceeds to cut down hundreds of thousands of acres of Borneo forest, as it has so many other forests in the Pacific Basin, one remains unmoved. The wood is needed for homes. The objective data dominate when only objective data can be communicated.

Meanwhile, sitting in our dark rooms ingesting images of Borneo forests, we lose feeling even for the forests near our homes. While we watch Borneo forests, we are not experiencing neighborhood forests, *local* wilderness or even *local* parks. As forest experience reduces to television forest, our caring about forests, *any* forest, goes into dormancy for lack of direct experience. And so the lumber company succeeds in cutting down the Borneo forest, and then, near to home, it also succeeds in building a new tract of condominiums where a local park had been.

In my opinion, the more the natural environment is conveyed on TV, the less people will understand about it or care about it, and the more likely its destruction becomes. Ecologists would be wise to abandon all attempts to put nature on television.

Programs concerned with the arts, programs concerned with many religions and all programs concerned with non-Western cultures are similarly distorted by television's inability to convey their sensual aspects.

Theater, music, dance, if they are to be fully understood and appreciated, require exquisitely fine visual and aural reproduction as well as exquisitely tuned sense reception in the viewer. The experience of them on television is only the barest approximation of the direct experience of the performance. The information loss is enormous, and it is the most critical and subtle information that is lost.

Some people argue that television delivers a new world of art to people in, say, Omaha, who might otherwise never see the Stuttgart Ballet or the New York Philharmonic. They say this stimulates interest in the arts. I find this very unlikely. Information received with only two senses, especially in the limited range of television, and considering the other dulling aspects of the medium, is simply not the same at the receiving end as it would have been in the theater or concert hall.

On television the depths are flattened, the spaces edited, the movements distorted and fuzzed-up, the music thinned and the scale reduced. This would have to affect the level of understanding and limit the quality of the experience. The human senses cannot experience what is not there. If television delivers a drastically reduced version of an art experience, then this is what the senses must deal with, and if one has never directly experienced the real thing, how is one to know that the reality is richer than the television version? Reading *Moby Dick* as a comic book does not inspire one to read *Moby Dick* in the original. Quite the opposite. And so seeing the Stuttgart Ballet performing on television leaves one with such a reduced notion of ballet as to reduce the appeal of ballet itself. The result is likely to be boredom and switched channels. To say that such a program stimulates new interest in arts is to believe, as Howard Gossage put it, "that it's possible to convince an eight-year-old that making love is more fun than ice cream cones."

And so it goes in all areas. The religions of the world, from Tibetan Buddhism to many forms of Catholicism, are deeply rooted in the rich interplay of the human mind and senses. On television they must be understood through fixed cerebral channels, leaving description, but no feeling. The same can be said for most cultures of the world, still immersed in the sensory relationships between human and environment. There is no way to effectively convey African cultures, as was mentioned, through images disconnected from the other senses, and certainly not through logical analysis. More often than not these cultures and others are sensually or mystically based and can be deeply understood only in those terms. Unfortunately, television makes the effort to explain them anyway, just as it claims to convey nature, the arts, the news and the details of human feeling.

Human beings who view these attempts are led to believe that these fuzzy little pellets of information about our rich, subtle, complex and varied world constitute something close to reality. What they really do is make the world as fuzzy, coarse, and turned-off as the medium itself.

XIV

IMAGES DISCONNECTED FROM SOURCE

I N his novel *Being There,* Polish writer Jerzy Kosinski describes a man who is born and raised in a house that he never leaves. His only contacts with humans are occasional encounters with a half-crazy maid, a crippled, senile old man confined in a room upstairs, and a television set. He watches television constantly.

In middle age the hero is suddenly thrown out of the house into the city. Attempting to deal with a world which he has seen only as reproduced on television, he tries to apply what he has learned from the set. He adopts television behavior. He tries to imitate the behavior of the people he has seen on the screen. He speaks like them, moves as they do, imitates their facial expressions. However, because these people were only images to him, and he has never experienced *real* people, save for the crazies in his house, he does not know anything beyond the images. He does not know about feelings, for example. He adopts the movements of the images but can't connect this with anything deeper inside himself. Because he has not exchanged feeling with a live human, his ability to feel has atrophied. He is a mechanical person, a humanoid. He is there physically, but like the television images, he is also not there.

I wonder if you would be willing to try another little experiment. Please go look into a mirror. As you gaze at yourself, try to get a sense of what is lost between the mirror image of you, and *you*.

You might ask someone to join you facing the mirror. If so, you will surely feel that other person's presence as you stand there. But in the reflection, this feeling will be lost. You will be left with only the image, possibly an expressive one, but only an image. What is missing from the reflection is life, or essence.

Finally, place an object in front of the mirror: a hair dryer, a chair, a vacuum cleaner, a comb. What is lost? I won't say nothing is lost in the reflection, a mirror image does slightly alter the dimension and the color of an object. But life has not dropped out, because the object did not have any life in it. Nothing emanates from it.

More information is lost in the reflection of a living thing than of an object. In the living creature, there is something which can be experienced only in person, no matter how vivid the attempt at visual reproduction. The inanimate object, on the other hand, has only its form. This can be reflected, if not perfectly, at least very well in the mirror image.

What applies to a mirror applies even more to a photograph or a film, and still more to a television reproduction.

Because television cannot convey the essence of life, it makes sense for television producers to concentrate on information in which life essence is not required for the message to be communicated. You don't need to "feel" the essence of a football player or a bomber pilot or a police attack squad to follow the action. And you surely don't need to feel the life in the product that is advertised, since the product has no life to begin with. And so football games, action dramas and product commercials, in which the image can carry the story, obtain a degree of communications efficiency that is not possible with humans, animals and plants.

The Elimination of "Aura"

Thirty years before McLuhan, a German critic, Walter Benjamin, wrote what is still the classic essay on the way the media affects what it attempts to convey: "The Work of Art in the Age of Mechanical Reproduction" (reprinted in *Illuminations,* a collection of his essays).

Benjamin's central argument is that *all* technical reproduction of art, nature, and the human image deletes what he calls "aura." (At the time he wrote, photographic reproduction, including film, was the main topic under discussion. But the argument applies to television as well.) Benjamin:

"One might subsume the eliminated element in the term 'aura' and go on to say: that which withers in the age of mechanical reproduction is the aura of the work of art."

Benjamin reminds us that before the age of mechanical reproduction, art objects did not exist in a context outside of their original use. If a religious object were carved in bronze, this piece of bronze gained its meaning from its context, that is, the place and time of its use. When it is dug up by archeologists two thousand years later, it may have intellectual meaning and be informative or beautiful, but it will not have retained the quality of its original power. This depended upon its connection to time and place. When it is then put behind glass in a museum, it has still less power. When it is photographed and reproduced ten thousand times on postcards, although it can then be found in ten thousand homes, it is so many times removed from its original shell that it conveys nothing. At this point, it could be used by anyone for any purpose, including advertisement. Meaning must be invested into it, as it no longer has any of its own.

Benjamin notes that what is true for art objects is even more true for natural, living beings. The art object, once separated from its source in time and place, loses the powers invested in it. The human being loses humanness itself.

Benjamin describes the plight of the performer in a film, for example, who has the job of conveying him or herself through machinery which is predisposed not to allow such a conveyance.

"This situation might be characterized as follows: for the first time—and this is the effect of the film—man [the actor] has to operate with his whole living person, yet foregoing [his] aura. For aura is tied to his presence; there can be no replica of it.

"The feeling of strangeness that overcomes the actor before the camera . . . is basically of the same kind as the estrangement felt before one's image in the mirror. But now [with photography and film] the reflected image has become separable, transportable. . . . The film responds to the shriveling of the aura with an artificial build-up of the 'personality' outside the studio. The cult of the movie star, fostered by the money of the film industry, preserves not the unique aura of the person but the 'spell of the personality,' the phony spell of a commodity."

Mechanical reproduction of images is the great equalizer. When you reproduce any image of anything that formerly had aura (or life), the effect is to dislocate the image from the aura, leaving only the image. At this point, the image is neutral, it has no greater inherent power than commodities.

Products have no life to begin with, neither did they have any aura that attached to some original artistic or religious use at a certain place or time. There is no original car or vacuum cleaner, at least not among those that are advertised. They are all duplications of each other, like the fiftieth copy of a photograph. So products lose virtually nothing when their images are reproduced mechanically or electronically, while original art objects lose their contextual meaning, and human beings and other living creatures lose virtually everything that qualifies as meaningful. Humans become image shells, containing nothing inside, no better or worse, more or less meaningful than the product images that interrupt them every few minutes.

By the simple process of removing images from immediate experience and passing them instead through a machine, human beings lose one of the attributes that differentiate us from objects. Products, meanwhile, suffer no such loss and effectively obtain a kind of equality with these aura-amputated living creatures shown on television. These factors conspire to make television an inherently more efficient and effective medium for advertising than for conveying any information in which life force exists: human feeling, human interaction, natural environment, or ways of thinking and being.

Advertisers, however, are not satisfied with equality. Leaving their products in their natural deadness would not instill any desire to buy. And so the advertising person goes a step further by constructing drama around the product, investing it with an *apparent* life. Since a product has no inherent drama, techniques are used to dramatize and enliven the product. Cuts, edits, zooms, cartoons and other effects, to be discussed further in Chapter Sixteen, have the effect of adding an artificial life force to the product. These technical events make it possible for products to surpass in power the images of the creatures whose aura has been separated from them by the act of mechanical or electronic reproduction.

So television accomplishes something that in real life would be impossible: making products more "alive" than people.

Walter Benjamin draws important political and psychological conclusions from the disconnection of humans and art from their auras.

He argues that in destroying aura via the mechanical reproduction of art, all art as well as humans and nature lose their grounding, their meaning in time and place. At this point, like the product in the advertisement, the art image or the human image can be used for any purpose whatsoever. The disconnection from inherent meaning, which would be visible if image, object and context were still merged, leads to a similarly disconnected aesthetics in which all uses for images are equal. All meaning in art and also human acts becomes only what is invested into them. There is no inherent meaning in anything. Everything, even war, is capable of becoming art, and we are back to Werner Erhard, *Solaris* and *1984*.

To illustrate the problem, Benjamin quotes Filippo Marinetti, one of the founders of Italian Futurism:

" 'For twenty-seven years we Futurists have rebelled against the branding of war as antiesthetic. . . . Accordingly we state . . . War is beautiful because it establishes man's dominion over the subjugated machinery by means of gas masks, terrifying megaphones, flame throwers, and small tanks. War is beautiful because it initiates the dreamt-of metalization of the human body. War is beautiful because it enriches a flowering meadow with the fiery orchids of machine guns. War is beautiful because it combines the gunfire, the cannonades, the cease-fire, the scents, and the stench of putrefaction into a symphony. War is beautiful because it creates new architecture, like that of the big tanks, the geometrical formation flights, the smoke spirals from burning villages, and many others. . . . Poets and artists of Futurism . . . remember these principles of an aesthetics of war so that your struggle for a new literature and a new graphic art . . . may be illumined by them.' "

Benjamin says this loss of the inherent meaning which is connected to art, humans and nature furthers the notion that all experience is equal, leading in short steps to fascism: "[Fascism] expects war to supply the artistic gratification of a sense perception that has been changed by technology. This is evidently the consummation of 'l'art pour l'art.' Mankind, which in Homer's time was an object for contemplation of the Olympian gods, now is one for itself. Its self-alienation has reached such a degree that it can experience its own destruction as an aesthetic pleasure of the first order."

The Bias toward Death

Ronald Reagan once said, "If you've seen one redwood, you've seen them all." A movie actor and politician, Reagan had doubtless struggled with the question of the reproducibility of himself. Perhaps he, like other commodities, lost his essence in reproduction and so did not notice that all redwoods are *not* the same.

At the time of his remark, I was working with the Sierra Club on the campaign to keep some of the virgin redwoods, many of which had been growing since before the time of Christ, from being cut down by logging companies. Everyone thought the Reagan statement typical of the problem. A great many human beings could not understand that there is a difference between the original, old-growth trees and the replanted redwoods the companies would exhibit on their tree farms.

Not caring about the old trees, the lumber companies could put out pamphlets that discussed the trees in cosmetic terms. One horrible example was their argument that "all most people really want is for the trees along the highway to be saved, so they can stop their cars, and pose for snapshots next to a redwood."

The lumber companies may have been more right than

wrong. Removed from direct contact with the old trees, their aura, their power, their life, their message about the potentialities of the planet, many people may have found Reagan's statement and the lumber company position plausible.

To offset this, we worked to convey a sense of what was being lost. We attempted to do this through the media. We carried around photos of the great old groves: moody, magical, somber, awesome, and attempted to place them in newspapers, magazines and on television.

Some outlets carried them and some did not, but it was clear that it didn't really matter whether they were reproduced in the media. They didn't "work." Too much was lost in the translation. More than anything, they lost their "aura," the mood that surrounds them and the quality of their existence that can be captured only in their presence.

Then we started doing the opposite. We carried around photos of acres of stumps where hundreds of redwoods had been cut down. I don't know if you have ever seen a field of tree stumps, but it is a horrific sight, not unlike a battlefield. Fortunately, however, it has very high visual definition, conveys a broad-band emotion—horror—and does not have the problem of conveying aura, since everything is dead.

When we carried these latter photos around, the media grabbed them. They even dispatched their own crews to redwood country to expand on what we'd brought.

That is the moment I learned that death is a much better subject for television than life. And so when television decided to concentrate upon images of dead bodies in Vietnam, it came as no surprise to me.

In the cases of both redwoods and Vietnam, images of death finally aroused the public. Images of life—whether the trees themselves, or the finely tuned Vietnamese culture and sensibility—accomplished nothing. They were far too complex, too subtle. They involved too many senses. Most of all, they required a conveyance of aura. Since none of this was possible on television, they only put people to sleep.

Separation from Time and Place

In separating images from their source, thereby deleting their aura, television, photography and film also remove the images from their context of time and place.

The images which arrive in your home may have been shot yesterday or a week ago, on location or in a studio. By the time you see them, they are not connected to those places or those times. They have been separated from all connection. All the images arrive in sequence with equal validity. They exist only in the here and now. They are floating equ. 'y in space.

This situation inevitably provides another advantage fur advertising relative to virtually any other kind of television information.

Human beings and living creatures exist in process. From one year to the next they are different. What's more, human culture, government, religion and art are also in process. Explaining a human being or a culture or a political system requires at least some historical perspective. Explaining a product requires no such historical understanding. Products do not grow organically, they are fashioned whole and complete in the here and now. You see them in one stage of their life cycle. That is their *only* stage until they start falling apart in your home. This is not to say that products have no history. A new Cadillac with a V-8 engine represents a historical change from a Model T. But you don't need to know the history to understand the Cadillac. And the Cadillac itself, the one you buy, does not grow or change.

Products can be understood completely and totally in the here and now. They are pure information, free of time and

291

free of place. When product images are placed on television in sequence with real events of the world, whose contexts of time and place are deleted by television, products obtain an equality they'd otherwise lack. This gives products far more significance in the viewer's mind than any direct experience of them would.

That advertising achieves a validity effectively equal to that of real events of the world is only one bizarre result of the separation of images from time and place. Another is that it becomes impossible for a viewer to be certain that the information which is presented on television ever actually happened.

Do you remember the Howard Johnson's shoot-out in New Orleans a few years ago? I watched it all on television.

The regular programming was interrupted to take me to New Orleans where a wildly murderous band of black revolutionaries had taken over the upper floors of a Howard Johnson's hotel. They were systematically murdering the white guests. This was a truly frightening story. Images of race war ran through my mind.

The announcer said that a massive police assault was underway, and I saw helicopters, police with drawn guns, and a lot of tense faces.

I didn't see any murderous black revolutionaries, although I certainly imagined them, and they were described for me by the police on the scene. The death toll was uncertain.

A few hours later, the news reported that the siege was continuing but that the police had reduced their estimate of murderous black revolutionaries to two or three and that the death of only one white guest had been thus far confirmed. However, a number of policemen had been killed by the murderers. The death toll was still uncertain but it could be as high as a dozen.

Back to the regular programming.

By the morning, the siege was over, and the police were able to find only one of the revolutionaries, who apparently had been dead for quite a while, long before the assault was halted. There was still only one dead white guest but there were eight dead police, killed by the band. Police were baffled as to how the other members of the murderous group had eluded them.

A week later, after an investigation, the New Orleans police department reported that they had found that only one white guest had been killed, only one black man had been involved in the killing, that this one man was not a black revolutionary but a crazy person. He had been dead for several hours while the invasion of the hotel continued, and all of the dead police had been killed by each other's ricocheting bullets. The story was carried in the back pages of the newspapers; I wasn't able to find it in any television news reports.

It turned out that virtually all of the facts as reported on television were totally wrong. Ignoring for the moment that television did not correct its own report, newspapers did, I was given the opportunity to straighten it all out in my mind. There were no murderous revolutionaries; there was only a crazy man. The police had all shot each other. But even now, several years later, I can recall the images of the police assault. Brave men acting in my behalf. The images of the murderous band. I can recall them now even though the information was completely false.

In April of 1976 the Chicago *Daily News* reported that Central Intelligence Agency operatives located in parts of the world where there are no journalists—central Africa, South American jungles, and so on—had been feeding totally fictitious stories to two hundred newspapers, thirty news services, twenty radio and television outlets and twenty-five publishers, all foreign owned. These stories, sometimes concerning fictitious guerrilla movements, would be reported as real in these countries and then would be picked up by the American media. Eventually you read these stories in your newspaper or saw them reported on the evening news. The purpose of the false stories was to manipulate information so that foreign governments and our government would think some event was happening when it wasn't or vice versa. Policy decisions would be made based on this information. Public understanding would be distorted. The course of world politics would be altered.

Can you recall the *Mayaguez* incident of 1975? Walter Cronkite announced that Ford had authorized Kissinger to undertake a rescue off the coast of Cambodia because the crew of the Mayaguez had been assaulted and seized. Kissinger sent the air force to bomb some island where the crew was presumably detained (but actually wasn't). Did you stop to realize at any point in following this story or in developing your opinion about it that every person and detail in it were media images describing media actions concerning other media images based on earlier media information?

Tragically, this is the case with virtually all news that is carried in the media. It exists outside of your life. Often it exists outside the lives of the people who report it and the government officials who act upon it.

However, for most people sitting at home viewing the news, there is no way at all to know what is true or correct and what is not. If the news has a certain logic to it, we believe it is right. We can determine the logic of one day's events if it seems to follow from the logic of the previous day's events, also carried in the media.

Under such circumstances, it becomes possible for news to exist *only* within the media and nowhere in the real world. That was the situation that Orwell posited in *1984*. Did Goldstein exist? Was there a war between Oceania and Eastasia?

How could anyone possibly know, since it all concerned events in distant places, and it all arrived on television.

With information confined to the media, totally separated from the context of time and place, the creation of reality is as simple as feeding it directly into our heads. An earlier lie can become what Werner Erhard calls the "ground of reality" for the newer lie. We don't need the CIA to prove the point. Any evening's news is filled with information that we can't possibly know is true. How could we know? The only way to know for sure if something happened is to be present at the time and in the place of the event. If not, you are taking the information on faith.

This problem of uncertainty, caused by disconnection from time and place, applies to all media. For example, some chapters ago, I described a correspondence I'd had with an anthropologist friend, Neal Daniels, concerning the importance of light in many cosmologies. I also described a trip to Micronesia and a conversation with a man I met there. I also told you about a woman at an environmental conference, using her words to support my arguments. How can you know if any of these things happened? How could you *possibly* know? Well, you could go to the American Anthropology Association, track down Neal Daniels, and ask him. If he exists. You could write the University of Michigan and ask for a roster of attendees at that environmental conference, seeking a woman who fit my description. You could do that only if the conference itself happened. But would you? What a lot of trouble that would be.

And yet, perhaps I made up those stories to fill out some points. Perhaps I made up one of them. How can you know?

Whenever you engage with the media, any media, you begin to take things on faith. With books you are at least able to stop and think about what you read, as you read. This gives you some chance to analyze. With television the images just come. They flow into you at their own speed, and you are hard pressed to know a true image from one which is manufactured. All of the images are equally disconnected from context, afloat in time and space.

Condensation of Time: The Bias against Accuracy

With events separated from the time and place in which they occur, it becomes possible to condense them in time. It is not only possible but inevitable that this be done. Unlike print media, or even film, television information is inherently limited by time. It is impossible to present all of most events, so what is presented is always condensed. Most of the event is squeezed out. The result of this condensation is distortion.

If you have ever participated in a public event of any sort and then watched the news report of it, you are already aware that the news report barely resembles what you experienced. You are aware of this because you were there. Other viewers are not aware. When television describes events that happened at some other historical time, no one can know what is true.

The best article I ever read on the inevitable distortions resulting from television's inherent need to condense time was written in *TV Guide* by Bill Davidson (March 20, 1976). Writing about the new spurt of "docudramas," which represent themselves as true versions of historical events, he said, "Truth may be the first victim when television 'docudramas' rewrite history."

Davidson analyzes some half-dozen docudramas for inaccuracy and distortion and then asks, "Does this mean that docudrama is more drama than docu? Probably yes. Is the American public deliberately being misled by representations that these films are in fact true stories? Probably yes."

In fact, however, the distortions are less deliberate than they are inevitable.

Davidson interviewed David Rintels, who wrote the docudrama *Fear on Trial*, which purported to be a true account of the blacklisting of John Henry Faulk in 1956. He quotes Rintels as saying:

" 'I had to tell a story condensing six or seven years into a little less than two hours, which means I could just barely hit the major highlights. I did what I think all writers should do—present the essence of the facts and capture the truth of the general story. . . . Attorney Louis Nizer's summation to the jury took more than 12 hours. I had to do it in three minutes.' "

Davidson also quotes Buzz Aldrin, the ex-astronaut whose life story was the subject of "Return to Earth" on ABC. " 'On the whole, I'm satisfied with the picture, but condensation sometimes alters the truth.' "

The need to condense is inherent in a medium which is limited by time. The process of condensation, however, has the effect of eliminating the sort of nuance which is as important to historical accuracy as the action that *is* included.

Davidson points out that since television docudramas have condensed such complex subjects as the career of Joseph McCarthy, the Attica prison riots, and the life of Martin Luther King, Jr., the problem is virtually beyond control. Davidson quotes psychologist Dr. Victor B. Cline of the University of Utah, who says: " 'The very real danger of these docudrama films is that people take it for granted that they're true and—unlike similar fictionalized history in movies and the theater—they are seen on a medium which also presents straight news. . . . I think they should carry a disclaimer to the effect that the story is not totally true but based on some of the elements of what actually occurred.' "

I think so too. But if there should be disclaimers for docudramas there should be many *more* for news. As prominent San Francisco journalist Susan Halas once put it: "There is no news, there's only media." Where docudramas reduce an event to an hour or two, distorting truth, the news may reduce the same event to thirty seconds, eliminating most of the information that a reasonable, thinking person would consider necessary to any understanding of events in process. What is left is the skeleton of events, making only scraps of knowledge available for people's perception and understanding.

The inevitable need to condense information in time is the cause of this. The *way* the information is condensed—what is left in and what is deleted—will be described further at the end of the next chapter, where we discuss highlighted moments and their application to news.

XV

ARTIFICIAL UNUSUALNESS

THE technical limitations already described conspire to create a far deeper and much more serious problem for television: It is inherently boring.

With information confined to only two sensory modes, with sensory synesthesia shifted, with low-definition imagery, with the total loss of context (aura and time), and with viewers whose thought processes are dulled, the producers of television programs begin with a difficult task. How to create interest through a medium that is predisposed to turn people off?

My friend Jack Edelson has put it this way: "It's the most curious thing; when I watch television I'm bored and yet fixated at the same time. I hate what I'm watching and I feel deeply disinterested but I keep watching anyway." His statement was echoed by dozens of letters I have received, and children describe their TV experience in similar terms.

The hypnotic-addictive quality of the medium goes a long way to keep the bored viewer fixated before the screen. So does the fact that our mediated environments don't offer much by way of stimulation. TV is the only action. However, there is much more to this bored fixation than that. Television producers and directors, deeply aware of the inherent limitations of the medium, have developed a vast technology of tricks—a technology of attachment, actually—that can succeed in keeping a viewer engaged despite the lack of any real desire to be watching. Most of the techniques were originally developed by advertising people, who have always had vast amounts of money available for experiments and whose *raison d'être* is to develop technologies to fixate the viewer.

Most of the techniques are rooted in an exploitation and inversion of a single emotionally based human tendency: interest in "highlighted moments."

Instinct to the Extraordinary

I described the Amazon Indians' means of discovering, understanding and interacting with their forest environment. The events that caused them the greatest alarm were the unique, the out of the ordinary: a broken twig that could not be explained, or a distant sound that had not been heard before. It is the unusual that stimulates heightened attention.

You can experience this yourself the next time you're out walking. Whether in a city or in a country meadow, the field of images, sounds, smells proceeds into you without your particularly noticing them. Then, an extraordinary event will occur. A bird will dive nearby, a boulder will roll across the path, a car will screech to a halt. You snap into a more alert condition, a decision may be required. A thought results.

Obviously being alert to the unusual moment is useful for survival. But aside from survival, the sensory interest in the unusual is a means toward gaining knowledge and pleasure.

Knowledge is gained by discerning change, by noting the event that is different from all others, by making distinctions and establishing patterns. The fiftieth time you watch a field of daisies you can still learn something new about natural form since no two observations are alike. Then there is the clearly special event: the single ten-foot daisy or the hole appearing where none had been the day before.

In both cases, the extraordinary induces notation, study, and eventually knowledge. "Sometimes in a field of daisies," one might say, "one daisy will grow abnormally large." That is knowledge. "It is the same with bears and foxes." This is a second level of knowledge. "Perhaps animals are like plants; I must watch for further examples of this." A process of self-education about planetary patterns has begun. The observation of *differences* is at the heart of the knowledge.

The senses are just as attuned to differentiation as the mind. We notice water or someone else's skin against our own because the moment of the touch is different from the moment before the touch. As the same touch is repeated over and over, we slowly sink back into automatic pilot. Although there can be comfort and security in the routine and the repetitive, the most stimulating event is the creative one, the new one.

Television is an exceedingly odd phenomenon. On the one hand it offers non-unique, totally repetitive experience. No matter what is on television, the viewer is sitting in a darkened room, almost all systems shut down, looking at light.

But within this deprived, repetitive, inherently boring environment, television producers create the fiction that something unusual is going on, thereby fixing attention. They do this in two ways: first, by outrageously fooling around with the imagery; second, by choosing content outside of ordinary life, thereby fitting the test of unusualness.

These two tactics combine to create a hierarchy of production standards that in the trade are lumped together as "good television." As we shall see, the term applies more to a quality of manipulation than a quality of content. I shall take these one at a time.

The Bias toward Technique as Replacement of Content

When you are watching television, you are seeing images that are utterly impossible in nature. This in itself qualifies the imagery for your attention, even when the content within the image is nothing you'd otherwise care about. For example, the camera can circle the subject. It can rise above it or go below it. It can zoom in or back away from it. The image can be changed in size or made to fade and reappear. Editors make it possible for a scene in one room to be followed instantly by a scene in another room, or at another time, or another place. Words appear over images. Music rises and falls in the background. Two images or three can appear simultaneously. One image can be superimposed on another on the screen. Motion can be slowed down or sped up.

None of these effects is possible in unmediated imagery. When you lift your eyes from this paper and look around your room, it doesn't become some other room or some other time. It could not possibly do that. Nor does your room circle around you or zoom back away from you. If it did do that, you would certainly pay one hell of a lot of attention to it, just as you would to anything new and unexplained that appeared in your field of vision.

Through these technical events, television images alter the usual, natural imagery possibilities, taking on the quality of a naturally highlighted event. They make it seem that what you are looking at is unique, unusual and extraordinary.

Attention is stimulated as though something new or important was going on, such as landslides, gigantic boulders or ten-foot daisies. But nothing unusual is going on. All that's happening is that the viewer is watching television, which is the same thing that happened an hour ago, or yesterday. A trick has been played. The viewer is fixated by a conspiracy

302

of dimmed-out environments combined with artificial, impossible, fictitious unusualness.

❖   ❖

To get an idea of the extent to which television is dependent upon technical tricks to maintain your interest, I suggest you try the following experiment, which I call the Technical Events Test.

Put on your television set and simply count the number of times there is a cut, a zoom, a superimposition, a voice-over, the appearance of words on the screen—a technical event of some kind.

You will find it goes something like this.

You are looking at a face speaking. Just as you are becoming accustomed to it, there's a cut to another face. (*technical event*) Then there might be an edit back to the first face. (*technical event*) Then the camera might slowly draw back to take in some aspect of a wider scene. (*technical event*) Then the action suddenly shifts outdoors to the street. (*technical event*) Intercut with these scenes might be some other parallel line of the story. It may be a series of images of someone in a car racing to meet the people on that street we have just visited. (*technical event*) The music rises. (*technical event*) And so on.

Each technical event—each alteration of what would be natural imagery—is intended to keep your attention from waning as it might otherwise. The effect is to lure your attention forward like a mechanical rabbit teasing a greyhound. Each time you are about to relax your attention, another technical event keeps you attached.

The luring forward never ceases for very long. If it did, you might become aware of the vacuousness of the content that can get through the inherent limitations of the medium. Then you would be aware of the boredom. If, for example, the camera made no movements and there was no cutting in time and place; if one camera merely sat in one place and recorded the entire length of a conversation, including all the pauses, redundancies, diversions, inaction—the way conversations happen in real life and real time—you would be disinclined to watch for very long. The program would have to be hours long before much of anything happened. Television can't wait for this, so it stimulates your interest technically.

Once you actually try the Technical Events Test you will probably find that in the average commercial television program, there are eight or ten technical events for every sixty-second period. That is, the flow of natural imagery is interrupted eight or ten times every minute, sometimes much more often than that.

You may also find that there is rarely a period of twenty seconds without any sort of technical event at all. That may give you an idea of the extent to which producers worry about whether the content itself can carry your interest.

One can only guess at the effect upon viewers of these hyperactive images, aside from fixating attention on the television set. Dr. Matthew Dumont, mentioned earlier, says these technical effects help cause hyperactivity among children. They must surely also contribute to the decline of attention span and the inability to absorb information that comes muddling along at natural, real-life speed.

To be constantly buffeted by bizarre and impossible imagery cannot help but produce stress in viewers. To have one's attention interrupted every ten seconds must jar mental processes that were otherwise attuned to natural, personal informational rhythms in which such interruptions would be literally maddening.

Leaving the television set to go outdoors, or to have an ordinary conversation, becomes unsatisfying. One wants action! Life becomes boring, and television interesting, all as a result of a system of technical hypes.

Meanwhile, the speed and activity of commercial programming are further exaggerated in advertising.

When you try the Technical Events Test on a few thirty- or sixty-second television commercials you will find that advertising has roughly twice the technical action of the already hyped-up programs that the ads interrupt. On the average, a thirty-second commercial will have from ten to fifteen technical events. There is almost never a six-second period without a technical event. What's more, the technical events in advertising have much more dimension than those in the programming. In addition to the camera zooms, pans, rolls and cuts, they are far more likely to have words flashing on and off the screen, songs going on and off, cartoon characters doing bizarre things, voice-overs, shots from helicopters and so on.

If regular television programming is hard-pressed to maintain your attention without tricks, advertisers have the problem many times over. In regular programming at least there are stories or news, *something* of interest. Within television's limits, regular programming has the option to present relevant content. Advertising content has no inherent interest at all. The content is always the same. The image may be a seascape and the product is beer. Or it may be a landscape and the product is cars. Or it may be a home and the product is coffee. Whatever the setting, the content of advertising is always a sales pitch. There is nothing inherently interesting in this. It is worse than boring; it is annoying. So tricks *must* be used in every advertisement. Maxwell Arnold, a San Francisco advertising man who is one of the industry's few outspoken critics, once told a radio interviewer: "Who the hell would choose to watch ads if there wasn't something going on aside from the content?" In the absence of interesting content, technical style is the name of the game.

Advertisers spend staggering amounts of money to achieve their technical successes. The average production budget for a minute of advertising is roughly ten times the cost of the average minute of programming. It is not at all unusual for a thirty-second commercial to have a production budget of fifty thousand to one hundred thousand dollars, enough to cover the total costs of many half-hour programs. This money is spent in techniques, and research upon techniques, to obtain your interest where there would otherwise be none. The frequently heard comment, "You know, I sometimes think advertising is the most interesting thing on television," is a testament to the success of these expenditures.

Advertisers are the high artists of the medium. They have gone further in the technologies of fixation than anyone else. But the lesson has also been learned by producers of the programs, and finally, by politicians.

During the Ford-Carter presidential campaign, at the point that Ford was gaining on Carter with incredible rapidity, the technical-events ratio between the commercials of the two was about four to one in favor of Ford. If Ford had spent a little more advertising money, and if the campaign had gone on another few days, I believe he would have passed Carter, no matter what the messages within their commercials. Because of the central role television now plays in campaigning, advertising technique has become more important than content in the American political arena.

The fact that advertising contains many more technical events per minute than commercial programming is significant from another, more subtle perspective. Advertising starts with a disadvantage with respect to the programming. It must be *more* technically interesting than the program or it will fail. That is, advertising must itself become a highlighted moment compared with what surrounds it.

If advertising failed to work on television, then advertisers would cease to sponsor the programs, leading, at least as things are presently structured, to the immediate collapse of television's economic base. If the programs ever become too interesting, that will be the end of television. The ideal relationship between program and commercial is that the program should be just interesting enough to keep you interested but not so interesting as to actually dominate the ads.

This applies to technique as well as content. On the rare occasion when something real or gripping appears on television—the SLA shootout, President Kennedy's funeral, an emergency presidential address—and the viewer is awakened from lethargy by the emergence of *real* highlighted content, as opposed to technique, advertisers make every attempt to cancel their spots. They will say they are doing this because it is in "bad taste" to advertise in such moments.

But when is advertising *not* in bad taste? Do they mean that interrupting people's lives to start hawking products is not rude and offensive behavior at any time? If someone came to your door every night to do that, you would soon call the police. Advertising is always in bad taste. What advertisers mean when they use the "bad taste" excuse is that when something really real happens on television, it may affect how well the ad works. In the context of concrete reality, advertising can be understood as vacuous, absurd, rude, outrageous. Advertising can succeed only in an environment in which the real merges with the fictional, and all become semireal with equal tone and undifferentiated meaning. In that context advertising can use its technical tricks to jump forward out of the medium, creating its artificial unusualness. The best environment for advertising is a dull and even one, where *it* can become the highlighted event.

This explains the tendency to sponsor programs that have that quality of even tone, from Walter Cronkite to Archie Bunker to Kojak. They all merge with each other, making an appropriate backdrop for the advertising. In probably the most brilliant article that has ever been written on television ("Sixteen Notes on Television," reprinted in *Literature in Revolution*), Todd Gitlin said: "The commercial is the purpose, the essence; the program is the package."

The program is only the excuse to get you to watch the advertising. Without the ads there would be no programs. Advertising is the true content of television and if it does not remain so, then advertisers will cease to support the medium, and television will cease to exist as the popular entertainment it presently is.

What about noncommercial television? Is this an exception to the rules of artificial unusualness?

Popular wisdom holds that noncommercial public television competes so ineffectively, in terms of audience ratings, because of the "low tastes" of the viewing public. I have heard many a liberal put it that "we need to educate people to appreciate better sorts of programming." I can barely restrain my anger at the arrogance, cynicism, and ignorance of this position.

If you will go back to your television set and apply the Technical Events Test to your noncommercial channel, you will find that except for documentary footage there are usually only two or three technical events in every minute of programming and that these are more likely to be of the simpler sort: camera switching, panning and zooms. Because they are not as well funded as their commercial competitors, noncommercial television producers can afford only about 25 percent as much technical gimmickry as the commercial stations. In the end, the ratio works out about this way:

Advertising: 20–30 technical events per minute.

Commercial program: 8–10 technical events per minute.

Public television: 2–3 technical events per minute.

The technical events are surely not the sole determinants of viewer interest and appeal, but they are far more logical an explanation for the popularity of certain programming than the assertion that people demand violent programs. What people desire is involvement and interest. In a world where real involvement and unique events are more and more remote from direct personal experience, and in a medium that is inherently dulling, it's a wonder that any people at all are able to make their way through *any* noncommercial programs with their small degree of technical effects. In fact, I find it a rather moving testimony to the vitality of people that they continue to seek content that has not been jazzed up and packaged.

This is all aside from the question of whether public television programs *are* any better than commercial programs. In fact most public television producers have the same system of values as their commercial counterparts and for the same reasons. Recognizing that hype is needed for ratings in such an intrinsically turned-off medium, and that the ratings are just as much a determinant for funding in public television as commercial television, they put as much money as possible into technique. They operate out of the same standards of "good television." They even gain support from the same corporations that dominate commercial television: oil companies and chemical companies.

It is sometimes considered a mitigating factor that the commercial message in public television is limited to a low-key acknowledgment at the beginning and the end of the program. But these companies are not attempting to achieve exactly the same effect on public television as they do on commercial TV. There is a different level of benefit to corporations who insinuate themselves into this so-called noncommercial environment. The benefit is company identification rather than product identification. This has long-run value in public relations terms rather than short-run gains in sales. In addition, having the name repeated in a noncommercial format can still set off the neuronal billboard that has been previously implanted in the brain by commercial programs. Finally, the cost of these low-key acknowledgments is negligible. To have its name appear on the screen before and after a half-hour program may cost a corporation only a few thousand dollars.

Underwriting an entire half-hour program on public television usually costs less than one sixty-second spot in commercial television.

Aside from these differences, public television is similar to the rest of television. Competing for many of the same dollars, the same ratings, the same markets and operating in the same medium with the same technical limitations, the noncommercial producer must make very similar choices.

The best proof can be found in the most successful public television shows. *Sesame Street*, for example, the most popular program in public television history, has a technical events ratio equal to and sometimes larger than its commercial competition.

It is not well enough appreciated, I think, that *Sesame Street* was conceived, designed and executed from its inception by ex-advertising people. Using every technique they learned in advertising—rapid cutting, interspersing of songs and cartoons, very short time spans—their show has been found more "interesting" than any public TV program that preceded it. This "interest" is based on *technique* and these are the same techniques used in advertising.

In Favor of "Alienated" Viewing

The Technical Events Test is extremely subversive to television. This is one reason I have asked you to do it. As people become aware of the degree to which technique, rather than anything intrinsically interesting, keeps them fixed to the screen, withdrawal from addiction and immersion can begin. I have seen this happen with my own children. Once I had put them to the task of counting and timing these technical events, their absorption was never the same.

When viewers become alert to the technology being used upon them, they can separate technique from content. With the effects of technique stripped away, the true content of the program has to stand on its own. In the case of advertising, it falls apart. Regular programming also assumes its true worth and it is often even less than you may have imagined was possible.

As you become able to pull back out of the immersion in the TV set, you can widen your perceptual environment to again include the room you are in. Your feelings and personal awareness are rekindled. With self-awareness emerging you can perceive the quality of sensory deadness television induces, the one-dimensionality of its narrowed information field, and arrive at an awareness of boredom. This leads to channel switching at first and eventually to turning off the set.

Any act that breaks immersion in the fantastic world of television is subversive to the medium, because without the immersion and addiction, its power is gone. Brainwashing ceases. As you watch advertising, you become enraged.

The great German dramatist Bertolt Brecht used the term "alienation" to describe this process of breaking immersion. Writing during the early thirties, Brecht used the term to mean the shattering of theatrical illusion. By breaking immersion in the fantasy the theater-goer becomes *self-aware* and attains a mental attitude that allows discernment, criticism, thought and political understanding of the material on display. Without "alienation," involvement is at an unconscious level, the theater-goer absorbing rather than reflecting and reacting. Brecht argued that becoming lost or immersed in the words, fantasies and entertainments of theater was preparation for similar immersion in words and fantasies of theatrical leadership: Hitler.

Brecht, like Walter Benjamin, felt that the entire development of art during the thirties furthered ways of mind suitable for autocracy.

Brecht developed his concept of "alienation" in order to break the *form* of the theatrical relationship. To accomplish this, he would interrupt the line of the theatrical action; or have the actors step out of their parts to speak directly to the audience personally or politically; or add such elements as placards. In films, he would put words on the screen to explain the meaning of a scene that might otherwise have been received as "entertainment," thereby shattering unconscious absorption.

In Brechtian terms, if an actor developed a character in such a way that the audience became absorbed in the character rather than the *meaning* of the character, then the actor would have failed. The goal was that each member of the audience become aware that he or she is in a theater, that actors are performing, that the characters are created on purpose to convey a message, and that the message applies directly to each person in the audience. In this way, theater had the capacity to become educational in a revolutionary way, capable of moving people to action. Without this shattering of illusion, Brecht felt, theater remains an example of mindless immersion within an autocratic format. And yet, because theater involves a live public performance, the possibilities for technically created illusion are far fewer than in film or television.

It is this very quality of "alienation" from the illusion, the experience of self-awareness, that advertisers and program producers go to such lengths to avoid. They may not actually be thinking to themselves: "I have got to keep these viewers hyped and away from boredom or I'll lose them." Instead, they define some production values as "good television" and others as "bad television." They will do anything they can to develop and keep your fixed gaze and total involvement. They've found that technical tricks do better than content because, as we have seen, the content loses too much in the translation through the medium to be engrossing on its own.

However, they *do* also choose content for its immersive and hyperactive value. In addition to shattering your normal perceptual patterns by artificially unusual imagery, dragging your mind and awareness forward, never allowing stasis or calm or a return to self-awareness, producers must also make program choices that fit the process.

The Bias to Highlighted Content: Toward the Peaks, Away from the Troughs

At one end of what we might think of as the spectrum of personal experience, there is the occasional momentous event. Emotionally engulfing. Intellectually overpowering. These experiences happen to everyone, but they are relatively rare. Between these "highs," life moves along from routine experience to routine experience, flowing one into the next, developing the overall pattern that is life's true content.

When you sit down in a café with a friend, you don't need to have an orgasm for the experience to be worthwhile. Perhaps nothing will happen in that hour or two. No exclamations of passion. No news of dire events. No shoot-outs at the next table or in the street. Perhaps you will merely converse or watch the passing parade. Perhaps you will explore some obscure detail in your friend's feelings or personal history. Perhaps you will muse about fashion. Most coffeehouse conversations, like the rest of life, will go more or less that way.

Ordinary life contains peaks and valleys of experience, highs and lows, long periods of dormancy, many periods of quiet, indecision, ambiguity, resolution, failed resolution. All of these fit into a wide pattern that is the way life is actually lived. Included within this pattern are occasional highlighted events: great shocks, unexpected eruptions, sudden achievements. Life would be frustrating without such catharsis and excitement, but life would be bizarre and maddening if it had too many of these peak events.

Much of the nervousness in the world today in both individual and national life may be attributable to the density and power of the experiences that are prearranged for our consumption. Too much happens too fast to be absorbed and integrated into an overall pattern of experience.

It is no accident that the world outside television has concentrated increasingly on large and cathartic events. All artificial environments and the consumer life encourage focus on peak events. When nature is absent, so is natural subtlety. Personal attunement to slower, nature-based rhythms is obscured. We focus on the "hits" that are provided, and these reduce more and more to commodities. Every commodity is advertised as offering a bigger and better and more powerful experience than the one that preceded it. Since life's experiences have been reduced to packaged commodities, like the chimpanzee in the lab, that is what we seek.

Television, in addition to being the prime exponent of the commodity life, makes a direct contribution to distorting life in the direction of highlighted experiences by choosing its contents to fit this pattern. It is a technological necessity that it do so.

Since television is such a vague and limited medium, so unlikely to produce much of any response in a viewer, producers must necessarily divide all content into two distinct categories: peaks and troughs, the highlighted and the routine, always choosing the former and not the latter. In this way, the choices in content match the technical bias toward artificial unusualness and also the tendencies of the wider commodity-based, artificial environment.

The programming bias is always toward the more vivid, more powerful, more cathartic, more definite, "clean" peaks of content. The result, not the process. The bizarre, rather than the usual.

In 1973, a wealthy young man leased a small suburban television station near San Francisco and tried the most curious experiment.

He presented only two programs every day. One occupied most of the day with images of ocean waves rolling to shore. One camera, no editing, no zooms. It just sat there and transmitted whatever the ocean did.

Then he switched to another single camera in an empty studio facing a blank wall. He invited everyone to do whatever he or she wished in front of the camera. Some people spoke into it; others tried more sensational behavior.

The first thing that was revealed by this experiment, which was practically an inversion of the usual television fare, was the extent to which the medium depends upon its technical events. A single stationary camera, picking up whatever passes through the frame, in real time, without alteration, will only bore people. If a professional producer-editor had gotten hold of that ocean footage, she or he could have created more interest in it. She or he could have zeroed in on details, shot from a helicopter following the waves forward, switched to a camera on the beach looking outward, and so on. With a little music, a nice little art piece might have been made out of it. But it would be engaging only for a short while.

No matter what technical tricks are used, ocean footage will *not* work for very long on television. It does not fit the test of highlighted moments. The experience of looking at oceans is beyond television's ability to deliver. To enjoy an ocean, one must be in a timeless condition, contemplative yet alert to the small changes in the sea and the life it supports. If you are looking for action and catharsis, watching an ocean will only bore you. Watching it on TV is even worse. You lose the salt smell, the wind, the lazy detail of the foam and light on wet sand and the sense of vast time and space. Television would also lose the nuances of a commonplace visit to a coffeehouse. The mundane conversation and people moving around or reading the paper would be profoundly boring to viewers sitting at home in their living rooms, *unless,* of course, some clown appeared and started tripping over everyone's feet while dropping trays. and then someone began to throw pastries around or spilled cappuccino on people's heads, or a bakery truck loaded with lemon meringue pies came crashing through the glass window. Now we're getting somewhere. Action.

In practice, no TV producer would ever seriously consider either oceans or coffeehouses as subject matter. They are intrinsically and obviously wrong subjects for the medium, "bad" television.

On the other hand, there are a lot of talking shows on television. Some people think this is odd since television is supposed to be a visual medium. Well, since television is so indistinct a medium, and since so little visual information can get through it, most of what we receive from television really comes in the words. This is especially true of news shows. We see some action—fires, wars, picketing—but we can't really make much of it until a reporter tells us what is happening and orients our minds to perceive what we are actually not seeing at all. In many ways television is really radio. The only real effect of the imagery is to fixate us.

Another reason why there is so much talking on television is that you *can* see faces. Faces talk. So naturally there is a bias toward talking. Within the talking there is a bias toward a kind of highlighted conversation.

Television talking is very pointed. Subject oriented, rather than generalized. Focused, rather than free-ranging. This is particularly the result of time limitations and the need to be sure that something happens beyond the kind of talk that takes place in grocery stores.

On television people tend to skim along the highlights of the conversational material. Blank spaces, pauses, personal comments, asides, changes of mood, changes of attitude, changes of subject—all of the rhythms of ordinary conversation—are rarely allowed into television talk. To do otherwise would defy the medium's demand for frequent catharsis, repeated highlight and achieved goals.

Therefore talk show dialogues take on the same rhythms and

follow the same values as dramatic programs or situation comedies or quiz shows or news. The dialogue moves from loaded line to loaded line, headline to headline, important pronouncement to important pronouncement, punch line to punch line, like Bob Hope's humor.

Verbal troughs are often written into dialogue shows. Many acting schools teach these. Talk show hosts and guests indulge briefly in "patter" which is pseudoaimless. But the process never advances very far. The goal remains a *laugh* or a *point* or a *contention* or an *outrage* or a *shock*. The conversation is never allowed to settle down to the rhythms of real life, because if it did, there'd be no point in having the television on at all. One could have aimless conversation with someone at the bus stop.

And so, as with the technically created artificial unusualness, content itself is usually chosen for its hyperactive effect. The survival of this dull, indistinct, inherently boring technological failure called television depends upon this effect.

Compared to football, baseball is an almost oriental game, minimizing individual stardom, requiring a wide range of aggressive and defensive skills, and filled with long periods of inaction and irresolution. It has no time limitations. Football, on the other hand, has immediate goals, resolution on every single play, and a lot of violence—itself a highlight. It has clearly distinguishable hierarchies: heroes and drones.

Baseball is virtually a process game. Not that baseball is a process the way oceans and coffeehouses and conversations and love are, but in the context of sports it is more process oriented than many.

Soccer has even fewer peaks than baseball. The action flows over an immense field. Moments of focused concentration are rare. There is very little resolution from minute to minute.

Boxing, on the other hand, is very focused, involving constant action, frequent resolution and peaks of personal catharsis. Basketball, although it is a flow sport like soccer, is played on a small field and involves highlighted events—baskets—every few seconds.

Naturally football has totally overpowered baseball on television, and so have boxing and basketball. Meanwhile, soccer is rarely presented, and when it is, it communicates almost nothing.

Television, which is better suited to football and boxing than to soccer, is also better suited to *any* sporting event than to probing of alternative consciousness or natural environments, or any delving into relationships, all of which require emphasis on process: the in-between spaces.

Within the range of all human experience, and all possible programming, *any* sport contains more clearly highlighted action than, say, 99 percent of human relationships, except for those with a sexual or violent orientation.

The dramatic programs, featuring jealousy, hatred, desire, fear, humiliation, ebullience, are not only the most visible on television, they are also the most emotionally loaded, with the larger cathartic payoffs, like home runs or touchdowns or wars. They pass the test of highlighted content, providing visibility in a dimmed-out medium.

Television presents relationships in crisis; those that stand out from the usual fare of everyday life, which is not so explosive and dramatic most of the time. In the television world, relationships involve the same huge cycles of feeling as sports shows: big joys, great losses, ups and downs, sudden shocks and surprises, explosive passions, frequent catharsis. We get soap opera, Mary Hartman, *Roots*. Without crises, television drama would not be able to deliver any feeling. Conversation or smaller feelings—love, friendship, camaraderie—do not deliver on television. Violence does. It delivers fear. Producers and sponsors are well advised to make choices in favor of such programs. Fear qualifies as a bona fide pseudoexperience. It can fool viewers into believing that when they are watching television, some actual living is going on, when it isn't. In the long run, experiencing artificial fear over and over again when nothing dangerous is actually going on eventually dulls one's responses. One becomes less subject to television fear while at the same time more paranoid about the real world one actually experiences less and less.

The bias toward the peaks of content is possibly most tragic when it comes to news. Since much of life is now removed from our direct experience, the news that we get from afar becomes our *total* information on the forces that shape and move our lives. That makes the distortions in it a very serious matter.

When Walter Cronkite says, "And that's the way it is," he is surely aware that that's the way it is only within the very narrow range of world events that are communicable through television news, and within *those* events, only in those aspects that fit the standards of "good television."

Edward Epstein, in *News from Nowhere,* says, "Presenting events exactly as they occur does not fit with the requisites of television news. . . . Given the requirement that a network news story have definite order, time and logic, it would be insufficient in most cases to record from beginning to end the natural sequence of events, with all the digressions, confusions and inconsistencies that more often than not constitute reality . . .

"Cameramen seek out the most action-packed moments; and editors then further concentrate the action. Even when an event is characterized by an unexpected low degree of activity, television can create the illusion of great activity. The relatively unenthusiastic reception General MacArthur received in Chicago during his homecoming welcome in 1951 thus appeared to be a massive and frenetic reception on television because all the moments of action were concentrated together. . . . In collapsing the time frame of events and concentrating the action into a continuous flow, television news tends to heighten the excitement of any group or other phenomena it pictures, to the neglect of the more vapid and humdrum elements.

". . . 'Our job is to cut out all the dead wood and dull moments,' one NBC editor commented. The procedure involves routinely eliminating the intervals in which little of visual interest occurs, and compressing the remaining fragments into one continuous montage of unceasing visual action. For instance, an attempt by the SDS faction at Columbia University to block the registration of students in September of 1968, involved, according to my observations, a few speeches by SDS leaders, hours of milling about, in which the protest more or less dissipated for lack of interest, and about one minute of violence when five SDS leaders attempted to push their way past two campus patrolmen. The hours of film taken that day by an NBC camera crew recorded various views of the crowd from 9:00 A.M. until the violence at about 2:00 P.M., and the minute or so of violent confrontation.

"However, when the happening was reduced to a two-minute news story for the NBC Evening News, the editors routinely retained the violent scenes, building up to them with quick cuts of speeches and crowd scenes. . . . The process of distilling action from preponderantly inactive scenes was not perceived as any sort of distortion by any of the editors interviewed. On the contrary, most of them considered it to be the accepted function of editing; as one chief editor observed, it was 'what we are really paid for.' "

The results of the bias toward highlighted news content were put even more succinctly by John Birt in *TV Guide* (August 9, 1975). He points out that some elements of news fit the needs of the medium more directly than others, and the result is a serious "bias in understanding . . . trying to come to grips with the often bewildering complexity of modern problems . . . is a formidable task, even without trying to put the result on television; and the failure rate is high. The realities one is seeking are abstract—macroeconomic mechanisms, political philosophies, international strategies—and cannot be directly televised like a battle zone or a demonstration."

Even when an effort is made to cover subtle or complex material, Birt says, the decision is made to choose only the most televisable elements. So a specific case of, say, a starving family will be chosen, rather than an overall look at its cause, which is more complicated and less televisable. The latter, Birt says, "runs the risk of being boring. A well-made report on a famine, or even on one starving family in Appalachia, will be more watchable than a report on the world food problem. A program on living conditions in Watts or Harlem will be more diverting than a report on housing policy. . . .

"I believe that the various forms and techniques of TV journalism can all too easily conspire together to create a bias against the audience's understanding of the society in which it lives."

Birt suggests that the problem could be solved by lengthening the time devoted to the "main stories of the day," so that a more comprehensive understanding of them might develop. Of course this would result in giving less time to the stories that are *not* the "main" ones, and so his recommendation seems to contradict his earlier remarks. In effect, it would leave *some* news highlighted to an even greater extent, while background stories or more minor events were dropped out. Would this build greater understanding of events in the world? Obviously not. It would leave people even more transfixed by the out-of-context information which is chosen.

I wonder why Birt reversed himself in the middle of an argument? Perhaps he couldn't bear to face the implications of what he was saying. To face the inevitable drift of his own reasoning would lead straight to the observation that news, like all other information on television, is inevitably and irrevocably biased away from some forms of content and toward others. If this is true, then we really *don't* know which end is up and which is down. We take things as they come.

XVI

THE PIECES THAT FALL THROUGH THE FILTER

As a way of drawing together the technical limits and tendencies of television technology so that a pattern emerges, I would like to offer a list, a sort of potpourri. A number of the items in it have been touched on earlier. They are included here again so that we can gain a unified impression of the medium, what kind of world it must inevitably transmit.

Thirty-three Miscellaneous Inherent Biases

1) War is better television than peace. It is filled with highlighted moments, contains action and resolution, and delivers a powerful emotion: fear. Peace is amorphous and broad. The emotions connected with it are subtle, personal and internal. These are far more difficult to televise.

2) Violence is better TV than nonviolence.

3) When there is a choice between objective events

323

(incidents, data) and subjective information (perspectives, thoughts, feelings), the objective event will be chosen. It is more likely to take visual form.

4) Cars (and most commodities) are more visible on television, and come across with less information loss, than any living thing, aside from human faces. The smaller a plant or creature, or the more complex an image it presents, the harder it is to convey and the less likely it is to be chosen. Cars, like most urban forms, offer a clean, straight, uncomplicated message. They communicate their essence more efficiently than plants do. We are bound to have more images of cars and urban forms on television than natural environments and creatures.

5) Religions with charismatic leaders such as Billy Graham, Jesus Christ, Reverend Moon, Maharishi or L. Ron Hubbard are far simpler to handle on television than leaderless or nature-based religions like Zen Buddhism, Christian Science, American Indians, or druidism, or, for that matter, atheism. Single, all-powerful gods, or individual godlike figures are simpler to describe because they have highly defined characteristics. Nature-based religions are dependent upon a gestalt of human feeling and perceptual exchanges with the planet. To be presented on television, they would need to be too simplified to retain meaning.

6) Political movements with single charismatic leaders are also more suitable and efficient for television. When a movement has no leader or focus, television needs to create one. Mao is simpler to transmit than Chinese communism. Chávez is better television than farm workers. Steinem is better than women. Graham is better than Christianity. Erhard is better than the "human potential movement." Hitler is easier to convey than fascism. Nader is easier than consumerism. Nixon is better than corruption.

324

7) The one is easier than the many. The personality or the symbol is easier than the philosophy. The philosophy requires depth, time, development, and in some cases, sensory information. This remains true unless the many are made into copies of each other. Then, the one is the same as the many.

8) For the same reasons, hierarchy is easier to report upon than democracy or collectivity. The former is focused and has a specific form: leaders and followers. Only the leaders need to be interviewed. Democratic or collective forms involve flow processes with power constantly shifting. Television reporters don't have time to interview everyone.

9) Superficiality is easier than depth.

10) Short subjects with beginnings and ends are simpler to transmit than extended and multifaceted information. The conclusion is simpler than the process.

11) Verbal information is easier to convey than sensory information since television can deliver words with little information loss. Sensory information is easier to convey than intuitive information, if the former is confined to the two operative senses of television. Intuitive information, which has no form at all, can barely be sent or received.

12) Feelings of conflict, and their embodiment in actions, work better on television than feelings of agreement and their embodiment in calm and unity. Conflict is outward, agreement is inward, and so the former is more visible than the latter.

13) Lust is better television than satisfaction. Ebullience and anxiety are better than tranquility. On the other hand, anger is better than anxiety. Jealousy is better television than acceptance. All of these work more easily than

love. Passionate love is more communicable than brotherly and sisterly love.

14) Competition is inherently more televisable than co-operation as it involves drama, winning, wanting and loss. Cooperation offers no conflict and becomes boring.

15) Materialism, acquisitiveness and ambition, all highly focused attitudes, work better than spirituality, nonseeking, openness and yielding. The medium cannot deal with ambiguity, subtlety and diversity.

16) Doing is easier to convey than being. Activity will always be chosen over inactivity.

17) When dealing with primitive peoples, objective events such as hunting, building, fighting or dancing are easier to convey through television than subjective details of qualities of experience, ways of mind, alternative perceptions. The latter qualities, which form the heart of life for primitive people, are dropped out in favor of the former.

18) Loud is easier to televise than soft. Close is easier than distant. Large is easier than small. Too large is harder than medium. The narrow is easier than the wide.

19) Linear information works better on television than information that comes as a matrix or has dimension. The singular is more understandable than the eclectic. The speculative is easier than the ambiguous.

20) The fixed is better than the evolutionary; the static is better than the fluid.

21) The bizarre always get more attention on television than the usual.

22) Facts concerning the moon are better television than

poetry concerning the moon. *Any* facts work better than *any* poetry.

23) The tree is easier to convey than the landscape. The bus is easier than the street. The street is easier than the forest path. The river is easier than the mountain. The flower is easier than the field. The road is easier than the river.

24) The specific is always easier than the general.

25) The expression is easier than the feeling, and so crying is better television than sadness. Verbal is always better than nonverbal.

26) The desires of black people for jobs, housing, integration makes for better television, because they are objective desires, than the conveyance of black culture itself, which is subjective, multifaceted and sensory.

27) The business relationship to natural landscapes as resources is easier to present than the Indian relationship to nature as the source of being.

28) The advertising relationship to life as consumption is easier to get across on television than the spiritualist relationship to life as expression.

29) A rocket scientist's understanding of the space and cosmos can be filtered through the medium; a mystic's understanding of space and cosmos as creature, or power, cannot be.

30) Quantity is easier than quality.

31) Calisthenics are easier than yoga since they can be visually copied in movement; yoga needs to be felt.

32) The finite is easier than the infinite.

33) Death is easier than life. It is specific, focused, highlighted, fixed, resolved and has meaning aside from context. Life, on the hand, is fluid, ambiguous, process oriented, complex, multileveled, sensory, intuitive. Cutting down redwood trees is better television than trying to convey their aura and power. Body counts of dead Vietnamese work better on television than appreciations of Vietnamese life or the complexities of the Vietnamese political struggle.

During February of 1977, public television carried a National Geographic special, "The New Indians," which was billed as exploring the emerging attitudes among Indian people who, while recovering their civil and political rights, also wish to rediscover and reaffirm the old Indian ways. Robert Redford narrated.

The first five minutes of the program attempted to convey a sense of the beauty of traditional Indian life-style and perception. The camera panned to mountains, rivers, fields of grass dotted by circles of teepees. Redford spoke of the Indian conception of the "oneness of things," the equality of all creatures, the desire to keep in harmony with the Great Spirit. We heard Indian chanting and drumbeats.

Sitting in my living room, I kept track of the technical events. No single shot lasted longer than ten seconds. Keeping the images jumping was a very wise decision on the part of the producers, because the mountains were too far away to be seen in anything beyond outline, the rivers were only a blur, and the fields of grass became a background haze in which the teepees were the only visible highlight. If we had been left to gaze at these images for more than ten seconds, an awareness of boredom would have developed. It was impossible to get a sense of the mountains, rivers, and fields which, so the narrator said, were the central forces in Indian awareness.

Neither did the chanting and drumming have much effect. If you have ever heard *real* Indian chanting and drumming, you know that they create their effect only after many hours of sitting within their rhythms as the repetition and the beat slowly seep into your bones. On television, they were only thematic, and used for that purpose, artifact.

The story cuts to Chicago. A group of bright-looking young people are loading their car. These are city-raised Indian kids, packing up for a cross-country drive to British Columbia, where there's to be a gathering of young Indian people and traditional Indians. The idea is to merge the activist energy of the young with the traditional knowledge of the old. The enthusiasm of the young people comes through. They laugh. They joke. They tease. They remind me of the kind of jovial, good-hearted people you see on *Sesame Street*: All-American, although not exactly white.

At the meeting in Canada, the city kids struggle to learn how to build a teepee, how to start a fire with sticks. We watch an old medicine man explain to the Chicagoans how a field of flowers reveals natural cycles. We hear him speak of natural balances; we watch the kids listening intently. His words are clear, the beauty of his face is moving, but the flower he is holding in his hands, and its seeds, the subject of his example, are impossible to see.

Later in the program we see some rare footage of the Potlatch ceremonies of the Kwakiutl people, which were suppressed by the Canadian government until recently. We see Indian dances; people dressed as animals; Indians in canoes led by an eagle-man, his arms flapping in a mock attempt to move the boats forward. We watch totems being carved. The goal is to immerse us, the viewers, in the Indian experience, to convey the beauty and mystery of their art and its organic, naturalistic meaning. But on television, cut at an average of ten technical events per minute, the ceremonials are practically impossible to follow. They are as fuzzy as the natural surroundings from which they have emerged. We get no sense of the dance. It passes in and out of the frame of the camera. We see only this piece of it or that one. The fine details of the costumes blur like the tiny seeds of the flower. We cannot smell the burning fire or the sweat of the dancers' bodies or the dirt of the floor. We cannot feel the coldness of the air.

Our exposure comes in ten-second pieces, at most. Whatever understanding we develop comes from Redford's words, which describe what we cannot actually see or intuit.

As I sit at home in my living room, watching these scenes with my family, the program takes on the quality of carnival or Mardi Gras or gigantic costume party. A reenactment. It looks like a production staged by the local museum auxiliary. Its reality is impossible to get. The whole ceremony enters the realm of artifact.

The information loss is virtually total. Aura is utterly destroyed. Time is fractured. The sensory information is lost. The context is deleted. The gestalt of intuitional experience is cracked. The details are gone. The mood is impossible to convey. The process is invisible, as is the source. No magic. Not enough is conveyed to develop any feeling of caring about what might happen to these people because the heart of their belief remains invisible, despite the attempt to convey it to me. This is not to say I don't care what happens. But I cared before I saw these scenes. If these scenes had been my total exposure to these cultures, they would only have confirmed the uselessness of trying to sustain cultures that obviously don't fit the world today.

The program shifts. We go to a Navajo reservation in the American Southwest. A group of young Indian lawyers are struggling to prevent the expansion of power plants in the Four Corners area. The traditional way of life of Navajo sheepherders, suddenly disrupted by roads, noise, soot and ash from the power plants, would be sacrificed to the expansion. The camera follows an old woman, a shepherd, whose land is threatened. The narration says, "She and the land move as one . . . she wants to keep her life as it is . . . she came from the land and she is part of the land." We hear the woman say, "We live in harmony with the Great Spirit."

What Great Spirit could she possibly be talking about? I couldn't see any great spirit there. Could she mean that fuzzy-looking desert, or the scrawny sheep? Could she mean that little mud house with no wiring? Really. What does she expect? It's nice to preserve cultures, but how can a few highways bother that?

We go to the government hearings. We see the young Indian lawyers arguing in behalf of this old woman. The lawyers decry the outrage. They cite the brutality wrought on Indian ways. We hear them charge the commissioners with failure to understand the Indians; failure to appreciate their way of life or that a way of mind is being threatened. We see the government commissioners, fat white men wearing suits and ties and looking bored. We learn that the only compensation this woman has had for the loss of her land was a $369 payment years before.

Okay. *Now* we get it. Conflict. Rules. Arguments. Laws. Right and wrong. Rip-off. Rights. Entrenched interests. Brutality. Lack of due process. Oppressors. Oppressed. Heroes. Downtrodden. It all comes flooding through.

Why didn't they get to this part earlier and drop all this "way of life," "way of mind," Great Spirit junk? It's only muddying things up. It's a civil rights issue. It's about economic rip-off. Let's hear it for those lawyers!

The program that followed immediately after "The New Indians" was called *In Search of America,* hosted by Ben Wattenberg. A six-part series, the show was intended to look at the bright side of America. "How can a nation that believes

331

it hasn't done anything right or bold or creative in the recent past, do anything right or bold or creative in the immediate future? . . . All we hear today is that big business rips us off, the blacks are losing ground, work is meaningless, we're feeding a bloated military-industrial complex and that we oppress developing countries and rape their resources. All that is mostly inaccurate," Wattenberg said.

The program concentrated on the virtues of big business. "For all its flaws, big business has provided more people with more needs and more luxuries."

Compared with what preceded it, this was quite a simple show; narrow in conception, direct, featuring very simple, straightforward imagery: Wattenberg talking, interviews with corporate economists, and, amazingly, actual footage from advertising commercials, showing how much research corporations undertake in order to improve their products on behalf of all of us. No sweeping (incomprehensible) vistas, no attempts at conveying ways of mind, no talk about Great Spirits. This show was about "needs" (products; easy to photograph); research for a better America (we saw Gillette engineers working night and day to improve our shaving); freedom of choice (twenty-one "shaving systems"); and the satisfaction of American "tastes." The show, of course, was about life-style, but it was a life-style that couldn't have been simpler to convey. And it was conveyed simply, clearly, boldly; the way it is in commercials. No information loss. It was a highly efficient program. Whereas the life-style of Indian people was delivered via muddy images, vague and incomprehensible references to alien realities—subjective, sensory, requiring an acquaintance with natural cycles—*this* life-style was objective, economic, product oriented.

There *was* conflict. Wattenberg told us we could choose either the life-style the corporations provided, and the economic benefits they spread out through the whole population, or we could choose central economic planning. We know, he

332

said, that central economic planning doesn't work. It hasn't worked in Sweden or England, for example. (Russia and China, though not named, were included by implication.) Here in America if corporations fail to provide what "we want," then they die. He toured with us through a graveyard of headstones, carved with the names of the corporations that had not kept up with Americans' changing needs. This was proof that we the people control the corporations, not vice versa. Corporate manipulation was a fiction.

The show only took a half hour. A nice, tight package. Within the terms of its definition, it worked. When I turned off the set and closed my eyes, laying my head back against the pillows of the sofa, the images that came to mind were of this Wattenberg person, his graveyard of dead corporations, the Gillette research labs . . . and I heard an internal recording of his voice: "Planners say it would be nice if we all lived in apartments, but most people prefer to live in their own single-family houses. And American business, sparked by the profit motive, is providing them. The same with mass transit. People prefer their own cars, manufactured by big business, providing what people want."

I also saw some images of that eagle-man, flapping his huge, furry wings as the canoeists rowed some Pacific bay. I saw some pictures in my head of the Southwest desert and a lonely Navajo woman on horseback, herding sheep. Cars, razors, Navajo deserts and Ben Wattenberg whirled in my mind.

I had wanted the Indian show to dominate, but I already knew that it couldn't and it didn't. A stupider, grosser, more simplistic but cleaner and clearer (more highlighted) presentation—better suited to the medium by several orders of magnitude—had achieved an equality, actually a superiority, even in my own biased mind. I reminded myself for the fiftieth time that if there are polar opposites in what television can communicate and what it cannot, at the pole of noncommunication would be cultural forms such as the American Indians'. At the pole of total communication would be cultural forms such as American business's.

Naturally, television has been used more successfully for the latter cultural forms than the former. Also naturally, the American population develops more of a feeling for products and a life-style suitable to business than it does for a sensitive, subtle and beautiful way of mind that theoretically offers an alternative. The more people sit inside their television experience, the more fixed they become in the hard-edged reality that the medium can convey.

In 1973 I helped organize an all-day press conference in Washington, D.C., hosted by Ralph Nader on behalf of Indigena, an organization devoted to creating a pan-Indian movement in the Western Hemisphere. Indigena gives particular attention to the struggle of South American Indians, who are presently suffering a fate previously visited upon the tribes of our own Great Plains and elsewhere. They are being slaughtered and driven off their land or, in the more "enlightened" countries, driven onto reservations and forced to assimilate. Speaking in cultural terms, it's death either way. All of this is done to make way for mineral exploration and development.

Before the press conference Nader advised the Indians and sympathetic anthropologists to be specific: to give the names of the corporations doing the dirty work, name the government officials, offer details of actual events. Understanding the bias of the media, Nader advised (correctly) that the information should be short, specific and punchy.

However, the people from Indigena believed, also correctly, that the only way the members of the press could possibly *care* enough about Indian people to attempt to give a viewing audience a real sense of Indian-ness, and therefore what was being lost, was to attempt to convey some Indian-ness at the press conference itself.

So, ignoring Nader's advice, the Indians devoted the first hour or so of the conference to ceremonies, prayers, songs, stories, testimonies to the Great Spirit. About 90 percent of the press left during these goings-on.

Next, the anthropologists got up and told rambling stories about the impact on an Amazon tribe when helicopters start flying overhead speaking to the Indians via loudspeakers, or when machinery is brought in. They described how a culture that has been functioning well for two thousand years can be destroyed in only one generation of technological assault.

A little before the lunch break Nader spoke, rattling off the facts and figures, the corporate names, the government policies, the American collaborations and so on. It was too late, most of the press had left.

By the time the lunch break was over, the audience was composed mainly of Indigena supporters and friends. Four hours' worth of new information on the conditions of Indian people in Paraguay, Colombia and Venezuela was shared among these friends, but as far as the press was concerned it never happened. There was no press there at all.

The net result of the press conference, which had taken months to organize and had cost several thousand dollars in travel, telephone and printing, was that not one story appeared on radio or television. Only two media outlets—*The New York Times* and *The Washington Post*—carried any mention of it at all. Both these stories were carried in the back pages of the paper, were about six inches long, and quoted entirely from Nader. In the case of the *Times* story, an equally long report ran alongside, quoting Brazilian government officials denying the truth of every single point Nader had made. The Great Spirit was not mentioned.

When I tell this story to political-activist friends, their answer, more often than not, is that the Indians have got to

335

be trained in how better to get their stories through the media. In other words, they must drop one cultural mind-set and function in another. Only then can they preserve the former. And yet, in learning the linear model, the technological communication patterns, the objectified forms that modern media honor and disseminate, the Indian herself or himself undergoes internal change to fit the form.

The question is this: Is it possible to adopt the hard-edged, fact-fascinated, aggressive, gross form in order to preserve a way of thinking that is completely alien to this model and cannot be conveyed through it?

To use the computer, one must develop computer-mind. To use the car, car-mind. To build the bomb, bomb-mind. To manipulate the media, one must be manipulative. To use television, which broadcasts flatness and one-dimensionality, it is necessary to think flatly and one-dimensionally.

The struggle of Indian people today is as much a consciousness struggle as it is a civil rights battle. To the extent that it is framed exclusively as a civil rights issue, the Indians lose, at least in cultural terms. Individual Indians may win a job, or a right, or a small payment for previous injustice, but their children and Indians of the future will not be Indians anymore; they will have been moved inside nationwide artificial reality with the rest of us. Since television itself is an outgrowth of the prevailing consciousness, it is logical that the outcome of an issue argued within it would be predetermined.

But imagine for a moment that television did not exist. Let's say that only print media existed.

It so happens that print media, while not perfect, can convey a lot more about Indian ways of mind than electronic media can because print can express much greater depth, complexity, change of mood, subtlety, detail and so on. Books, especially, can be written in much slower rhythms, encouraging a perception that builds, stage by stage, over the length of a long reading process that may take many hours, or days.

Of course, publishers, these days, also riding the rapids of modern life and responsive to commodity-mind, discourage books that move at deliberate speed, preferring those that are punchy, fast-reading, highlighted, riding the tops of the waves, like television sitcoms, or advertising.

Yet many books do exist that are solely devoted to states of feeling or expressions of intuition, or that deal in the realm of subjective reaction. There are books which are exclusively ritualistic or which have a mythic quality. And so such works as *Book of the Hopi, Lame Deer: Seeker of Visions, Black Elk Speaks, Seven Arrows, Indian Tales,* and others are able to convey more on an imagery level, a sensory level, and an evocational level than all the TV specials combined.

This is not to say that these books are sufficient. Only direct experience is. But if the battle were fought in books, Indians might win. If print were the only media in the world, the natural advantage of today's dominant forms—corporate, military, technological, scientific—over concrete ways of thinking would be vastly diminished. In a wider information field, the Indian mind would have greater validity. So people who are interested in celebrating and saving Indian cultures, like people interested in the arts or ecology or any nonhierarchical political forms, might be well advised to cease all efforts to transmit these intentions through television and devote greater effort to undermining television itself and accelerating the struggle within other information fields.

Am I actually saying that television is utterly useless? There are the old examples of the destruction of Joseph McCarthy, the exposure of the Vietnam War, the undoing of Richard Nixon, the civil rights movement. We cannot deny that television has occasionally served what appears, even to me, as a progressive purpose.

And yet what ties all of these together is the extent to which they were framed in the sort of objective terms that television can handle.

McCarthy, Vietnam, Nixon were exposed because the issues were lies, deceits, corruption—objective matters. These are all "good television."

But, finally, I want to get back to the civil rights movement because it is the exception that proves the larger point about the medium.

At the time of the early civil rights demonstrations, led at first by anonymous and brave black people, within incredibly hostile environments, and then by Martin Luther King, Jr., Malcolm X, Stokely Carmichael and others, television had only recently come into its own. The wiring-in of everyone was nearing completion. As a result, what happened in obscure Southern towns was visited upon millions of living rooms. People could see red-neck sheriffs beating people. Everyone had to face the hard reality of racism. Its appearance on television ignited the movement beyond the South. A new national attitude developed. The obvious rightness of the struggle could not be avoided.

In turning the television telescope upon this movement, the powers that be in television were not acting out of any deep moral or political enlightenment; they were following the inexorable dictates of the medium itself.

The luckiest, or if it was conscious and deliberate, the smartest aspect of the civil rights movement was that it was confrontational. From the time of the early sit-ins, it expressed conflict.

There was a good deal of violence. The issues were framed in objective terms: rights, opportunities, jobs, housing, schools. There were good guys and bad guys. It was simple to tell which was which because they even came in different colors. There were inspired leaders who stood bravely against dazzling odds. There were mass demonstrations.

All of these were the ingredients of "good television." They had action, they had highlight, they were highly visible, they were people-centered, they did not deal with sensory or subjective information, they did not require contextual understanding, they were "issues." No aura!

The civil rights struggle was about power and rights. And now we find black children in schools with white children, black people living in white neighborhoods, black people in high public office, black people on boards of big corporations. There are even black people reporting television news.

But there is something odd in the quality of this success. I'm sure it has not escaped you that the black television news commentators and the Asian ones, as well as the women, are inseparable in tone of voice, phrasing, attitudes, style of clothes, overall behavior patterns and apparent political perspective from the hundreds of white men who preceded them in those roles. The color and sex are more varied now, but the message is the same. Is it nit-picking to point this out? I don't think so.

The average black person, three or four generations removed from Africa, raised in a transplanted culture in the Deep South, kept isolated until very recently from the dominant white culture and its forms, is likely to have retained something of a way of feeling and being different from the Judeo-Christian European.

But this average black person—the one who retains a rich cultural perspective that is not yet fully Americanized—is not the one who is chosen for the network television show or the corporate vice-presidency. He or she would not be chosen because, in so many ways, this person would be ill suited for the objective, mental, aggressive, unfeeling styles that are rewarded in corporate life. Instead, the corporations pick the rare black person (or Chicano or woman or Indian) who is more like the white males who already occupy the center stage.

What is true for television commentators and corporation

executives is also true for government officials. As the personnel within the institutions change, the institutions maintain their inflexible form. The balance of power among races and sexes begins to alter, but the power arrangements themselves—some people on top, other people on the bottom, other people totally excluded—are not threatened. As more diverse people occupy the central control systems, the systems do not become more diverse. The *people* lose their diversity and start to be transformed by the systems. The systems remain the same. The perceptual patterns that have been excluded remain excluded. If alternatives to the life-style of the systems exist, they are not represented.

None of this is to argue that black people, Indians, women, or any other group which has been denied access should not seek the successes they are presently beginning to achieve in the objective world of money and power. In their shoes I would certainly do the same. It is only to remark that the subtle pressures of technological and corporate form create an archetypal Faustian bargain. In winning rights or money or power, the diverse elements in American culture lose their unique identity, their cultural roots. They become what they oppose.

And so the real power is revealed as existing in the institutions and the technology itself. For proof, you have only to watch the occasional black cultural program on Sunday morning television. It might as well be *Happy Days* or *Mr. T*. As with *Roots,* a way of mind is reduced to the exigencies of soap opera and sitcoms. As for white "culture," presumed to be the oppressor, it does not exist either. It is itself subordinate to corporate culture, or corporate consciousness, commodity life and the channelization of all behavior and thought into a nice package that suits a machine.

❖   ❖

January 1977. It's 8:15 A.M. The phone rings.

JERRY: Hello.

VOICE: My name is Fred Jones [name changed] and I'm the producer of the *Yesterday Show* [name changed]. We've heard about your book and we're very excited about it.

JERRY: You are?

PRODUCER: Yeah, you know we love controversial material. We wonder if you'd like to come on? You've got a great idea there, getting rid of TV. (He laughs.) Listen, I think we could do a really good job for you, and it'd sure sell copies of the book. I know you might have a few misgivings about coming on television (He laughs again.). . . .

JERRY: Yes, you're right about that. Listen, how much do you know about what I'm doing?

PRODUCER: Well, a lot of people around here have been talking about it. But I'd love to know more. Can you tell me in a few words why you want to eliminate television?

JERRY: Well, actually I really can't tell you in a few words. It looks like it takes me about a hundred thousand words to tell it.

PRODUCER: Well, I know, but what are the main points?

JERRY: One of the main points is that television can only deal with main points so only certain kinds of things can get through. I think my arguments are probably among those which couldn't be conveyed. Especially not in a talk show format.

PRODUCER: Why do you say that? We really like controversy. We'll give you lots of time to string it out.

JERRY: Look, I'm not trying to be difficult, but I made

myself a promise that I would never go on television. To get this material requires a really slow process, argument by argument. I'm not good television, neither is this book. Well, parts of it are good television. The fact that I want to get rid of it is pretty hot . . . but then, you know, commercials would come on, you'd have to tell jokes to liven things up.

PRODUCER: We'll take care of the jokes.

JERRY: I know, but it all starts to fit inside the form itself; it will get seen a certain way; it all washes out. I saw that happen to Marie Winn. Nothing will change. It'll have no meaning. Anyway I want people to stop watching television. Somebody has to keep information outside that system.

PRODUCER: Well, for Christsake, how are you going to sell your book? Do you know how many people watch our show? Aren't those your market? How are you going to sell it otherwise? I'm asking if you want to talk to ten million people.

JERRY: It's tempting, but I know what would happen. I've been on television before. First of all, going on television makes me nervous as hell. Talking into cameras is totally weird . . . but aside from that, I know what would happen to the material. It would all be about research. You'd have two psychologists and two media experts on there and we'd have a lively discussion back and forth and in the end the people watching the show wouldn't have learned a goddam thing. It would all reduce to who's the better arguer, when the point is really about experience. There's no way I can do it on television; if I could, I probably wouldn't have bothered to write the book. If this information gets sifted through that form of yours, it will be ruined. I don't know, maybe I'll run an ad. Ads for me are sort of like publishing. I control the context, and there are no commercial interruptions.

PRODUCER: I can't believe this conversation. I'm talking about free time and you're buying ads.

JERRY: Well, I'll let you know. I'll think about it. I realize it would be an interesting shot for you, but for me, I'm not so sure.

POSTSCRIPT

IMPOSSIBLE
THOUGHTS

XVII

TELEVISION TABOO

ACCORDING to librarians I have asked, approximately six thousand books have been written on the subject of television. Of these, I have been able to locate only one—a slim and superficial novel, *The Day Television Died* by Don McGuire—which even contemplates the notion that television could or ought to be eliminated. What makes this such a difficult idea?

❖   ❖

In the three years this book was in preparation, at least one hundred people must have come up to me at parties or in cafés, and after expressing their support for a book which deals harshly with television would ask, "Are you really going to advocate its elimination?"

"Yes," I would say, "once you really pay attention to it, you see that it's a totally horrible technology, irredeemable; we'd all be much better off without it."

"I couldn't agree with you more," would be the invariable response, "but you don't really expect to succeed, do you?"

This last question always filled me with the most uncomfortable feeling. The people who asked it had just admitted to hating television and yet I was left with the impression that

347

they also hated the idea that I might actually believe it possible to get rid of television. It made me seem weird to them in some way.

Well, it's a point, I suppose. How can I expect to succeed when even those people who loathe television find the idea of eliminating it so utterly impossible? But *why* is it so unthinkable that we might eliminate a whole technology?

If the arguments of the preceding pages are even partially correct, then television produces such a diverse collection of dangerous effects—mental, physiological, ecological, economic, political; effects that are dangerous to the person and also to society and the planet—that it seems to me only logical to propose that it should never have been introduced, or once introduced, be permitted to continue.

It is not as though Americans have no precedent for action against things that are proven dangerous. We have seen various levels of legal control put upon tobacco, saccharin, some food dyes, certain uses of polychlorinated biphenyls, aerosols, fluoroscopes and X rays to name a few. These have all been thought too dangerous to allow and yet their only negative effect is personal, they seem to cause cancer. It is at least possible, judging by some of the material in Chapter Nine on the potential effects of the narrow spectra of television light, that television also causes cancer. But is it only on the basis of cancer that we are able to think of banning something? Consider a few of television's other effects:

Television seems to be addictive. Because of the way the visual signal is processed in the mind, it inhibits cognitive processes. Television qualifies more as an instrument of brainwashing, sleep induction and/or hypnosis than anything that stimulates conscious learning processes.

Television is a form of sense deprivation, causing disorientation and confusion. It leaves viewers less able to tell the real from the not-real, the internal from the external, the personally experienced from the externally implanted. It disorients a sense of time, place, history and nature.

Television suppresses and replaces creative human imagery, encourages mass passivity, and trains people to accept authority. It is an instrument of transmutation, turning people into their TV images.

By stimulating action while simultaneously suppressing it, television contributes to hyperactivity.

Television limits and confines human knowledge. It changes the way humans receive information from the world. In place of natural multidimensional information reception, it offers a very narrow-gauged sense experience, diminishing the amount and kind of information people receive. Television keeps awareness contained within its own rigid channels, a tiny fraction of the natural information field. Because of television we believe we know more, but we know less.

By unifying everyone within its framework and by centralizing experience within itself, television virtually replaces environment. It accelerates our alienation from nature and therefore accelerates the destruction of nature. It moves us farther inside an already pervasive artificial reality. It furthers the loss of personal knowledge and the gathering of all information in the hands of a techno-scientific-industrial elite.

Television technology is inherently antidemocratic. Because of its cost, the limited kind of information it can disseminate, the way it transforms the people who use it, and the fact that a few speak while millions absorb, television is suitable for use only by the most powerful corporate interests in the country. They inevitably use it to redesign human minds into a channeled, artificial, commercial form, that nicely fits the artificial environment. Television freewayizes, suburbanizes and commoditizes human beings, who are then easier to control. Meanwhile, those who control television consolidate their power.

349

Television aids the creation of societal conditions which produce autocracy; it also creates the appropriate mental patterns for it and simultaneously dulls all awarenes that this is happening.

Taking into account all these effects and the dozens of others described in the body of this book, is it really necessary to show that television causes cancer in order to get rid of it? Is it not possible to outlaw a technology based on its political or economic or psychological effects? For if even a small portion of these arguments are valid, then in the long run they are surely more important than the fact that a percentage of people get sick. Why does banning such a technology seem bizarre?

One answer to this question lies with the absolutely erroneous assumption that technologies are "neutral," benign instruments that may be used well or badly depending upon who controls them. Americans have not grasped the fact that many technologies determine their own use, their own effects, and even the kind of people who control them. We have not yet learned to think of technology as having ideology built into its very form.

A second explanation is that once any technology of a certain scale is introduced, it effectively becomes the environment of our awareness. While we may imagine life without X rays or aerosols, we cannot imagine life without concrete or cars or electricity. These are so ubiquitous that they literally spread themselves around our awareness. We are contained within them, and as McLuhan puts it, "the fish is the last creature which is capable of understanding the water." So it is the most pervasive of the technologies that become invisible to us. Television is an extreme example of this pervasiveness and confinement. It becomes not only the external environment for an entire population, it also projects itself inside us. Television has so enveloped and entered us, it is hard for most of us to remember that it was scarcely more than a generation ago that there was no such thing as television, or that four million years of human evolution somehow took place without it.

A third reason we don't believe it possible to control technological evolution is that, in fact, for most of us it is *not* possible to do so. The great majority of us have no say at all in choosing or controlling technologies. These choices, as I've described, are now solely within the hands of this same technical-scientific-industrial-corporate elite whose power is enhanced by the technology they create. From our point of view the machines and processes they invent and disseminate just seem to appear on the scene from nowhere. Yet all life adjusts accordingly, including human systems of organization and understanding. We don't get to vote on these things as they are introduced. All we get to do is pay for them, use them and then live within their effects.

On the very rare occasions when we do perceive a technology's negative effects, we find it takes a herculean organizing effort to do anything about it. I have given the example of the SST. Though that is a technology which is surely among the most absurd, wasteful, useless and elitist ever invented, it took thousands of people years of effort to ban its production in this country. Despite this, foreign-made SSTs are being permitted to land in American airports.

I have also used the nuclear power example. This technology is so dangerous, not only for our own generation but for the next several thousand, that it should not be its banning that is unthinkable but its existence. Yet, just as I was completing work on this book in mid-1977, Dr. James Schlesinger of the National Energy Administration was saying, "If Californians wish to eliminate nuclear power, then we'll have to find a way around this desire of theirs, our need for that energy is too great."

Similar stories could be told about genetic engineering, satellite communication systems, microwave technology, neutron bombs, laser technology, centralized computer banks, and a thousand other processes, including many about which we may not even have heard.

We believe ourselves to be living in a democracy because from time to time we get to vote on candidates for public office. Yet our vote for congressperson or president means very little in the light of our lack of power over technological inventions that affect the nature of our existence more than any individual leader has ever done. Without our gaining control over technology, all notions of democracy are a farce. If we cannot even think of abandoning a technology, or thinking of it, affect the ban, then we are trapped in a state of passivity and impotence hardly to be distinguished from living under a dictatorship. What is confusing is that our dictator is not a person. Though a handful of people most certainly benefit from and harness to their purposes these pervasive technologies, the true dictators are the technologies themselves.

David Brower, president of Friends of the Earth, has argued that unlike human beings accused of crimes, all technologies should be assumed guilty of dangerous effects until proven innocent. No new technology should ever be introduced, he has said, until its ultimate effects are known and explained to the population. This is necessary, he feels, because once it has been introduced, getting rid of any technology is practically impossible—so much of life gets reorganized around it and so much power and vested interest attaches to its continuance.

Of course what Brower envisions is itself practically impossible. Many technologies are too technically complex for the average person, like myself, not technically trained, to understand them. Also, in many instances it is impossible to identify all effects of a technology in advance of its introduction, especially those which do not lend themselves to scientific proofs and evidences. But where does this leave us? Since it is impossible fully to grasp or explain many technologies, do we then go ahead with them? Do we trust our industrial leaders? Do we merely let them shoot craps with our existence? And if we do foresee undesirable effects from a technology, what means exist for then getting rid of that technology? Are there any? And what does all of this mean to the ultimate control of our lives?

In Chapter Four I raised the possibility of an alternative way of thinking about the problem. If we believe in democratic processes, then we must also believe in resisting whatever subverts democracy. In the case of technology, we might wish to seek a line beyond which democratic control is not possible and then say that any technology which goes beyond this line is taboo. Although it might be difficult to define this line precisely, it might not be so difficult to know when some technologies are clearly over it. Any technology which by its nature encourages autocracy would surely be over such a line. Any technology that benefits only a small number of people to the physical, emotional, political, and psychological detriment of large numbers of other people would also certainly be over that line. In fact, one could make the argument that any technology whose operations and results are too complex for the majority of people to understand would also be beyond this line of democratic control.

Can we really say any longer that a reason to go ahead with a technology is that it is too complex for people to grasp, or too clumsy or difficult to dismantle? Either we believe in democratic control or we do not. If we do, then anything which is beyond such control is certainly anathema to democracy.

At the moment our only choices are personal ones. Though we may not be able to do anything whatever about genetic engineering or neutron bombs, individually we can say "no" to television. We can throw our sets in the garbage pail where they belong. But while this is an act that may be very satisfying and beneficial, in making this act we must never forget that, like choosing not to drive a car, it is no expression of democratic freedom. In democratic terms, this individual act is meaningless, as it has no effect at all upon the wider society, which continues as before. In fact, this act disconnects us from the system and leaves us *less* able to participate in and affect it than before. Like Huxley's "savage," or like today's young people who drop out to rural farms, we find ourselves even further removed from participation in the central processes that direct our society, our culture, our politics, and our economic organization. We are struggling in a classic double bind.

Because eliminating television seems impossible, and personal withdrawal is in some ways not enough, at least at a systematic level, most of us naturally attempt to reform matters. In the case of television we have worked to improve and democratize its output.

But a central argument of this book is that television, for the most part, cannot possibly yield to reform. Its problems are inherent in the technology itself to the same extent that violence is inherent in guns.

No new age of well-meaning television executives can change what the medium does to people who watch it. Its effects on body and mind are inseparable from the viewing experience.

As for the political effects, if we switched from the commercial control of television to, say, governmental control, as in Sweden or Argentina or Russia, this would not change the essential political relationships: the unification of experience, the one speaking to the many, the inevitable training in autocracy that these conditions engender.

Similarly, no change in programming format from the present violent, antisocial tendencies to the more "prosocial" visions of educators and psychologists will mean much compared with the training in passivity, the destruction of creativity, the dulling of communicative abilities that any extended exposure to television inevitably produces. This is even assuming that the programming *could* be substantially changed which, as we have seen, is highly doubtful.

No influx of talented directors or writers can offset the technical limits of the medium itself. No matter who is in control, the medium remains confined to its cold, narrow culverts of hyperactive information. Nothing and no one can change this, nor can anyone change how television's technical limits confine awareness. As the person who gazes at streams becomes streamlike, so as we watch television we inexorably evolve into creatures whose bodies and minds become television-like.

True, if we banned all advertising, that would allay many negative effects of the medium and diminish the power of the huge corporations that are re-creating life in their image.

True, if we banned all *broadcast* television, leaving only cable systems, that would reduce the effect of the centralization of control. More kinds of people might have access to the medium, but they would still have to submit to the dictates of the technology. As they used the machine, they would find their material and their own consciousness changing to suit the technological form. The people who use television become more like each other, the Indian who learns television is an Indian no longer.

If we reduced the number of broadcast hours per day, or the number of days per week that television is permitted to broadcast, as many countries have, that would surely be an improvement.

If we eliminated all crime shows and other sensational entertainment, it would reveal what an inherently boring medium this is, producing awareness of artificial fixation despite boredom.

If we banned all nature shows or news broadcasts from television, due to the unavoidable and very dangerous distortions and aberrations which are inherent in televising these subjects, then this would leave other, better-qualified media to report them to us. The result would be an increased awareness of far more complex, complete and subtle information.

If we outlawed networks, there would be a new emphasis on local events, bringing us nearer to issues upon which we might have some direct personal effect.

All of these changes in television would be to the good, in my opinion, and worthy of support, but do you believe that they'd be any easier to achieve than the outright elimination of the whole technology? I don't think so. Considering how difficult it has been merely to reduce the volume or the kind of advertising that is directed at our children, and considering the overwhelming power of the interests who control communications in this country, we might just as well put our efforts toward trying for the hole in one. It will take no greater amount of organization and it does not suffer the inhibitions of ambiguity.

Imagining a world free of television, I can envision only beneficial effects.

What is lost because we can no longer flip a switch for instant "entertainment" will be more than offset by human contact, enlivened minds and resurgence of personal investigation and activation.

What is lost because we can no longer see fuzzy and reduced versions of drama or forests will be more than offset by the actual experience of life and environment directly lived, and the resurgence of the human feeling that will accompany this.

What is lost by the unavailability of escape from what may

be the painful conditions of many people's lives, might be more than offset by the concrete realization that life has been *made* painful, more to some than to others, and the desire to do something about this, to attack whatever forces have conspired to make this so.

Once rid of television, our information field would instantly widen to include aspects of life which have been discarded and forgotten. Human beings would rediscover facets of experience that we've permitted to lie dormant.

The nature of political process would surely change, making possible not only more subtle perspectives, but also the possibility of content over style. Political and economic power, now more concentrated than ever before in American history, would surely shift somewhat in the direction of more decentralized, noncapitalistic, community-based structures.

Learning would doubtless reemerge to substitute for brainwashing. Individual knowledge and the collective knowledge of communities of friends and peers would again flower as monolithic, institutional, surrogate knowledge declined.

Overall, chances are excellent that human beings, once outside the cloud of television images, would be happier than they have been of late, once again living in a reality which is less artificial, less imposed, and more responsive to personal action.

How to achieve the elimination of television? I certainly cannot answer that question. It is obvious, however, that the first step is for all of us to purge from our minds the idea that just because television exists, we cannot get rid of it.

Thank you.

SAN FRANCISCO
July 3, 1977

ACKNOWLEDGMENTS

M OST OF ALL I am grateful to my immediate family for their involvement, their patience, their love and affection throughout three unusually strained years.

My children, Yari and Kai, not only provided much of the basic research for the book and a large part of the motive for doing it, but the very deliciousness of their presence, their sanity, and their humor kept me centered in many a difficult moment.

My wife, Anica Vesel Mander, while finishing work on two books of her own and teaching a full schedule at Antioch College, found time to give detailed study to the manuscript in its various drafts, adding ideas and suggesting some very major improvements. These, together with the constancy of her love and support, made it possible to survive what became an all-consuming task.

John Brockman, my agent, was far more than that from the very start of the project. More as a friend than anything else, he convinced me to undertake the book, even going so far as to sit me down in his apartment and personally talk me through it for hours, until a coherent outline emerged. Then, he stayed closely in touch throughout the writing process.

James Landis of William Morrow & Company exhibited an amazing sensitivity to nuance, as well as meticulousness, brilliance, patience, speed, efficiency and, not the least of his attributes, toughness, an unbeatable list of qualities for an editor to have.

No less important to the successful completion of this project was San Francisco writer and editor Mary Jean Haley. In addition to accomplishing much of the early research, during the final month of the book's preparation she worked with me daily, tightening, editing, even rewriting here and there as needed, until a manuscript which was far too clumsy and long became manageable.

Six close personal friends participated continuously, not only through the quality of their support and affection through many crises, but also with specific research, editing ideas, and manuscript criticism. My thanks, love and appreciation, therefore, go to Ernest Callenbach, Cherie Cullen, Jack Edelson, Carole Levine, Anne Kent Rush and Nina Winter.

Another person deserving special mention for her many long hours on this project is Patricia Rain. In addition to doing a considerable amount of research, she typed this manuscript twice, becoming so intimate with many points that her editorial suggestions were among the most useful I received.

Very important research, particularly on the various medical and biological effects of television, was gathered by Mickey Friedman. Mitch Cohen was the person who found that amazing article by Viktor Tausk. Paul Kaufman, of the National Center for Experiments in Television, contributed a whole compendium of important articles, as well as providing me valuable criticism of many of the manuscript's technical details. For other useful research and/or manuscript feedback, thanks to Stefan Dasho, Alvin Duskin, Roland Finston, Susan Lyne, Stephanie Mills, Karen Payne, Barbara Richter, Tom Turner, Joseph Vesel and Judith Williams.

Financial survival, an extreme problem when holed up for three years, was made possible by grants from Friends of the Earth Foundation, the Laras Fund, and the Foundation for

National Progress. For making these grants possible, I would like to thank in particular, Dan Noyes, Mary Anna Colwell, Barbara Hunter and David Hunter. Thank you also Don Aitken, Diana Dillaway, Mark Dowie, Lois Crozier Hogle, Godfrey Reggio, Natalie Roberts and Mela Vesel.

I was happy to have a chance to reacquaint myself with the immaculate graphic work of my former advertising colleagues, Marget Larsen and Robert Freeman, who are responsible for the elegant jacket design and the inside layout of the book.

While I am speaking of my former advertising colleagues, I want to say a word about the contribution made by one of them, Howard Gossage, who died many years before I even thought to do this book. Gossage exposed me to a way of thinking about media, its power and its absurdities, which probably affected my own perceptions more than any other single person or source. Often while working on this project, I found myself mentally checking things with the way he would have seen them, his mind remains that alive to me.

Finally, for contributions of hot leads and miscellaneous good ideas, I would like to thank Larry Adleman, Rina Alcalay, Obie Benz, Jeff Brand, Stewart Brand, Susan Brockman, Neeli Cherkovski, Sheldon Davis, Libby Edwards, Mali Gesmundo, Todd Gitlin, Rubin Glickman, Colette Goerner, Arlene Goldbard, Rasa Gustaitis, Jim Harding, Janet Kranzberg, Ann Kyle, Marie Hélène Laraque, George Leonard, Leo Litwak, Jerry Lubenow, Joan Lubenow, John Magnuson, Jane Margold, Susan Margolis, Katinka Matson, John Mattson, Jeannie Milligan, Albert Morse, Stewart Mott, Mike Murphy, Michael Nolan, Mark Obenhaus, Zev Putterman, Michael Shamberg, Michael Singer, Dick Shouse, Sara Urquart-Duskin, Henry Weinstein, and the folks at the Ant Farm, Optic Nerve and Malvina's.

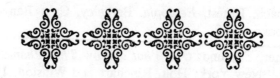

BIBLIOGRAPHY

Arlen, Michael, *Living Room War*. New York: Viking, 1966.

Baillie, Gil, "Next Question: Taboo," in *Planet Drum*, Planet Drum Foundation, P.O. Box 31251, San Francisco, 1975.

Barnet, Richard and Ronald Muller, "Global Reach." *The New Yorker*, December 2, 1974, pp. 53-128, and December 9, 1974, pp. 100-159.

Bateson, Gregory, *Steps to an Ecology of Mind*. San Francisco: Chandler, 1972.

Birt, John, "There Is a Bias in Television Journalism. It Is Not Against Any Particular Party or Point of View—It Is a Bias Against Understanding." *TV Guide*, August 9, 1975, pp. 3-7.

Benedict, Ruth, *Patterns of Culture*. Boston: Houghton Mifflin, 1971.

Benjamin, Walter, *Illuminations,* ed. Hannah Arendt. New York: Schocken Books, 1969.

Bierhorst, John, ed., *The Red Swan*. New York: McGraw-Hill, 1976.

Bradbury, Ray, *Fahrenheit 451*. New York: Ballantine Books, 1953.

Callenbach, Ernest, *Ecotopia*. Berkeley, Cal.: Banyan Tree Books, 1975.

Carpenter, Edmund, *Oh, What a Blow That Phantom Gave Me!* New York: Holt, Rinehart and Winston, 1972.

Chait, Lawrence G., "Four Vital Ingredients of the Coming Revolution in Consumer Marketing, 1970–2000." Speech, 1968, published by Lawrence G. Chait, 641 Lexington Avenue, New York, N. Y. 10022.

Clark, David G. and William B. Blankenburg, *You and Media: Mass Communication and Society*. San Francisco: Canfield Press, 1973.

Comstock, George A., Eli A. Rubinstein, and John P. Murray, eds., *Television and Social Behavior*, Vols. I–IV. U.S. Department of Health, Education and Welfare, National Institute of Mental Health. Washington, D.C.: 1972.

Conrat, Richard and Maisie Conrat, *The American Farm*. San Francisco: California Historical Society/Houghton Mifflin, 1977.

Cowen, Robert J., "A Note on the Meaning of Television to a Psychotic Woman." *Bulletin of the Menninger Clinic*, Vol. 23 (1959), pp. 202-3.

"Creativity and Television—A Depressing Picture." *Psychology Today*, November 1973, pp. 14-15.

Davidson, Bill, "Fact or Fiction." *TV Guide*, March 20, 1976, pp. 4-8.

De Angulo, Jaime, *Indian Tales*. New York: Hill & Wang, 1953.

Debord, Guy, *Society of the Spectacle*. Detroit: Black and Red, Box 9546, 1973.

De Novais, Carmem, "Amazon Indians—Sharing Knowledge with the World." *Indigena,* Winter, 1975–76, p. 10.

Ellul, Jacques, *Propaganda.* New York: Alfred A. Knopf, 1965.

————, *The Technological Society.* New York: Alfred A. Knopf, 1964.

Emery, Fred and Merrelyn Emery, *A Choice of Futures: To Enlighten or Inform?* Canberra: Centre for Continuing Education, Australian National University, 1975.

Enzensberger, Hans M., *The Consciousness Industry.* New York: The Seabury Press, 1974.

Epstein, Edward J., *News from Nowhere.* New York: Random House, 1973.

Esser, Aristede H., "Environment and Mental Health." Speech at World Mental Health Congress, Sydney, Australia, October 1973.

Fink, Donald G. and David M. Lutyens, *The Physics of Television.* New York: Doubleday, 1960.

Freire, Paulo, *Pedagogy of the Oppressed.* New York: The Seabury Press, 1970.

Gerbner, George and Larry Gross, "The Scary World of TV's Heavy Viewer." *Psychology Today,* April 1976, pp. 41-89.

Gitlin, Todd, "Sixteen Notes on Television and the Movement," in George White and Charles Newman, *Literature in Revolution.* New York: Holt, Rinehart and Winston, 1972.

Glatzer, Robert, *The New Advertising.* New York: Citadel Press, 1971.

Gotz, I. L., "On Children and Television." *Elementary School Journal,* April, 1975, pp. 415-18.

Holt, John, *Escape from Childhood.* New York: E. P. Dutton, 1975.

Huxley, Aldous, *Brave New World.* New York: Harper & Brothers, 1932.

Illich, Ivan, *Energy and Equity.* London: Calder & Boyars, 1974.

————, *Medical Nemesis.* New York: Random House, 1976.

Johnson, Nicholas, *How to Talk Back to Your Television Set.* Boston: Atlantic Monthly Press, 1970.

Kaplan, Donald M., "The Psychopathology of TV Watching." *Performance,* July–August 1972, pp. 21-29.

Kelso, Louis O. and Patricia Hetter, *How to Turn Eighty Million Workers into Capitalists on Borrowed Money.* New York: Random House, 1967.

Kosinski, Jerzy, *Being There.* New York: Harcourt Brace, 1971.

Kroger, William G. and Sidney A. Schneider, "An Electronic Aid for Hypnotic Induction." *International Journal of Clinical and Experimental Hypnosis,* Vol. 7 (1959), pp. 93-98.

Krugman, Herbert E., "Brain Wave Measures of Media Involvement." *Journal of Advertising Research.* February 1971, pp. 3-9.

Kuleshov, Lev, *Kuleshov on Film,* ed. Ronald Levaco. Berkeley, Cal.: University of California Press, 1974.

Lacey, Louise, *Lunaception.* New York: Coward, McCann, 1974.

Lamb, F. Bruce, *Wizard of the Upper Amazon*. Boston: Houghton Mifflin, 1971.

Lame Deer, John and Richard Erdoes, *Lame Deer, Seeker of Visions*. New York: Simon & Schuster, 1972.

Lefebvre, Henri, *Everyday Life in the Modern World*. New York: Harper & Row, 1971.

Lem, Stanislaw, *Solaris*. New York: Walker, 1971.

Lesser, Gerald S., *Children and Television*. New York: Random House, 1974.

Lyons, Nancy, and Letitia Upton, "Basic Facts: Distribution of Personal Income and Wealth in the United States." The Cambridge Institute, 1878 Massachusetts Ave., Cambridge, Mass., 1972.

McGuire, Don, *The Day Television Died*. New York: Doubleday, 1966.

McLuhan, Marshal, *Gutenberg Galaxy*. Toronto: Univ. of Toronto Press, 1962.

————, *Understanding Media*. New York: McGraw-Hill, 1964.

Marcuse, Herbert, *One Dimensional Man*. Boston: Beacon Press, 1964.

Meerloo, Joast, "Television Addiction and Reactive Apathy." *Journal of Nervous and Mental Disease*, Vol. 120 (1954), pp. 290-91.

Mulholland, Thomas B., "Training Visual Attention." *Academic Therapy*, Fall 1974, pp. 5-17.

Murchie, Guy, *Music of the Spheres*. New York: Dover, 1961.

The Network Project, *Notebook*, Vols. I–VII. 101 Earl Hall, Columbia University, New York, 1973.

"New Insights Into Buying Explored," *Investments in Tomorrow,* No. 16. Menlo Park, Cal.: Stanford Research Institute, Summer 1975.

Niehardt, John G., *Black Elk Speaks.* New York: William Morrow, 1932.

Nielsen Television, 1975. Chicago: A. C. Nielsen, 1975.

Olson, David and Richard Parker, "Why Prices Go Up When Jobs Go Down." *Mother Jones,* February 1977, pp. 11-12.

"One Hundred Leading Advertisers." *Advertising Age,* August 18, 1975, pp. 156-57.

"One Hundred Leading Advertisers." *Advertising Age,* August 23, 1976, pp. 90-91.

Ornstein, Robert, ed., *The Nature of Human Consciousness.* San Francisco: W. H. Freeman, 1973.

Orwell, George, *1984.* New York: Harcourt Brace, 1949.

Ott, John N., *Health and Light.* Old Greenwich, Conn.: Devin-Adair, 1973.

————, *My Ivory Cellar.* Chicago: Twentieth Century Press, 1958.

————, "The Eyes' Dual Function." *The Eye, Ear, Nose and Throat Monthly,* July, 1974, pp. 42-50; August, 1974, pp. 24-35; November, 1974, pp. 48-53.

Patterson, Thomas E. and Robert D. McClure, "Political Campaigns: TV Power Is a Myth." *Psychology Today,* July, 1976, pp. 61-90.

Pawley, Martin, *The Private Future.* New York: Random House, 1974.

Peper, Erik and Thomas Mulholland, "Occipital Alpha and

Accommodative Vergence, Pursuit Tracking and Fast Eye Movements." *Psychophysiology,* No. 5 (1971), pp. 556-75.

Point Blank! Contributions Towards a Situationist Revolution. Published by Point Blank!, P.O. Box 2233, Station A, Berkeley, Cal., 1972.

Poznanski, Z. and M. Pawlik, "Epileptic Seizures Provoked by Television." *Polish Medical Journal,* 8 (1969).

Rush, Anne Kent, *Moon, Moon.* Berkeley, Cal.: Moon Books/Random House, 1976.

Samuels, Mike and Nancy Samuels, *Seeing with the Mind's Eye.* Berkeley, Cal.: Bookworks/Random House, 1975.

Scheer, Robert, *America after Nixon.* New York: McGraw-Hill, 1974.

Schiller, Herbert I., *Mass Communications and American Empire.* New York: Kelley, 1969.

————, *The Mind Managers.* Boston: Beacon Press, 1973.

Schwartz, Tony, *The Responsive Chord.* New York: Doubleday/Anchor, 1973.

Schwartz, Zarea L., "Photogenic Epilepsy. A Study of the Sensitivity to Photic Stimulation." *Neurologia,* Vol. 11 1966), pp. 539-48.

Shamberg, Michael and Raindance Corporation, *Guerrilla Television.* New York: Holt, Rinehart and Winston, 1971.

Slater, Philip, *The Pursuit of Loneliness.* Boston: Beacon Press, 1971.

Smith, Kendric C., "The Science of Photobiology." *BioScience,* January, 1974, pp. 45-48.

Smythe, Dallas W., "Communications: Blind Spot of Western Marxism." Paper delivered at West Coast Critical Communications Conference, Stanford University, December, 1975.

Sontag, Susan, *Against Interpretation*. New York: Dell, 1961.

Stavins, Ralph L., ed., *Television Today: The End of Communication and the Death of Community*. Washington, D.C.: Communication Service Corp., 1969.

Stewart, Kilton, "Dream Theory in Malaya," in C. Tart, ed., *Altered States of Consciousness*. New York: Doubleday, 1972.

Storm, Hyemeyhosts, *Seven Arrows*. New York: Harper & Row, 1972.

Suinn, Richard M., "Psychology for Olympic Champs," *Psychology Today*, July, 1976, pp. 38-42.

Tart, Charles, *Altered States of Consciousness*. New York: Doubleday, 1972.

Tausk, Viktor, "On the Origin of the 'Influencing Machine' in Schizophrenia," in Robert Fliess, ed., *The Psycho-Analytic Reader*. New York: International Universities Press, 1967.

Thurow, Lester C., "The Distribution of Wealth and Earnings." *Public Interest Economics Newsletter*, December 1975, pp. 2-3.

Toffler, Alvin, *Future Shock*. New York: Random House, 1970.

Wald, Carol and Judith Papachristou, *Myth America*. New York: Pantheon Books, 1975.

Waldman, Anne, *Fast Speaking Woman*. San Francisco: City Lights Books, 1975.

Waters, Frank, *Book of the Hopi*. New York: Viking, 1963.

Willett, John, ed., *Brecht on Theatre*. New York: Hill & Wang, 1964.

Williams, Raymond, *Television: Technology and Cultural Form*. New York: Schocken Books, 1975.

Winn, Marie, *The Plug-In Drug*. New York: Viking, 1977.

Worth, Sol and John Adair, *Through Navajo Eyes*. Bloomington, Ind.: Indiana Univ. Press, 1972.

Wurtman, Richard J., "The Effects of Light on the Human Body." *Scientific American*, July 1975, pp. 69-77.

Young, Arthur M., *The Reflexive Universe*. New York: Delacorte Press/Seymour Lawrence, 1976.